Middle-Class Culture in the Nineteenth Century

Middle-Class Culture in the Nineteenth Century

America, Australia and Britain

Linda Young

palgrave
macmillan

Published by
PALGRAVE MACMILLAN
Houndmills, Basingstoke, Hampshire RG21 6XS and
175 Fifth Avenue, New York, N.Y. 10010
Companies and representatives throughout the world

PALGRAVE MACMILLAN is the global academic imprint of the Palgrave
Macmillan division of St. Martin's Press, LLC and of Palgrave Macmillan Ltd.
Macmillan® is a registered trademark in the United States, United Kingdom
and other countries. Palgrave is a registered trademark in the European
Union and other countries.

ISBN-13: 978–0–333–99746–8
ISBN-10: 0–333–99746–8

This book is printed on paper suitable for recycling and made from fully
managed and sustained forest sources. Logging, pulping and manufacturing
processes are expected to conform to the environmental regulations of the
country of origin.

A catalogue record for this book is available from the British Library.

Library of Congress Catalog Card Number: 2002074993

Printed and bound in Great Britain by
CPI Antony Rowe, Chippenham and Eastbourne

To my mother and father

Contents

List of Illustrations

Acknowledgements

It is very satisfying to acknowledge the assistance and encouragement of so many people in the development of this book: I am grateful to you all. It began as a PhD thesis at Flinders University of South Australia, supervised by Lyndall Ryan and Bob Holton. It grew into a book thanks to a Post Doctoral Fellowship in the History programme of the Research School of Social Sciences, Australian National University, facilitated by Paul Bourke and Pat Jalland. Throughout the whole business, the University of Canberra and my colleagues in the Cultural Heritage Management programme, especially Brian Egloff, provided a great environment in which to work.

Old friends contributed much to the idea, the thesis and the book, and I made some new friends in pursuing its byways. Pim Allison, Grace Karskens, Joan Kerr, Susan Lawrence, Ros Russell and Shirley Wajda have been inspiration as well as fun.

A history is only as good as its sources. I treasure the librarians and archivists who helped me use the collections of the University of Canberra, the Australian National University, the National Library of Australia, the State Library of New South Wales, the Historic Houses Trust of New South Wales, the British Library, Winterthur Library, the National Archives of Scotland and the Public Archives of Delaware.

My sources also lay in museums and historic houses, where I catalogued, researched and learned from good colleagues. Specially important were the Museum of Applied Arts and Sciences, Sydney; the Western Australian Museum, Perth; and the National Trust of South Australia.

The illustrations are critical to the meanings of the book. Jane Hingston of the University of Canberra processed most of them, with style and insight. For assistance with reproduction and permission costs I am very grateful for a grant from the Australian Academy of the Humanities.

A book takes a lot of emotional energy. Shirley Young advised and encouraged more than she knows. David Young perhaps knows what he is owed, having sustained both book and me all the way.

Introduction

The simple, physical presence of historic objects can be both inspiring and overwhelming as a means of direct contact with the past. You can touch the very things that historic people did (if you're allowed), or at least gaze on the forms and spaces that were familiar to them, and loose your imagination by being in the presence of something that has been then and still is now. Humans come and go, but some kinds of material things last forever (or for a very long time) and thus contain the special quality of witnessing the past to the present. But the sheer presence of the antique is not self-explanatory. Modern people know the past in a multitude of ways – through sentiment or awe, as education or entertainment – but we can never know it as did the people who lived 'back then'. The human way of perceiving the physical world is grounded in such a multitude of conscious and unconscious phenomena that we can hope only to grasp elements of it. Nonetheless, to encounter the past is a challenge that enchants many people.

Museum curators are specially privileged to have access to historic material which the public must usually enjoy more vicariously, and it was in a museum, handling objects in order to catalogue them, that this book began. The caretakers of historic objects begin their work by studying each item, describing it in terms of fabric, manufacture, style, function and provenance, comparing it with other examples in the collection or in illustrated books. The goal of the process is to identify objects, to verify their authenticity – and often that is the end of it, an end in itself. This is largely because the concept of the value of historic material, while conventionally acknowledged as a potential source of knowledge and a public benefit, drifts easily into the realm of financial value because there is a lucrative market in certain kinds of ancient objects. Cash equivalence is a vivid, handy way of appreciating value, and few people are immune to the aura of something worth a lot of money. By contrast, the intellectual reasons why objects can be called valuable are often opaque. Recognizing the value in an old laundry iron ('we had one of those') or a grotesque mantel ornament ('I wouldn't want that in my house') requires specialized knowledge.

The fact is, the meanings of historic objects are complex and elusive. In the view of students of material culture, objects are not merely instrumental use values which enable humans to function in the physical world. More than this, objects mediate much of human life; objects are integral and interactive in human culture. They express meanings in social relationships such as nurturing and entertaining, and in environmental accommodations such as housing and cleanliness. These contexts suggest how meanings can be understood from the ways that people select, present, employ, exchange and value objects. Historic change in economy and technology has an evident bearing on the production of objects, and shifts in belief and behaviour affect the history of how people need, desire and consume goods. It is relatively easy to research the history of production if capital investment is involved, for money always leaves records. It is much harder to trace the history of cottage industries and home-based production. It is positively difficult to investigate the personal context of consumption since it requires literate individuals whose records survive the risks of time. But when consumer change occurs on a large enough scale, it is sometimes apparent that it was motivated by social tastes which indicate new ideas. It's clear we need a very large framework of research to delve into the meanings of historic objects.

Then there are practical constraints in studying material culture. If and how objects last through time depends on a lottery of factors: physical durability, continuing value (for whatever reason), size (very small and very large things tend to survive), location (isolated, secret or forgotten places are good conditions for object continuity) and sheer chance. Things survive in private or commercial ownership, but only when they reach museums, the archives of material culture, do they become accessible for public study. Yet having endured time, they are culled again at the gate of the museum, this time by intellectual criteria. Most objects collected by museums are acquired for their significance to the present, being judged to be important in the context of the day. Meaning is understood by contemporary standards, as can be seen in collections made by previous generations, where the structure is shaped by different beliefs and agendas. Thus only since the rise of social history in museums (somewhat later than it arrived in academe) have institutions collected, for instance, the apparatus of everyday life in the past. Before the 1970s, mundane objects weren't considered important enough to be in museums, unless they were associated with some great man, famous event or quaint local tradition. All these conditions whittle down the quantum of historic material culture available for analysis and comparison.

Further constraints of management and habit also shape collections, and thus potential understanding, of historic material culture. The inherent consequences of selecting which among many objects to acquire ('you can't collect everything') mean that the material that makes it into museum repositories can only ever be a fraction of the total universe of goods. The limits of selection are often determined by the availability and long-term cost of storage space, which mandates that out of any range of items just one, or sometimes a representative sample, is collected. This makes it difficult subsequently to understand historic objects that once existed in multiples, such as sets of underclothes or tools. Material collected from its original context can be documented on site to provide evidence of the relationships between objects in their setting, but it's rarely collected *in toto*. The logistic problems of conserving whole assemblages tends to be resolved by selection, which inevitably isolates and decontextualizes the chosen objects. Through such trials, objects eventually enter the formal register of the museum and become 'historic'.

An antidote to these necessary evils is the preservation of entire houses complete with the fittings, furnishings, equipment, decoration and sometimes the outbuildings and gardens that made them working human systems. The reasons why houses have been conserved as museums are various and not always for the sake of the totality of everyday material they might contain; collections of art treasures or the lingering spirit of a great man are more common origins of house museums. An entire house is expensive to maintain as a museum, as well as difficult to present in other than static ways which risk the popular perception of a dead past. But those with intact domestic collections of everything are specially precious as time capsules of material culture. They have the additional virtue of representing aspects of historic experience that are not always found in museum collections, straddling private life and its public dimensions, and situating especially the daily experience of women, children and other subaltern figures such as extended family and servants.

I have had the good fortune to catalogue two intact house museums and to work in many more. Steeped in the repetitive minutiae of domestic collections, it is hard to resist a feeling of special intimacy with and understanding of the various owners and users of the material. But there are always mysteries – incomprehensible gaps, extraordinary additions – to remind one of the idiosyncrasy, the difference, of people in the past. One has only to think of the serendipity of one's own possessions, based on logical need as many of them are, but shaped by personal taste, opportunity and occasion: I have sometimes blanched at the thought of some bright young curator sifting through my household to interpret my life a hundred years hence. Still, in the name of historical knowledge we engage with the evidence of the past, and note the discrepancies which alert us to the limits of archaeological-style investigation. It points to the need for comparative and contextualizing research to take us as close as possible to grasping the past.

That context is the subject of this book. It is nearly twenty years since I catalogued my first historic house, and I tried out various methodologies and interpretations before coming to the culture of gentility.[1] Researching gentility has been something of a burden, for while I can say it with a straight face, the word makes most people titter. It's a giggle of nervousness rather than humour, which suggests that the concept of gentility touches some anxious spot in the modern psyche. Modern people feel gentility cannot be genuine. It suggests spurious or affected behaviour, artificiality in an age when to 'act natural' is the ideal. Perhaps the nervous response rises from secret consciousness that there is plenty of artifice in nature, that to act naturally is often as carefully constructed a style as Victorian formality was.

As I understand the culture of gentility that surged at the turn of the nineteenth century, it was essentially a product of self-control. Self-possession in public was a primary aim, and ideally in private life as well, especially in the socialization of children but also in intimate personal practice. People adopted self-controlled gentility for strategic reasons to find personal identity in group affiliation, and to live 'nicer' as well as better in both physical and emotional aspects. Assisting them was a new range of goods to enable and demonstrate the genteel person's capacity, from bath tubs to handkerchiefs to silver (or silver-like) knives and forks to matching suites of furniture. Once available only to the uppermost reaches of society, such objects began to be produced at many price levels, as demand rose among ordinary people to live in the style of their aspirations. Yet possessing the goods was not sufficient to be acknowledged as genteel; they had to be used with the correct discipline: the bath brought out every day, the handkerchief employed discreetly, the cutlery held just so, the furniture upholstered in grand but not flashy fabric. The knowledge to make the right use of the necessary equipment could come at mother's knee, in an advice book or by imitation of others, in that order of effectiveness. Knowledge – the resource of cultural capital – plus goods – underwritten by a certain level of income – generated the genteel lifestyle.

Many of the forms of gentility followed aristocratic models, but certain fundamentals of the condition were so new and different that the late eighteenth/early nineteenth-century manifestation should not be considered merely derivative, but distinctive. The difference turns on the moral value of men working to make a living, which implicitly acknowledged the shame of limited means, redressed by women observing the niceties of leisured life to maintain the family honour of refined standards. To realize the lifestyle or 'habitus' of gentility, men and women worked the system of social performance codified as etiquette and the system of material consumption shaped by correct taste.

As a somewhat misleading shorthand, I call it Victorian gentility, though in fact it preceded Victoria's accession to the throne in 1837, and even her birth. The idea of the 'long' nineteenth century is not new, but is a convenient way to describe the period from about the 1780s to 1914. Victoria's century encompassed the flowering of genteel culture among people who were not only expanding in number but in geographical spread, thanks to British imperialism and American frontierism. Genteel standards persist in some degree today, though not by that name, and with merely a shadow of the cultural authority they possessed in the nineteenth century. Gentility may have become stultifying by (or even before) the turn of the twentieth century, yet it contained a dynamic that motivated, and an ideal which shaped, the lifestyle of what became the dominant fraction of English society in Britain, the United States and British colonies around the globe.

Gentility was the culture of the middle class, and can even be said to define it. This idea has some utility, since middle-class definition has been famously difficult to reach via the conventional criteria of work, income or political stance. Work is critical in separating out the middle from the upper class, the region where wealth comes from the labour of others, and enough of it to live in leisure. The middle class has to work to earn its living, though the kinds of work are diverse and common only in not being manual. The income that work brings in is also diverse, from a lot to a little. The politics of the middle class have never been unified, being individualist and self-interested, more ready to compromise than to resist. The absence of political struggle sends the definition of the middle class outside some of the standard ideas of class formation, and yet most observers recognize that modern western society contains something between those who control and those who do the dirty work. For many theorists, this idea of breadth and diversity makes the concept of a unitary Victorian middle class too broad for useful analysis; on the other hand, the search for intra-class distinctions misses the overall unity of inspiration and aspiration that impelled the rising middle class.

But whatever it is, the middle class is now deeply unfashionable. It has been condemned as reactionary for such a long time that no one wants to claim membership.[2] To find oneself studying the middle class is so politically incorrect, or at least irrelevant, that it's somewhat embarrassing. Yet the middle class is today the stock of almost all of us, and its history must have some call on modern attention. So middle-class history has a long way to go by comparison with the study of the virtuous working class and the glamorous nobility. A subject search in my university library reveals the following rate of historical investigations:

	Working class	*Middle class*	*Nobility/gentry*
Great Britain	252	22	98/17
United States	201	36	
Australia	84	6	

This tabulation shows that historians believe neither the United States nor Australia possessed a class of aristocrats in the British sense. As much as anything, this absence of a structural upper class is a reason why the middle class seems absurd: what is it in the middle of? Does it exist at all? Class is still a newish category of historical analysis in the United States, where democratic politics have been seen, practically from 1776, to make it different from all other national histories. Something of the same exceptionalism exists in Australia, where egalitarian, anti-authoritarian social attitudes were long thought to preclude class society. Nonetheless, these national frames of reference contain substantial literatures based on the analysis of class, and being a researcher in the smallest corner, I compared local conditions with overseas sources.

From the point of view of the historic house museums whose material I knew so well, connections with Britain and the United States were clear. Some furnishings were made in Australia, but the majority was British and American. The imperial agenda of supplying goods to the colonies shaped the domestic material culture of Australian life since

1788, especially in furniture, textiles, ceramics, glass and cutlery. American production strengths in machinery small and large, and domestic equipment from clocks to apple-corers, were familiar. Historic domestic assemblages in Australia featured certain characteristic localisms such as Aboriginal weapons worked into trophies and kangaroos applied as decorative motifs, but otherwise their form, character, material, arrangement and use appeared to share a great deal with middle-class material culture in Britain and the United States. Does the logic of similarity include the meanings of objects in common?

This question and its findings lead to the perspective of transnational history. Historians have taken the nation or its subsets as a basic framework of study for so long that it seems a given, and indeed, national society, economics and culture shape almost everyone's lived experience in the most mundane ways. The idea of national identity and its obverse – national difference – is so important that transnational views rattle many conventions. Yet evidence such as the similarity of household furnishings and the meanings they contained for the people who used them on far-flung continents suggests that the same history of values and practices informed middle-class societies in Britain, the United States and Australia. In the larger focus of transnationalism, the culture of the international middle class was neither 'British', 'American' nor 'Australian' but characteristic of 'Greater' Britain.

The perspective of Greater Britain is central to the subject of this book. It facilitates the argument for cultural continuities across space and time, a sticky topic to maintain because variations here and there are inevitable. It is much easier to note discrepancies than to identify the threshold of significant difference, and locating difference has had the advantage of confirming the taste for national exceptionalism, of asserting the unique character of the place where things diverge. Admitting to continuity seems to let down the spirit of the American Revolution, or to endorse the Old World values that despatched the poor and the criminal from the motherland to the antipodes.

In so far as the thesis of Greater Britain depends on the distribution of material goods, it has been criticized as representing merely the trading power of imperial Britain and commercial America, distributing (or dumping) cargoes of furniture and equipment on overseas markets for the locals to buy as they could afford and use as they needed. The critique implies that the goods have only utilitarian value and that the users are defined by their nation as necessarily different. Informed by the curatorial approach to the meanings of objects and by the transnational focus on their spheres of their use, a different conclusion emerges:

that the international trade in domestic goods was driven by demand for certain kinds of items which both enabled and expressed a common pattern of values, behaviours and beliefs: middle-class gentility.

The history of gentility is five hundred years older than the Victorian middle class, and its diffusion downwards from court society has been traced in most centuries before the nineteenth. The argument why the Victorian period merits yet another contribution to the topic is the substance of Chapter 1 of this book. Various traditions and frameworks for defining the middle class are discussed in Chapter 2, but it stresses that the identification of middle classness via cultural expression or habitus is not confined to the segment which most fully expresses the largest range of characteristics, namely the rich. The depth and complexity of Victorian genteel culture is explored in Chapter 3, showing that the new class depended profoundly on self-controlled behaviours. Adoption of some of the most characteristic values and practices is presented in Chapters 4, 5 and 6, describing the strategies and convictions that made people middle class; such adoptions also enclose people at the margins of gentility into this understanding of the middle class. This view of the middle class includes people who might have been derided for buying self-improvement handbooks; people who ate, dressed and furnished more stylishly than their betters thought they ought to; and people in provincial towns in Britain, industrial cities and republican frontiers in America and colonies in Australia and elsewhere. These perspectives identify a middle class unburdened by retro-myths of democratic egalitarianism, and a genteel culture constructed independently of the aristocracy.

It often seems to me that these topics were expressed definitively by Jane Austen and George Cruikshank, and subsequent comment is redundant. Still, I draw on their verbal and visual eloquence throughout the book, confident that both sufficiently inhabit the reader's imagination to burnish the otherwise plodding documentation of history with the bite of satire.

1
Cultural Baggage: the Genteel World

Let us begin with three drawing rooms of the 1830s–1840s, images by amateur or vernacular artists. An extended family occupies each room. Older members sit, though in a horizontal hierarchy showing the least important characters at the margins of each family and its picture. All the characters wear up-to-date clothes and hair styles; the furniture varies in fashionability. With no further information it is impossible to locate any of these images to a particular geography, other than the generalized 'European'.

Luckily, each picture has a provenance that indicates its origin. They are arranged in alphabetical order by province: England, New South Wales, New York. The first picture is by Charlotte Bosanquet, a watercolour painted in 1843, of her cousin's house, Clay Hill, at Enfield, Hertfordshire. Admiral Bosanquet was a senior naval officer, married to another Bosanquet cousin; they had three children, two shown here. Charlotte was the daughter of a London manufacturer.

The second picture is attributed to Edward Hawkins. It can be dated to 1830, give or take two years, by the extreme leg-of-mutton sleeves worn by every female in the scene. If the image shows the Hawkins family, it is probably the drawing room of Blackdown, a brick house near the inland town of Bathurst, settled and built by Thomas Hawkins in 1823, retired from the Royal Navy. Three generations are depicted: an aged mother-in-law at the right; Thomas and either his wife or daughter-in-law; four young adults and five children, of whom some proportion must be Thomas's seven offspring.

The third picture shows the silhouettes of an unidentified family, taken by Augustin Edouart, a master of the craft, in New York in 1842 and contextualized in a sketch of their drawing room. The central pair are flanked by their children and two grandmothers.

The conditions of the three images are not *quite* directly comparable, but they are notably similar.[1] The families pictured represent the inter-generational group usual before the twentieth century. The New South Wales furnishings are old fashioned for 1830; the Hertfordshire furnishings are modest; the New York equipage is comparatively rich. But a historical anthropologist would recognize each as a manifestation of the same culture.

That is the burden of this book. A new culture crystallized around the turn of the nineteenth century, defining an unprecedented middle class, identifiable throughout the Anglo world of Greater Britain in people's values, behaviours, social lives and material worlds. To become 'a better class of people' was the goal of countless eager, anxious, ever-more-aspirant individuals of the nineteenth century. They strove mightily in the ambition. They made themselves respectable through self-help. They adopted conservative values, adapted personal habits to new rules of self-presentation, acted out formal behaviours in public and in private. They shaped their lives to conform to new standards of expectation and reception. Assiduous and energetic, the early nineteenth-century middle class created itself by living the life of the middle class. In *doing*, they came to *be* middle class, making their own definitions of what was correct – for who was to say if they were or weren't?

The term 'middle class' dates to the teens of the nineteenth century, postdating 'ruling class' and predating 'working class'. The important point of this chronology turns on the concept of class, which in the twenty years either side of the turn of the nineteenth century overtook the former understanding of ranks, orders and degrees, the previous 'one class society' in whose cosmology one status system was univer-sally recognized.[2] Now people began to describe others, and indeed to call themselves, middle class, though what they meant and how they got to be that way has been argued over by sociologists and historians ever since. In the most simple telling, events in the late eighteenth/early nineteenth century either generated or differentiated an extensive and, by the time Queen Victoria ascended the throne, recognizably 'Victorian' middle class in Britain.[3] It also happened more or less simul-taneously in the United States, indicating that immediate political events were not the causal incidents of the new class formation; what both societies shared at this time were the large processes of industriali-zation, urbanization, the spread of wealth and the rise of evangelical religion. The new middle-class culture further took root in Britain's Australian colonies, established in 1788 and 1803. These were not just direct transplants, but new societies led and shaped by the rising middle class in the absence of either aristocracy or working class.

Drawing room life: a woman writes, children play.

Charlotte Bosanquet, 'Drawing Room, Clay Hall', 1843.

A family gathers to make music and conversation.
Anon, 'Interior in NSW', *c.* 1830.

Individuals pose in their finest room.

Auguste Edouart, 'A New York family in silhouette', 1842.

Boundaries to the middle class have always been difficult to define, but throughout the nineteenth century, the guardians and gatekeepers of the middle class were its own constituents. This paradox makes it clear that the middle class was not and could never be a homogeneous social bloc. Rather, the middle class was a highly stratified body composed of minutely refined layers of distinction, each stratum distinguishing its own adherents and excluding undesirables. This book shows how a corpus of values and behaviours can be employed to describe and differentiate the Victorian middle class by demonstrating its unity of aspiration and commonality of expression. Only degree, comprehensiveness or wealthier manifestation distinguished fine strata within the middle class; the totality can be identified as all those sharing the basic menu of ideals and actions.

This range of internal variations set up the hurdles of exclusive snobbery that constitute much writing about the middle class, ideas which were real enough, but were not as conclusive as many sociologists and historians think. Rather, there was always a tension in asserting and maintaining genteel status, for almost all acknowledged a stratum above their own, whether or not they expected to be admitted to it. In a society in which a constantly increasing number of people became eligible through the acquisition of discretionary money and/or education to participate, a constant struggle ensued to establish a position, to protect it from others, and perhaps to advance it without opposition: truly a conundrum of contradictory purposes. The very nature of middle classness was to better, and further better, oneself. Consequently middle-class status in the early nineteenth century was a fluid, dynamic state, always open for individuals to advance, while risking descent, and constantly contested. One attained middle-class success by acquiescence, through being acknowledged by those whom one sought to join, exemplified by, say, the events in *Pride and Prejudice* where Elizabeth Bennet's aunt and uncle Gardiner are greeted by Mr Darcy but sneered at by Mrs Hurst.[4] It was sufficient for aspirants to become middle class in the eyes of some, as long as it was the *right* some, for few were ever accorded unanimous recognition.

Distinctive middle-class structures formed the characteristic bourgeois culture, but historical understanding has been often subverted by the middle class's apparent adoption of the forms of the aristocracy: its fine table manners, ballroom pleasures and luxurious style. The stickiest step in understanding middle-class construction is to disentangle its relations with aristocratic culture, at once yearned for and yet moralized as decadent and unproductive. The imitative elements of middle-class culture are so obvious and so many that it is easy to assume the same conditions and values underpin them, but it was not the case. The imitative character of middle-class culture is a pointer to its essential drive: the urge of aspiration, of self-improvement, of upward mobility. In practice, it contained a hollow element of promise that good or at least correct behaviour would achieve the reward of higher status. In this lies the source of the dynamic structure of minutely differentiated levels of genteel practice, offering infinite possibilities to move up and up. When considered in critical retrospect, it is clear that very few individuals ever crossed the divide between middle class and aristocracy, but the promise (or the myth) of such possibility was very widely sustained. At the same time, the drive to adopt elegant standards motivated countless aspirants to improve their knowledge, social skills and income and to live ever more comfortable, genteel, middle-class lives in the process of trying.

The culture of gentility

The mechanism of demonstrating middle-class compliance was not driven by money, though certain financial resources were necessary. More critically, acceptance by peers required fluent participation in a core of beliefs and rituals. Such practice amounts to mastery of the culture, informed by possession of the cultural capital which enabled the agency of lifestyle: *gentility* is a name for the culture of the middle class. It was one term among many in contemporary use for the raft of values, beliefs and behaviours that united its practitioners and its use here does not preclude others such as respectability and refinement.[5] For the purpose of this study, gentility is taken to refer to the entire cultural system of the late eighteenth/early nineteenth century middle class, the ideology that characterized, identified and solidified it. Neither the name nor the synthesis of characteristics is in common use today, for it has lost currency, and now suggests false delicacy and exaggerated refinement. The *Oxford English Dictionary* notes: 'In seriously laudatory use [gentility] may now be said to be a vulgarism; in educated language it has always a sarcastic or at least playful colouring.' Doubt about the word surfaced early, though not consistently; Agogos ('Guide'), author of one of the most frequently reprinted advice manuals of the 1830s, *Hints on Etiquette*, recommends:

Never use the term *'genteel.'* Do not speak of *'genteel people;'* it is a low estimate of good breeding, used only by vulgar persons, and from *their* lips implies that union of finery, flippancy and affectation often found in those but one remove from 'hewers of wood and drawers of water.' Substitute 'well-bred person,' or 'manners of a gentle-woman' or of 'a gentleman' instead.[6]

[A bundle of disciplined values underpinned nineteenth-century genteel culture: self-control of the body, its desires, weaknesses and autonomic responses; self-control of the spirit and emotions; exquisitely structured control of the self in public; and control of the environment, extending from personal space to domestic shell to urban frame, carried into the country and across the sea to the colonies] Norbert Elias traces the history of these values and their expressive practices as 'the civilising process', represented by a rising threshold of the consciousness of shame in relation to others. He analyses the beginnings of genteel self-control in the power over individuals exercised by an absolute prince in the Middle Ages and progressing to an internally-sustained spirit of self-control inculcated in the young by late eighteenth-century middle-class styles of parenting.[7] For Elias's purposes, self-control was expressed in three major regions of behaviour: the control of appetite, excretion and social interaction. These controls came to be initiated by the self, but, as subsequent case studies will show, were mediated and buttressed by material goods and conventional systems such as knives and forks, handkerchiefs, chamber pots and prescribed etiquette. Some of these examples changed, and some emerged for the first time, in the sixteenth and seventeenth centuries, though faster and slower throughout Europe: the napkin, for instance, individualized the diner and separated his or her fingers from the common table and raised the social standard of cleanliness at the table.

In growing economies, [rich commoners sought to emulate the standards and practices of the court and so spread what Elias calls *civilité*] It was an elite culture, requiring possession of not only the correct appurtenances, but also the correct internalized character, learned through childhood education. As more and more people came to desire the comforts and pleasures of *civilité*, they sought to adopt its standards for themselves through self-education based on observation and imitation and on advice books published to meet their need. By the mid-eighteenth century, Britain (a late starter in the courtly culture stakes by comparison with Italy and France) contained a coherent class aspiring to what was still an essentially aristocratic code encircling the court of the king.

One reason the Victorian middle class has been found so awkward to define is its apparent dependence on the aristocracy for inspiration and legitimation, making it seem merely derivative, and in the post-Revolutionary United States, un-American. British social historians of the 1960s tended to assume that the middle class had overtaken the old nobility to become socially dominant by 1832, when the first Reform Act extended the franchise to men with more than £10 worth of property, followed in 1846 by the abolition of the Corn Laws, which curtailed the power of the great aristocratic landholders.[8] But in the 1970s came revisionist observations that the middle class had never established its own power with a political party, nor had the political power of the aristocracy ever been seriously challenged: reasons to suggest a thesis of the 'failure' of the middle class.[9] Both views become more amenable to understanding the relation of the middle class to the aristocracy in the early nineteenth century if considered in terms of its expressive culture.

For while the new middle class displayed a strong aspiration towards refined culture, it possessed the strategic flexibility to adapt its requirements to middle-class conditions. This book advances the view that in the processes of adaptation can be seen the distinctive shape of Victorian gentility, the particular character which made the turn-of-the-nineteenth-century middle class a new and different specimen from previous middling ranks. In summary, the most important constraint on the appropriation of refined culture was the absence of the wealth to afford untrammelled leisure, a prerequisite for participation in the high society of the court. [Inherited riches and rents based on land ownership had long been the means by which the aristocracy was freed from the necessity of working for an income, and leisure was therefore a key marker of rich, noble status; the opposite, the need to work, was the sign of ignobility.] The genius and novelty of the Victorian middle class was to invert this view of work and leisure, so that *not* to work became a standard of poor behaviour. As Leonore Davidoff and Catherine Hall show in *Family Fortunes*, the moral currency of personal worth became the critical measure of both the man and the woman.[10] It was a judgement that could be applied either up or down the social scale, for it condemned the idle rich as much as the feckless poor and so cast the middle class as distinctly separate from both.

At the same time, the desire to indulge in the cultivated activities enabled by a leisured life – making music, drawing and embroidery for women; hunting and shooting for men – was realized in a part-time compromise by keeping the female half of the middle-class family out of income-earning work and able to practise the idle arts of gracious living. This strategy contained the risk that women could be seen as shiftless for not working. To meet the charge, many female activities were promoted to the honourable status of work, though the tasks ranged on a scale of serious to frivolous from the work of dispensing charity to the poor, to managing the household accounts and personnel, to bringing up children, to painting fans and embroidering carpet slippers. The financial incapacity of middle-class men to maintain grouse moors and horses to ride to hunt told against them in the stakes of sheer status, but the medieval honour code as expressed in hunting was at the same time supplanted by a code of duty towards authority, family and God. The middle-class man could now find honour not only in work but also in service to ideals, but it was a bloodless vocation whose passivity smacked of emasculated energy. Later in the nineteenth century, competitive team sports came to fill the niche of honourable masculine contest, but in the early formation of middle-class gentility, even ritualized aggression was not countenanced. The prohibition on violence in any form introduced the earliest realization of the kind of civilized society that still shapes the ideal of western social standards.

The reconstruction of genteel culture by assigning new value to *work* as the substance of life and by apportioning elements of the family economy to the representational labour of keeping up appearances met the new conditions of contemporary capitalism. Genteel culture also introduced a new gendering of household work. Men went out into the public world to earn a living and make profits through daily labour in intellectual, not manual, fields. Women inhabited the private world of the home, where as domestic managers they demarcated the family's middle-class status via control of working-class servants. Women's society opened into a small world in which they performed social rituals of *civilité* to maintain honour on behalf of the family, in a world shaped by religion and philanthropy. The doctrine of separate spheres for men and women now became entrenched not only by moral imperatives about the rightness of men's and women's roles, but also by the requirements of status honour within the community.

At the same time, it can be seen that the chicken-and-egg circumstances of rising standards of living and the revolution in industrial production enabled ever more people to participate in the comforts, even luxuries, of new middle-class conditions. The evidence of forthcoming chapters shows how individuals manipulated those conditions via two mechanisms: consumption of the right goods and performance of correct standards of etiquette. The evidence exemplifies the systems of distinction constructed by etiquette and consumption, both composed of infinite units of difference. Thus choices among the immense range of possible actions in each system locate the practitioner in relation to others' choices. Such a relativist structure enabled unparalleled social mobility.

Of the two, etiquette was the purest system of difference. Etiquette had grown out of a five-hundred-year history of courtly courtesy whose original purpose had been the king's control of a potentially subversive aristocracy. But by the turn of the nineteenth century, etiquette was driven by the individual's internalized commitment to the correct construction of social relations. The semiotic potential of Victorian etiquette arose because not only did etiquette comprise a set of rules, but it also required interpretation of the rules situated in real life. Here clustered the possibilities for variation, in the decisions that directed action the right way or the wrong way. The correctness of the agent's choice could never be certain, being knowable only through its reception by peers or would-be peers. In this dialectic of actor to audience lay the dynamic of etiquette. Choice of etiquette performance was informed by possession of a degree or more of cultural capital. It could be enhanced by the right social origin, which made the native use of etiquette more natural and powerful than that of the self-taught aspirant; subtle distinctions could be drawn between natural-born or practised performances, both in contrast with the inadequacy of the unrehearsed.

The benefits of congenital skill also applied to the system of difference offered by the consumption of goods. The tremendous variety of goods available in the early nineteenth century and their range of material, colour and quality opened up a field of choices more concrete but not necessarily clearer than that of etiquette. The ownership of civilized comforts such as tablewares, furnishing textiles and furniture became available to more and more people throughout the nineteenth century, and not only at the richer end of the spectrum. Becoming democratized compared with the once exclusive privilege of the aristocracy, the field of consumer goods increasingly contained so many possibilities of choice that wealth alone was no longer the determinant of access. Knowing *which* item to acquire from among many emerged as another test of decoding the language of one's society in order to be included or to exclude others.

Class, culture and habitus

In these ways, E. P. Thompson's famous insight that the English working class was present at its own making might be applied to the almost

simultaneous manufacture of the middle class. The relationships negotiated among people were not mere expressions of class consciousness,
but actively constituted the middle class. This view contrasts with the
Marxist concept of class as a function of socio-economic relations of
labour and capital. The determinism of economic base structures over
ideology and consciousness makes it difficult to perceive the expressive
behaviour – the agency – of individuals. Hence Thompson's practical
view of class is specially apt in delineating an alternative view of the
Victorian middle class: 'something that happens' when individuals feel
a common identity between themselves; 'people who share the same
categories of interests, social experiences, traditions and value system,
who have a *disposition* to *behave* as a class.'[11] Believing like the middle
class, performing like the middle class, consuming like the middle class,
constituted agents *as* the middle class.

Kindred in meaning though very different in origin, Pierre Bourdieu's
view of social groups as difference-expressive communities further
enables conception of the middle class in cultural and representational
terms. Working in the tradition of Max Weber and Thorstein Veblen on
the use of symbolic material in social differentiation, Bourdieu demonstrates the social functions of taste on the basis that taste operates as a
class-marker, expressing a set of dispositions that generates 'meaningful
practices and meaning-giving perceptions', the constellation he names
habitus.[12] Habitus is said to mediate agency and structure, being sub-
jectively constituted but objectively observable in the similar but exclusive positions adopted by categories of people. In his most developed
exposition, Bourdieu expands on the relation of habitus to the objective world: 'The conditionings associated with a particular class of conditions produce habitus[es], . . . principles which generate and organise
practices and representations . . .', which are harmonized by material
conditions to coagulate recognizable classes of people.[13] In other words,
the choices people make in using symbolic material transposes their distinctions of taste into distinctions of class. It must be said that these
summaries of a large and complex theory do inadequate justice to
Bourdieu's thinking, but indicate the richness and utility of the idea of
habitus for this purpose. The summaries also suggest the mechanical
and tautological weakness of the notion of a structure that is both structured and structuring – yet it is a risk worth taking for its scope of the
mental and the material, the cause and its effect, the agent and the
structure.

In Bourdieu's system, the characteristic practices of classes are socially
contextualized as products of relations between habitus and field, that

is, the time and space determined by the distribution of resources. Thus the notion of habitus encompasses both the mindset that governs choice and the products of that choice, for example, not only the taste for, but also the expression of, certain spaces and furnishings in a house, garden, street or town, as well as the variety and mode of lives lived in them and the changes that occur in all these dimensions. The concept envisages resources as capital in various forms: economic capital or conventional wealth; cultural capital, essentially education, though not necessarily formal; and symbolic capital, the acknowledgement by others of individual prestige. All are mutually convertible.[14] This useful notion of the interchangeability of capital resources explains how change can occur within habituses. Applied to the formation of the Victorian middle class, economic capital could to some degree purchase cultural capital through self-education, though it often took a second generation fully to gain the symbolic capital of acknowledgement by new peers. Buying cultural capital (in the sense of superficial learning what is the right thing to do, the correct way to think and feel) has always had an unseemly aura, but the market has rarely hesitated to supply what demand requires. Hence the late eighteenth/early nineteenth-century period saw a surge of advice manuals and self-help guides for the would-be genteel, as well as a proliferation of music, dancing, drawing and elocution masters to tutor aspirants in the genteel arts. As noted above, adult learning was never as effective as learning at mother's knee, which amounted to the generational investment of cultural capital, with all the advantages of old money.

Accordingly the field of tastes can be mapped in quadrants defined by financial and cultural capital. The quarter high in both financial and cultural capital contains the wealthy, cultivated aristocracy and the quarter low in both indicates poor, ignorant peasants. The remaining quarters are occupied by the opposite states of wealth with no learning – the nouveaux riches – in the scheme of nineteenth-century gentility, the aspiring middle class; and learning with no wealth – the genteel poor. Beyond these apexes and nadirs, further permutations of culture and finance describe all tastes in between. The important insight given by the theory of habitus is to remove taste from the common-sense perception of being either a product of personal idiosyncrasy or purely a function of wealth; on the contrary, taste is as systematically defined as any of the conventions of social coherence. It is the basis 'whereby one classifies oneself and is classified by others.'[15] Acquiring, practising and maintaining the right taste in order to identify and be identified correctly was a matter of supreme self-control.

Charming and Astute Professor. – I ASSURE YOU, MRS. LUKYDYGAR, YOUR DELIGHTFUL LITTLE DAUGHTER IS A PERFECT PRODIGY.

Mrs. Lukydygar.—I DUNNO WHAT YOU MEAN BY A "PRODIGY," ME, GAMUT. THE ONLY ONE AS EVER I SEE, WAS KEP IN A BOTTLE O' SPERRITS AT A SHOW. BUT SHE DO PLAY BEAUTIFUL TO BE SURE.

Nouveau: Colonial wealth attempts to buy cultural capital – and succeeds?

Nicholas Chevalier, 'Mrs Lukydygar [lucky (gold) digger] and the music professor', *Melbourne Punch*, vol. 1 (Melbourne: 1855) p. 12.

This book applies Bourdieu's model backwards in time to the turn of the nineteenth century and its first half, to consider gentility as a pulsing, shifting field of distinctions that stretched and shrank according to the permutations of financial and cultural capital possessed by individuals. By signifying inclusion or exclusion from their sector of habitus both systems express the agent's command of cultural capital and its concomitant quantum of economic capital. The practice of both is, as Bourdieu writes, 'an act of deciphering, decoding, which presupposes practical or explicit mastery of a cipher or code.'[16]

The examples of self-controlled belief and behaviour discussed so far make a fair picture of the nature of gentility, but they can also be dissected systematically to expose its skeletal structure. Elias documents the medieval and early modern history of how the self grew to be controlled both privately in the body and emotions, and publicly in social interaction.[17] Richard L. Bushman's book *The Refinement of America* carries the theme of bodily control across the Atlantic and into the eighteenth and nineteenth centuries, as expressed in continuously more demanding attitudes towards cleanliness in housing, clothing, feeding and personal presentation, and in prescriptive standards of posture, which was subject to archetypal conflicting pressures to be both upright and yet at ease.[18] Control of the body was joined to emotional constraint in the prohibition of expressive feeling, whether negative or positive: anger was unacceptable, and so was joy. It is clear that this degree of emotional control imposed a stringent test of genteel propriety and, not surprisingly, it was the least successfully managed. Although artifice was despised as insincere formality, highly controlled social interaction was probably among the less stressful demands of all the prescriptions of gentility, for rituals of contact between people in the form of manners are fundamental structures in conducting human relationships. Nonetheless, as James Curtin shows in *Propriety and Position*, nineteenth-century etiquette was not a simple or obvious system and required constant attention and sensitivity to carry off correctly, not to mention the need for time spent in learning the rules.[19]

Drawing on Davidoff, Hall, and Bushman suggests the importance of Elias's three forms of the older *civilité* that became directly incorporated into middle-class gentility: deference to hierarchical authority, kindness towards women and other powerless groups, and piety. Deference is among the most critical characters of gentility, for it contains a notion of self-worth within a moralized power structure of people superior and inferior to one's self. Deference is easy to interpret as one of the traditional requirements of womanly behaviour. For men, the inherent shame of deference as a statement of powerlessness needed rituals such as chivalry and opportunities such as voluntary societies for doing good in order to make it palatable. The psychologist Erving Goffman analyses deference as a mode of devotion by which the agent celebrates and confirms his relationship with the subject, expressed mainly in rituals of presentation and avoidance, both of which employ a characteristic demeanour.[20] The deference of the genteel person was expressed in constant sensitivity to the status relationships of all social encounters, shaping tone, style and content. Deference is also critical to the worldview of social mobility, in recognizing a superior stratum of being to which the agent might aspire. Simultaneously, deference justifies the righteousness of the existing order. Yet deference is not self-abnegation, and therefore required a whisker-fine perception of the relative status of everyone else. The techniques by which individuals learned such sensitive information profoundly penetrated social contact in the form of small talk. At the same time, the possibility that small talk could be either important or demanding led to the pretence that it was insignificant, a fiction that solidified into mockery and condemnation in the post-Victorian, post-genteel world.

The other side of the coin of deference is charity or altruistic kindness. Charity may contain political assertions of right and responsibility in performing acts which assert status in relation to others, but it is the Christian aspect of humility and kindness in such contact which marks genteel charity. The chivalric code of protecting women, children, the halt, the lame and other species of marginal society was practised by the genteel to certain limits of tolerance, mainly demarcated by race (Irish, black, indigenous, according to circumstance), beyond which kind acts were noted as exceptional and even a bit doubtful. Another delicate line of risk haunted genteel behaviour in the fear of intruding one's self on others, with the consequence that there was always a fine line between desirable reserve and formal coldness. The potential for confusion was sometimes exploited as a means of rejecting social contact, but the difficulty of resolving the right measure created the quintessential character of the middle-class snob, another image that lives on to poison the historical reputation of Victorian gentility.

Both deference and kindness possess a variety of historical expressions in the realm of piety. The nineteenth-century middle-class expression of pious action had evangelical and revivalist roots and was significantly different in gendered practice. As Davidoff and Hall point out, the revivalist and dissenting churches endowed women with a new degree of autonomy and value, at first spiritual, but quickly taken up into the domestic and other spheres of practice; Mary Ryan shows how similar religious movements in America became associated with women's special role in middle-class formation.[21] Thus the new and characteristic 'cult of domesticity' was played out in a moral framework of Christian piety, and so was the middle-class practice of female philanthropy. Domesticity came to embrace far more than home-centred activity, through sacramental presentations of motherhood, and cross-class sacralizing practices such as household Bible-reading. The very language of domesticity borrowed the terminology of religion to describe everyday relations, special events and even furnishings: holy bonds, sacred duties, the temple of the home. For men, piety offered a status in relation to an authority even higher than the aristocracy whose presence counter-defined the middle class. God required service through discipline and duty, attentions which also served the needs of earning a living through work, thus neatly combining necessity and godliness. Masculine gentility was quintessentially pious, producing the serious, selfless man of integrity as the middle-class model.[22]

The religious agency permitted to women, especially in the dissenting churches, and the ways in which women seized and extended its possibilities, were prime sources of the undoubted improvement in female status associated with the emergence of the Victorian middle class and its genteel culture. The Christian principle that men and women are equal in the eyes of the Lord, though challenged by Biblical commands to women in their social conditions of wife and motherhood, still justified teaching girls to read so they could understand the Word, and in some congregations, justified women preaching and conducting their own ministries. Connecting this view to many studies of Victorian philanthropy shows that charity in the form of bringing religion to the straying and lost became conventionally permissible as a form of service to God. In fact, it soon proved a field of action and organization that women achieved so competently that their missions, even if bordering on the 'unsuitable', could not be gainsaid. In the mid to late nineteenth century, pious women's missions came to involve all aspects of public work, provoking some criticism for their moves into the masculine world of action, but piety and Christian purpose continued to justify female ambition and even adventure.[23]

It is not by chance that private and social life were the quintessential domains of women within the middle-class system of gentility; in these environments women undertook vitally necessary work as managers of class relations and agents of public representation of status. The traditional gendered separation of public and private life intensified in the late eighteenth/early nineteenth century period, and the separation of men's and women's spheres emerged as one of the most characteristic and defining social arrangements of the Victorian middle class. One of the accommodations made to adapt aristocratic practice to middle-class reality was the removal of women from productive work into the realm of the private home. In this way, the valorization of women as 'angels in the house' and of women's work (whether serious or trivial) connected crucially to the precepts of gentility, so that it can be seen as an essentially feminine culture. Indeed it was so in the view of some contemporaries, provoking real risk to traditional masculine identity.[24] That a woman became head of the British state at the same time was a stroke of fate whose importance to the influence of feminized culture cannot be underestimated: Victoria's struggles to maintain wifely and motherly duty while simultaneously exercising imperial authority illuminate some of the gender crises of gentility.[25]

As these graces spread in social practice, Victorian society became kinder and gentler than any before it in history, establishing many of the standards of manners and ethics valued today. This is not to deny that oppression and hypocrisy continued to blight the lives of many nineteenth-century people, or that lapses from the highest standards frustrated the vast Victorian project of social improvement, but to suggest that genteel values became the culture predominant among the most influential segment of the international Anglo population. As such, the habits and appurtenances of gentility became a model of the desire for self-improvement wherever economic opportunities offered.

Histories of gentility

Beside Norbert Elias's work, there is a small body of histories of gentility, or aspects thereof under various names. Many are histories of manners, written in chatty style more for amusement at the quaint habits of the past than as analyses of cultural meaning or change; they are, however, more or less useful repositories of evidence.[26] The history of the gentleman (incorporating the gentlewoman) is a more academic genre, usually with a British, and often a literary, orientation.[27] Two important American studies address the notion of gentility in the kind of cultural terms that inform the present work: John Kasson's *Rudeness and Civility*, and Richard Bushman's *The Refinement of America*.[28]

In codes of manners, Kasson sees statements about what people take to be their social identities, social relationships and social 'reality',

Queenly: The idea of queenliness informed middle-class women's family role, exemplified by Victoria herself, mother of nine children.

After F. X. Winterhalter, 'The Royal Family', 1846: lithograph by Alphonse Leon Noel (France: *c.* 1850).

arranged in 'dialectics of social classification'.[29] He observes changes in manners and social practice beginning in the early nineteenth century, which he associates with urbanization: new behaviours required in the urban environment, regrettably unsituated in class terms. Kasson's most interesting research into such change is his evidence that the new range of rituals of civility entered and reformed the internal self as well as permeating the external world of social interaction. This offers a unique nineteenth-century case study of Elias's focus on self-control, suggesting that the manner of easy mastery required in public could mask an anxious and conflicted identity grappling with the social changes of the move from rural or artisan employments to urban industrial or commercial life.

Bushman's immense study of 'the material world that was created to sustain genteel life' is informed by his scholarship of the eighteenth century, a perspective enabling him to trace a long history of gentility.[30] He establishes the concept of gentility as a major cultural expression on the evidence of new personal disciplines of behaviour and personal presentation, and of new controls exerted over form and decoration in buildings, gardens and town planning. From about 1790, he sees a great spread of genteel practice throughout American society, in a diluted quality he names 'vernacular gentility', or 'respectability'. However, the fetching idea of trickle-down gentility hides critical differences between the earlier and later gentilities, and these differences explain the residual problems Bushman notes as enduring contradictions.[31] If Victorian gentility is conceived as a subversion rather than an extension of the older aristocratic tradition, it can be seen to be much more accessible to the nineteenth-century working class, whom Bushman concludes were profoundly excluded by middle-class gentility. Further, the apparent disjunction of eighteenth-century gentility with religion, one of the major themes of American social history, is turned on its head through the role of evangelical piety in the formation of Victorian gentility. Lastly, the problem of a supposedly democratic, republican people rushing to adopt the lifestyle of aristocrats is resolved by understanding their desire as not for aristocracy, but for middle classness. [32]

Bushman offers a tremendous overview of the psychic and material dimensions of gentility, but in seeking its origins and effects, he is overwhelmed by a functionalist interpretation of its manifestations: that gentility came to unite (white) Americans, whatever their wealth, if they were willing to learn its precepts. This harks back to the mid-twentieth-century American discourse of consensus, in which liberal-progressivist analyses of conflicting interests in institutional history were overwhelmed by a broad, synthetic unity.[33] Class difference is a touchy category in American historiography; equally powerful traditions (though by no means all) deny its existence or, alternatively, assert it as a pervasive monoculture.[34] A better explanation for the rise of genteel values and behaviours in the United States is offered by the rise of a causal middle class.

Historians have rarely sought the culture of gentility in nineteenth-century colonial worlds because it is assumed to belong to an aristocracy who did not inhabit the extremes of empire: 'We are inclined to think of colonies as primitive and coarse and the mother country as refined and advanced from the beginning,' writes Bushman of colonial America.[35] The royal governors of Virginia before the American Revolution were unmatched in other settler colonies, where, by the turn of the nineteenth century, governors tended to be military or civil officials of new middle-class social origins. Yet the apparatus of colonial governance travelled with the governors' families, who established circles of genteel society in even the most unpromising environments, such as the penal colonies of New South Wales and Van Diemen's Land. In these extreme social conditions, elaborate rules of inclusion and exclusion developed, exemplified by the stratagems of Australia's 'pure merinos' (increasingly wealthy, land-owning sheep graziers) versus 'emancipists' (as ex-convicts preferred to be known). The tensions of status contest underlie many histories of colonial Australia, but have been taken as frames of reference only in academic work.[36]

The struggle for class

This book asserts the centrality of class in debates about gentility. More than that, it argues that, for the middle class, the aspirational forms of gentility constitute the very substance of class as experience, relationship and power.

Social theorists have found the middle class a problematic formation ever since the development of class society around the turn of the nineteenth century. Historians showed a great reluctance to engage with it until the late twentieth century. Both groups expose the gentrifying ambitions of their own, predominantly middle-class origins in a long trend of fashionable disdain for acknowledging the middle class by making it an object of research. The rise of social history elevated the study of the oppressed and exploited, and to some extent justified studies of the major exploiters – the circumstantially defined ruling class; both fields also satisfy the political sympathies of many left-liberal

academics. With neither oppressed virtue nor noble largesse or wicked-
ness to commend it, the middle class seemed absurd and hollow, especially to its own modern constituents. It was so ordinary, so normative,
that as one historian put it as late as 1991: 'the middle class comes to
be the history of nearly everything, and the phenomenon evaporates.'[37]
Such denial can be seen as a classic specimen of the power of the
aristocratic ideal in middle-class aspiration, shaping consciousness but
undermining class interest, observed since the mid-nineteenth century.[38] It may well explain the relative paucity of historical analysis of
the middle class.

Otherwise, the extent of historiographical resistance to the presence
and influence of the middle class in the nineteenth century is mysteri-
ous. Some limits follow from the tendency of scholars to frame new
work in the times and places of existing expertise, and from rare exposure to the prehistory or larger geography of topics. Still, citations and
bibliographies show that researchers are aware of a breadth of writing
which does not always seem to inform their own publications. This
could be a product of historical caution, or of fashion, but either way,
it contributes to the scarcity of middle-class studies.

Yet despite the long wishfulness of pretending the middle class didn't
exist or was not worth research, there was always an intuitive understanding that a social body of people lies between the upper class and
the bottom of the heap, however defined. Its historiographic time came
in the 1980s, when a rash of historians on both sides of the Atlantic
produced detailed studies from which substantive conclusions about the
particular nature of middle classness could be drawn. One of the first
was Mary Ryan's analysis, *Cradle of the Middle Class*, in which she traces
the formation of an American middle class through distinctive domestic values and family practices.[39] The meticulous studies by Davidoff and
Hall of middle-class people in industrializing and rural England in the
first decades of the nineteenth century demonstrate how central to the
larger stories of economic growth were kin networks in which otherwise invisible women maintained family enterprises and gave them the
credibility of genteel class. R. J. Morris's study of Leeds from 1820 to
1850 already locates his subject in this environment, pointing to distinctive forms of urban social organization that defined the middle class
by subidentification with like status-groups, political parties and religious denominations.[40] Stuart Blumin suggests that middle-class formation in the United States was specific to its urban industrial society in
the 1830s, identifying six major categories of experience as the defining sites of middle-class development at the turn of the nineteenth

century: work, consumption, residential location, formal and informal voluntary associations, and family organization and strategy.[41]

These studies employ the categories of consciousness and social organization, more or less under the influence of E. P. Thompson, to extend older, determinist views of class identity and formation. All demonstrate the presence of a self-conscious class-for-itself, maintaining and reproducing its characteristic culture within an arena of acutely self-controlled agency, via mobilization of financial capital within family and religious networks; investment in the cultural capital of the family through childhood socialization and further education; and maintenance of symbolic capital conducted in highly ritualized social interactions.

As described above, the historical category of a distinctive middle class in the United States emerged only in the last twenty years of the twentieth century, partly as a consequence of the relative absence of class analysis in American historiography.[42] Many American writers preferred to see their country as not-British, as uniquely republican and democratic, and therefore classless. Since the War of Independence is conventionally presented as an anti-royalist rebellion, the agents associated with the nobility of Britain had to be assumed to have been eliminated along with their machinery of power. Alternatively, following de Tocqueville, there is an American discourse of classlessness in which all citizens are middle class because there are few extremes of wealth and poverty.[43] This argument collapses quickly in relation to black America, and even for white society it appears to refer to a mythic pre-industrial golden age. Both views of supposed classlessness constituted blind spots, where the assumption of democratic equality in the United States hid the presence of characteristic class cultures, including a middle class complete with the characteristic apparatus of gentility. Thus, for example, Daniel Walker Howe's germinal essay, 'Victorian Culture in America', describes the conditions, connections and identity of the middle class in an inclusive sweep, all the while avoiding the name 'middle class' in favour of 'Victorian'.[44]

For different but not unrelated reasons, the middle class has been ignored or denied in the once-British colonies of Australia. Much historiographical energy was dedicated to explaining that the British middle class changed when it arrived in Australia, or indeed during the voyage out, into something different, characteristically egalitarian, and therefore not middle class.[45] In so far as recognition was acknowledged at all, the bourgeoisie tends to have been presented as small, pathetic or ludicrous.[46] Much of this dismissive tone arises from the powerful local tradition of labour history, focusing on working-class struggle as the defining dynamic of Australian history. The argument about Australian egalitarianism began to enlarge in the 1980s with studies showing emigrants' desires for social advancement which made them willing participants in the society of deference and rank.[47] But overall, it is clear that many writers preferred not to see a middle class as part of Australian colonial history.

The primal historical theorist of new societies, Louis Hartz, supports the exceptionalist views popular in both America and Australia, yet can be called on to subvert the nature of that received wisdom. Hartz describes the founding of colonies and their subsequent societies as the detachment and re-establishment of a fragment of the parent culture. Because the colonial fragment contains only a limited range of the original culture's characters, he argues that it develops differently from the parent, and the inhabitants eventually become a different people.[48] The model is grounded in the experience of groups leaving the parent culture, unified by opposition to a central authority, such as the Puritan emigration to Massachusetts: the resulting colony is highly cohesive within itself and maintains few official links with the old country. Hartz's argument suggests that without the range of oppositions contained in the entire society, the colonial fragment loses the stimulus to change and becomes conservative, even static. Its future is no longer the same as that of the original stock; it has a different potential. Accordingly, Hartz predicts that depending on the social stage at which the parent culture was abandoned, certain political styles do or do not develop in the colony.[49] Yet Hartz's model does not exclude the survival of cultural continuities in the social development of both the United States and the Australian colonies; there were certainly middle-class people among the fragments which emigrated at different times.

More than that, Jack P. Greene suggests an alternative, interactive model of the socio-cultural development of new societies.[50] He identifies an initial phase of simplifying the translated culture in order to cope with raw conditions; then, as stability emerges, the culture becomes elaborated and acculturated, thus establishing a new standard culture which is accepted and replicated. But the process is not simply linear: feeding back into all stages are further possibilities of inheriting more of the parent culture via metropolitanization (noted in the colonial United States case as re-anglicization in later generations), and of creolization born out of adaptive experience in the new location. The weakness of Greene's model is its predicate of a coherent community, unaffected by splits of class or other interest, but its recognition of the effects of further, top-up contact with the culture source is helpful. With that perspective, this book proposes the concept of gentility as a transnational culture.

Gentility as a transnational Anglo cultural system

On the historical evidence of Britain, the United States and Australia, the system of gentility can be seen as the common currency of an international, English-speaking middle class which shared a transnational identity as inhabitants of 'Greater' Britain.

The idea of Greater Britain was proposed in the 1860s as the basis of the imperial federation movement, a proto-Commonwealth of Nations (excluding the run-away United States) which never came to fruition.[51] The term was picked up in the 1970s by American historians of the colonial period, in work that traced the spread of ideas and culture in a sphere that had also been named the 'Atlantic archipelago'.[52] Simultaneously, a New Zealander, J. G. A. Pocock, called for a new 'plural' British history which would replace the concept of a monolithic parent society with that of 'an expanding zone of cultural conflict and creation', encompassing an oceanic unity of settler colonies, conquests and cultural influences.[53] Greater Britain has since received most attention from its initial advocates, American colonial specialists in the seventeenth and eighteenth centuries. There has been almost none from the native British side of the zone, which still takes the lofty Britain-centric view of the Empire, and likewise among the 'neo-Britains' of the former colonies.[54] From both sides come histories *of* the colonies and their subsequent nation-states, but few histories *with* the colonies. The habitual national frame of reference encourages historians to present British (in fact, usually English) culture as definitive, normative and central, and colonial culture as either peripheral and inferior or assertively different and national. The larger focus of a continuous, transnational Anglo culture avoids the perils of exceptionalism and opens up new understanding of some commonalties of history.

Gentility makes a fine example. It spread throughout the cultural dominion of Britain as Anglo people emigrated, willingly or unwillingly, and their offspring maintained their traditions, often depending on a continuing flow of British goods, material and cultural, to sustain the new societies.[55] Middling Anglo people became globally distributed throughout the seventeenth, eighteenth and nineteenth centuries, but despite drastic translocation, it is the argument of this book that their cultural practices remained more continuous than disrupted.[56] The middle class and its culture of values, beliefs and behaviours expressed in distinctive habituses survived, often stimulated by improved economic conditions. Even framed by the perspective of Greater Britain, this is a bold claim, inviting a multitude of qualifications. For the sake of the large argument, let us here acknowledge just three conditions of variance between Britain, the United States and the Australian colonies. In Britain, the presence of the nobility almost always kept a brake on middle-class advancement. In America, the 'peculiar institution' of the South and the increasing opposition to slavery in the North fundamentally disrupted the power bases of the middle class in each section. And in America and Australia the absence of the topmost class of the nobility, together with the opportunities offered by expanding economies, opened unprecedented doors to middle-class advancement.

The study of the transmission of intangible cultural practice is little documented in pre-twentieth-century history, though it is a staple of folklore studies. The topic received a fillip in the wake of ethnic consciousness movements of the later twentieth century, beginning with work showing how African-American cultures survived in expressive as well as attenuated forms despite the rigours of slavery.[57] Since then the whole gamut of cultures that emigrated to the United States has been documented for cultural persistence. Studies such as David Hackett Fischer's *Albion's Seed* shows how four distinctive British cultural continuities survived epochal American events including the War of Independence, even many generations after the initial migrations, concluding that the continuities of a parent culture are stronger than differences in environment.[58] In the modern world, sociological investigations document how emigrants hope, try and manage to retain the essentials of culture and lifestyle in places of new settlement.[59] In Australia, the cultural baggage of British emigration is often depicted as a 'cultural cringe', a pitiful search for confidence in the old world rather than an attempt to establish a vibrant new antipodean culture. This tabula rasa view is today reshaped by the concept of diaspora to appreciate the dual or multiple identities of migrants, and the multicultural respect for the survival of non-dominant cultures throughout the traumas of emigration – an important shift in values with implications for reinterpreting the impact of older transmissions of British culture.[60] Drawing on these examples, the principle of the survival of values and behaviours despite alterations in circumstance is central to this work.

The concept of the middle-class culture of gentility inhabiting the nineteenth-century globe has *nearly* been said many times, for at the most elementary level, it represents the cultural reach of Britain via its empire – an early specimen of cultural globalization. But the claim is not universally recognized. In Britain, though studies of the development of the nineteenth-century middle class are plentiful and informed, the cultural hegemony of gentility is masked by its connections to aristocratic values, standards which make middle-class culture seem nothing more than imitative. The classical writers on middle classdom, Asa Briggs and Harold Perkin, emphasize the middle class's connections to the work and wealth of the Industrial Revolution, necessary to fire the political movements required by the new interests, but they barely touch on social or cultural expression; nor does the recent monumental *Oxford History of the British Empire*.[61] The specialized literature on aspects of middle-class life tends to follow the materialist line that class is an economically determined formation.[62] The distortions of power make the social effect of the aristocracy in Britain blindingly all-pervasive: its style and forms were so influential in the construction of middle-class gentility that among British historians the differences between bourgeois and aristocratic culture tend to be lost to sight.

⌈A further barrier to recognizing the autonomy of nineteenth-century genteel culture is the long reach of pure snobbery, whereby the aspirational drive of the middle class was resisted with derision from on high, starting with the nobility. Indeed, to mock the would-be genteel is a stratagem of every stratum aiming to resist encroachment from below, usually in a judgement of how ill the aspirant carries off his imitative attempts. The effectiveness of this mechanism of distinguishing one's own desirable style or degree of cultural practice in contrast with lesser forms lives on as a vehicle of almost any discriminatory perspective: such are the informal devices of status gatekeeping. Even today it is de rigueur to mock the middle class, for the social conscience of the modern historian is more likely to identify with dispossessed groups at the bottom of the social scale than with aristocrat-emulators.⌋

The transnational dimensions of genteel culture may have seemed less evident to metropolitan observers and historians thanks to an imperial variation on snobbery. Among the tyrannies of the periphery is the expectation that far-flung culture must be a pale imitation, a watered-down trickle of the real thing – in a word, provincial, or, worse, colonial. If the provinces or colonies in question were small and poor, there were unlikely to be adequate financial resources to realize the full apparatus of the genteel habitus. On the other hand, prosperous provinces and colonies could enable more lavish grandeur than most could afford in the metropolis. Both views contain truth, but both miss the argument that middle-class gentility existed in a huge range of expressions, shaped more by cultural capital than by economic capital. The common element that unified the middle class wherever it lived was the desire, and some capacity, to live genteely.

The concept of global cultural flows is still young, and is predominantly used to exemplify cultural exchanges via ultra-modern instant communication technologies and post-Second World War migrations of guest-workers, refugees and travellers.[63] Views on the origins of cultural globalization differ; a major perspective observes that it is an ancient phenomenon of trade and conquest, now incomparably speeded up by telecommunications and travel technologies.[64] In this view, the European emigrations of the nineteenth century are situated at the cusp of the end of the ancient model and the beginning of the modern era. Emigrants were translated from the old world to the new by ideological persecution, the multiple ills of poverty, criminal sentencing or the restless dissatisfactions of ambition; they were transported by ever more advanced vessels and they stayed in touch with the old world by increasingly efficient communication systems. They travelled with the cultural baggage of their roots and they clung to old standards amid the stresses of making new lives in America, Australia and elsewhere. To cling is, however, an unstable posture. New circumstances induce accommodations, present opportunities, reshape previous grips. In some cases, such change bred hybrid expressions of parent cultural forms, which were condemned as bastards and used to justify the dominance of the true strain of metropolitan cultural authority, be it accent, clothing or manners. Subsequent nationalist rhetoric often seized these reshaped products and assertively named them evidence of a new cultural identity.

Yet some cultural forms remain more static than others, even, or perhaps especially, under stress. Gentility was one. Essentially conservative and exclusive, the middle-class genteel who emigrated for whatever reason had the active inducement of status protection to reproduce their former way of life. If they prospered sufficiently in the new world, they found themselves cultural leaders. People themselves fairly new to middle-class conditions, they became local models of desirable lifestyle, for thanks to higher standards of living in the republic or the colonies, genteel status became a goal for many who had been rural artisans or industrial labourers in the old country. In the new land, aspirants could buy elements of style such as a house, a carriage and a piano, which became cultural capital in the minds and hands of their children; thus the genteel habitus was translated wider in space and deeper in time. But if the gradations of genteel living were to continue to hold desirable value, the internal stability and consistency of the system had to be preserved, and without the hereditary apparatus of an aristocracy as a definitional boundary.

Gentility recognized no authoritative manifesto (though some advisory manuals claimed to be so), and in a fertile environment for new expressions of middle classness, variation in the body of knowledge and practice seems inevitable. It is therefore astonishing to survey international evidence of the two great mechanisms of gentility, consumerism and etiquette, to discover that they are, to all effects and purposes, the same. The same repertoire of parlour furniture and equipment for personal cleanliness, from fancy tables to bidets, is listed in middle-class household inventories from three continents; examples from Scotland, Delaware and New South Wales in the 1830s–40s make this point in the following chapters. At the same time, manuals published in Britain, the United States and Australia make little reference to local conditions or differences, often referring back to London or court practice. Identical books were published in local imprints, occasionally with an introduction that recognizes difference, as in the 1838 edition of the much-published *Hints on Etiquette* reprinted in Hobart: 'If the pen which produced this useful little book has stood the test of metropolitan criticism "at home", no apology can be required from the present publisher for re-printing Hints on Etiquette in Van Diemen's Land.'[65]

The reality of prescriptive literature in the arena of daily life is always questionable, but the advice books offer benchmarks of the kind used by practitioners to make judgements about other people's gentility. They can be read in the opinions of middle-class travellers, who were usually dismissive of provincial and colonial culture in the books they published back home. Typical is Fanny Trollope, who (among endless criticisms) described American women's style as 'a mixture of affectation and of shyness in their little mincing unsteady step' and called American men 'nearly all hollow chested and round shouldered'. Louisa Meredith found Australian men suffered from the same lack of physique and that 'a very large proportion of both male and female natives [Australian-born] *snuffle* dreadfully; just the same nasal twang as many Americans have.'[66] The common themes and language of this jeremiad on colonial culture mark it as a discourse of metropolitan disparagement, conducted from the point of view of gatekeepers, and anxious gatekeepers at that. Throughout their writings, Trollope and Meredith acknowledge the aspiration of the middle classes of the United States and Australia, and they express their dislike of status competition by dismissing it. But there can be no doubt that the competition was real.

This vision generates an international middle class of much larger dimensions than is usually theorized today. It is extensive not only in its global reach but in the vertical integration of its aspirants, which includes the very wealthy and cultured, the not very well-off and would-be cultured and the extremely poor but highly cultured. The difference and independence of the Anglo gentility described in this book proposes a satisfying explanation for the changes in middle-class nature and composition between the period of the late seventeenth to mid-eighteenth centuries, and the late eighteenth to early nineteenth centuries. Informed by a long-term perspective, some historians of early modern Britain and the United States trace the process of changes that erupted at the turn of the nineteenth century to origins in the late seventeenth century.[67] But most concur that the fifty years from 1780 to 1830 contain the profound disturbance in all dimensions and locations of Anglo life that altered society for the forthcoming century: witness the complex interactions of the growth of cities, industrial production and consumer spending, events bathed in the stern morality of religious revival. Responding to all these events and causally connected with them is what this work takes to be the central organizing principle of the difference from the past: the construction of the Victorian middle class and its cultural expression of gentility.

2
In between: the Problem of the Middle Class

The formation of the middle class in Britain, the United States and the Australian colonies is easier to document than to define. So many definitions have been written that some commentators conclude that the 'middle class' should be determined by self-definition as those people who considered themselves middle class and were acknowledged as such by their community, or even more simply, as a heuristic device for the purposes of history or sociology.[1] Nonetheless, doubt remains in some quarters, expressed in a continuing lament for 'the great difficulty in locating a self-referential value for the middle class.'[2] In this field of shifting interconnections and fuzzy boundaries, E. P. Thompson's view of class – that it is not a category but something which happens in human relationships, recognizable in relations between people – presents the way forward. This book analyses the expressive practices of self-control, consumption and performance to document a set of convergences which define a large but distinctive middle class.

The historiography of the middle class in Britain, the United States and British colonial sites around the globe has never been considered unitarily, and rarely comparatively. The differences in national economy, politics and society – not to mention regional variations within – are undeniably so significant that it seems risky to attempt to equate them. Can the emergence of the middle class in each of these environments be considered the same process, varying only in the timing at different locations? The large phenomena of industrialization and urbanization which fostered the growth of non-manual labour and entrepreneurial opportunity were never evenly spread through nations, let alone colonies. And yet considered as practice, by the early decades of the nineteenth century, the lived genteel experience of large numbers of people in England, Scotland, Wales, Ireland, New England, the mid-

Atlantic and southern states of America, New South Wales and Van Diemen's Land was remarkably similar. Nowhere is much conflict evident to shape a self-conscious class-for-itself, asserting its interests in competition with others; in fact, the community of shared values rose above an astonishing span of economic distinctions. Deference to those 'above' in the scale of status honour was central to the middle-class mentality even in a democracy, and so, generally, was confidence in being superior to those 'below'. The major field of status tension was inside the whole, expressed in a writhing competition to get (and stay) ahead, always at risk of sliding down a snake as much as rising via an opportune ladder. Throughout the Anglo world, knowing that one fitted in constituted what came to be condemned as the 'smug' bourgeois sense of identity.

The *Oxford English Dictionary* dates the term 'middle class' to 1812; other sources give a slightly longer chronology of use which shows it as a historical shift away from the terminology of 'ranks' and 'estates'.[3] The notion of a monolithic middle class has, however, always been regarded as inadequate, and a multitude of analyses exists proposing various subsets of the middle class. Upper and lower middle class are the most common divisions, sometimes measured by income, sometimes by occupation. Observing England in the 1840s, Marx theorized all capitalist society into just two classes: the bourgeoisie which owned the means of production and the proletariat which sold its labour. However, he acknowledged a difference between the magnate financiers and the petty bourgeoisie, whom he expected eventually to drift down into the proletariat. This division describes the common view of early nineteenth-century society as tripartite: upper or ruling class, middle class and lower or working class.[4]

Writing the history of the middle class

National traditions of history-writing, and the exceptionalist arguments made to distinguish the United States and Australia as different from the parent culture, constitute the normal framework of historiography; this is true of the middle class as much as any topic. Only with the rise of world history and interest in the history of globalization does the comparative perspective begin to identify aspects of social structure as diasporic rather than unique. In reviewing historical ideas about the middle class, then, it is important to search for similarities which have been suppressed in the search for differences, not with the aim of weaving a synthetic unity but to identify strands of motivation and

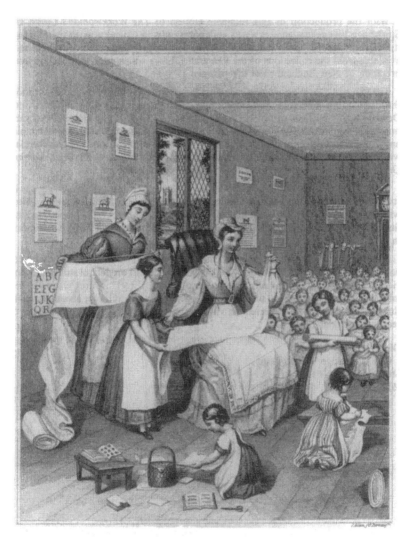

Class-conscious: Charity enabled genteel women to assert the hierarchy of middle-class power.

'She stretcheth out her hand to the Poor; She looketh well to the ways of her Household' Proverbs 31: *The Work Woman's Guide* (London: 1833), frontispiece.

expression that might be seen as a web rather than a fabric. Nonetheless, certain conditions and most chronologies of middle-class formation were different in Britain and the United States, and indeed were various within those wholes. This raises the question whether much the same processes occurred in each location but on different time scales, or whether the processes were significantly different but produced an apparently similar result. Analogous on both sides of the Atlantic, though starting somewhat earlier in Britain, were the large shifts of changing work patterns and urban growth due to industrialization, new styles of organizing the family and social networks, and unprecedented opportunities to develop relative wealth and hence consumption. Different were the political circumstances of monarchy and its aristocratic oligarchy, and the democracy established by the American Revolution. The economic situation of Americans was startlingly different to that of comparable Britons, illustrated by the extent of landholding: in 1798, nearly 50 per cent of free white men in America owned real property, as opposed to 10 per cent in England and 3 per cent in Scotland.[5] Historiographic trends have focused on each of these aspects of eighteenth and nineteenth century history, but the findings have rarely been synthesized.

Middle-class history is virtually absent in the first grand accounts of Victorian Britain written in the 1930s.[6] Thereafter came a generation of positivist analysts who constructed the history of the middle class as a drive to social dominance through political and social triumphs based on growing economic power. Until the 1960s, this view of the middle class described the rise of merchants and traders, seen as gradually supplanting the feudal order with commercial culture and flowering in the nineteenth century among manufacturers and bankers.[7] Next arrived more complex accounts, emphasizing the ideological success of the middle-class entrepreneurial spirit in contest with aristocratic power on the one hand and working-class activism on the other; this view usually argues that middle-class power continues into contemporary times.[8] These accounts present nineteenth-century British social change in terms of class formation, in which the ranks of the old order separate about 1800, transform through conflict into class society in the 1820s–40s, and thereafter jostle in constant, uneasy competition.

The new contrasts in social status are conventionally explained in three ways: inspired by industrialization and urbanization, by fear or hope of the French Revolution, or by new perspectives on common interests. Political accounts of the latter are the most frequent, exemplified by Asa Briggs's concept of the middle class as 'a class of movements', of campaigns against the old rank and order community which crystallized it into class society.[9] These discourses present distinct class-based views of the world: the ruling elite threatened by the execution of nobles in France and the rising self-consciousness of British workers; the emerging middle class recognizing a shared oppression in the tax burden of the Napoleonic Wars and a shared righteousness in the dignity of industry; and the workers experiencing both less dependence on patrons and more exploitation through the factory system. Such experiences are said to have generated a consciousness of class among the middle and working classes, though meanwhile the aristocracy continued to maintain its own ancient sense of hereditary caste. Within these broad contours of class division are many subtle gradations with elastic borders, thus enabling considerable individual mobility. At the uppermost end of the scale, upward mobility has been argued to be less than contemporary myth supposed, but at the edges of the fuzzy border between working and middle class, most opinion agrees there was substantial opportunity for 'the natural effort of every individual to better his own condition', as Adam Smith described it.[10]

This view of British middle-class power is challenged by an alternative view of middle-class 'failure' which enabled the landed aristocracy to maintain its dominant interests in the new capitalist world until at least the First World War. Two major explanations have been put forward for this argument. First, analysis of wealth throughout Britain shows a split between the commercial middle class of London and the manufacturing middle class of the north of England, undermining the possibility of united class action.[11] Second, a deep anti-commercial strand in the middle-class mentality has been identified by several writers, whereby the middle class chose aristocratic values rather than entrepreneurial ones, even at the expense of its own interest.[12] The revisionists presently hold the balance of orthodoxy in the debate about the 'success' of the British middle class, essentially on the grounds that the aristocracy continued to control political power well into the twentieth century. But from the point of view of cultural practice, this book argues that the establishment of characteristic values expressed in distinctive institutions enabled the middle class to negotiate its interests and contain its own internal conflicts in a convincing show of class solidarity – and this is the basis of the viability of making international comparisons.

The history of the middle class in America was long hobbled by a discourse of classless republican equality.[13] On the one hand, democracy was seen to produce independence, individualism and choice; on the other, vulgarity, materialism and rootlessness. A man of his time, de Tocqueville described all these characteristics in his observations of 1831, articulating a view already popular and enshrining it for the future: that the absence of aristocracy and peasantry, of extremes of wealth and poverty, of high culture and gutter ignorance, generated a mass middle class that cast the United States as a different kind of nation among all others.[14] The power of de Tocqueville's vision shaped the popular discourse of American egalitarianism well into the 1970s, when the limitations of his evidence came to be examined closely, but in the meantime, analysis of class stratification in the United States was mainly the province of sociologists.[15] The political ideal of equality became interpreted in historic practice as a society of the middling sort, a view that elided into the mid-twentieth-century 'consensus' of privatist, individualist values unifying all levels of American society. Interpreted by Louis Hartz not as a self-conscious class but as a liberal culture of the middle way, the consensus school promoted the long-standing view of the United States as bourgeois from its national inception.[16] But after the flush of optimism represented by the Jacksonian 'era of the common man', the middling sort also began to be criticized, condemned, even demonized, for its comfortable sins.[17] It was not rescued until the coming of labour historiography in the 1970s introduced the perspective of class consciousness to American history, beginning with the working class. Drawing on the surge of detailed studies of working lives and on Marxist theory via Anthony Giddens, Stuart Blumin began to publish material culminating in the first definitive explanation of the formation of the American middle class. He identifies a different and decided middle class developing in the industrializing cities in the 1820s–30s, characterized by specific forms of work, consumption, associations and family organization, which converged to form a consciousness of mutual interest.[18] Though criticized for drawing distinctions more firmly than in real life and for focusing middle classness as a local phenomenon, Blumin's work initiated and still frames the big picture of the history of the American middle class.

Elements of these ideas appeared in Australian historiography, but were constrained by the fond principle that Australians are different from their Anglo forebears, specially in the characteristics of communality and generosity, according to which all men are as good as each other if given a fair go. Despite a strong consciousness of subordinate class interests and the concomitant acknowledgement of a ruling class of varying description, the conviction that there never were many, if any, middle-class people in the early colonies is persistent from the

1930s to the 1980s; even when admitted, they are disparaged as un-Australian, 'straining after exclusiveness and gentility'.[19] John Hirst relocates this mighty effort to ignore the middle class into the argument about Australian egalitarianism, by showing that the social distinction most readily available to an emigrant on the make was that of becoming a gentleman, as determined informally by work status and income: in other words, which Hirst doesn't use, a middle class.[20] Continuing the tradition of sidestepping the m-word, but acknowledging the continuities with British social structure, Penny Russell analyses later nineteenth-century diarists' culture of feminine gentility but typically fails to problematize the idea other than as an ideological expression of the upper-class gentry.[21] It is still almost impossible to find historical studies of the Australian middle class explicitly recognized as such; they are equally rare in other former British colonies.[22]

Meanwhile, in Britain and the United States, middle-class historiography joined a similar track, with the proliferation of detailed accounts of middle-class experience, based on micro-studies of exemplary occupational segments and specimen cities. They propose that the middle class defined itself through various combinations of new and characteristic organization of religion, community and status within the context of industrialization and urbanization.[23] The concept of a discrete event named The Industrial Revolution was overtaken by a more complex history of new technologies and modes of work organization coexisting with old models in different places over a long period of time, and hence no longer viewed as decisive in the formation of either the proletarian or bourgeois conditions.[24] Nonetheless, the ripples of the new were recognized as contributing to a different kind of social environment, focused on the city. The demand for offices, factories and the accommodation of workers and managers changed the shape of towns, and the movement of people from rural work to urban industrial work altered the shape of the countryside. Different social relationships were formed by new propinquities according to class. Communities of middle-class people defined themselves with specialized activities, many grounded in religious commitment, expressed in the formation and operation of voluntary societies dedicated to particular aims: rescue of sinners, education of mechanics, improvement of water supplies, establishment of art galleries and so forth. These organizations were under no central authority but produced a network of social connections within which bourgeois culture and class consciousness flourished. Living in an urban environment enabled such activities thanks to the concentration of people and resources; the new ether nourished the new forms.

Two key texts develop the social history perspective with the important addition of women's agency. Mary Ryan's *Cradle of the Middle Class*, a study of Utica in upstate New York, shows new patterns of family organization and child-rearing producing distinctively middle-class people in a pattern to be found on both sides of the Atlantic. Utica people had participated passionately in the revivalism of the Great Awakening and again in the Second Great Awakening, fertilizing their minds with the mission to convert and improve humanity. Ryan identifies the central strategies by which the new class was constructed as limiting family size, socializing children (often with the aid of instruction manuals) into genteel habits, and extending their education and parental residence until they could form complete new family units themselves.[25] The powerful religious movements of the community and the central role of women in bringing up children focus the novel influences exercised on the formation of the middle class. Touching on similar ideas, Leonore Davidoff and Catherine Hall's *Family Fortunes* is grounded in the view that gender determined the particular shape of the English nineteenth-century middle class as much as its opportunity-seeking economics, in particular the separation of men's and women's lives into public and domestic worlds. These oppositions were unified by class consciousness and the practice of dissenting or evangelical religion, but were always stressed by the contradictions of gendered dependence and independence with religious modesty and entrepreneurial spirit.[26] Davidoff and Hall's special contribution to the study of middle-class formation is to show how women were essential participants in shaping the distinctive culture of the middle class via substantial though largely invisible labour in family businesses, investment of their own capital and networks of family support. Neither pawns nor dupes, women worked behind the scenes as managers, accountants and venture capitalists, as well as keeping up the domestic work of maintaining and reproducing the men who fronted business. Davidoff and Hall demonstrate that many middle-class women lived the stresses and risks entailed in building new enterprises, all the while keeping up bourgeois standards for the sake of public honour. In all these roles women shaped the emergent middle class as something distinct and different from other class formations, past or contemporary.

Ryan, Davidoff and Hall crested a surge of further studies of the middle class, stretching the techniques of social history applied to particular localities and, often, to particular fractions of the broader class. The highly specific products of these researches test and largely confirm the directions established by the pioneers.[27] Yet the very diversity of these studies, so variously structuring the events of middle-class formation, raises the question if and how such particularistic efforts can be synthesized. Each focuses on a geographic or occupational aspect of the middling experience, but makes regular common discoveries: the effects of family as a sphere of action; the inspiration of revivalist or evangelical religion; the communal activities of voluntary associations; and the influence, but separateness, of female agency. In case after case they affirm the presence of an assertive middle class composed of distinctive fragments: artisans transforming into small businessmen; retailers making a solo (or bigger) competence; professionals bringing formerly elite services to new clients; clerks and managers servicing the new economy created by the others. The sheer variety of such case studies leads a 1993 review of middle-class formation to conclude, as this book does, that the nineteenth-century middle class was heterogeneous and shifting, but with an integrity that justifies the concept of something more than residual in-betweenism.[28]

Meanwhile, feminist historians established a field of women's history employing gender as the fundamental category of analysis. It revised and enlarged traditional ideas about historical significance to include personal, subjective experience as well as public and political events.[29] Among them were Marxists who revised class histories to study the past through a 'doubled' view of the social order comprising not only societal structures but also psychic-sexual ones.[30] These directions transformed middle-class history with studies of the origins of sexist social structures, such as the 'cults' of true womanhood and domesticity.[31] In the United States, the early feminist accounts made causal connections between woman-centred phenomena and the development of a distinctive middle class, exemplified by the insight that the domestic ideal was integral to the consolidation of bourgeois power in the same way that men's self-identification depended on a construction of the feminine.[32] The important contribution of the feminist historians to understanding middle-class development was not to create any set of clearer boundaries to 'middle class', but to refocus the directions of study towards expressive and symbolic practice. The consequence is that the rise of the middle class can no longer be told as a story simply of politics and economics, but must now include values and beliefs, together with their social and material expressions.

The postmodernist focus on the representation of culture directs an epistemological shift away from emphasis on causes and towards an emphasis on meanings. Its reverberations are widespread but inconsistent. A few have cautioned that to reduce experience only to the meanings that shape it is to block understanding: 'in spite of the relative autonomy of cultural meanings, human subjects still make and remake the worlds of meaning in which they are suspended.'[33] This approach altered the groundwork of historical enquiries into the middle class. British writing of the 1990s on the nature and formation of the middle class engages with the notion that class may be neither as certain nor as central a category as the previous half-century of scholarship had assumed, even to the point of suggesting 'perhaps it is the case that [class's] significance has been . . . over estimated.'[34] The origins of the middle class now seem to lie much further back in time than eighteenth-century urban prosperity, reaching into the mid-seventeenth century. The 'rise' of the middle class simultaneously appears less smooth, with as many individuals slipping socially downwards to the proletariat as those becoming bourgeois over several generations of modest failure or success.[35]

With the dissolution of the old assurance that there is a bond between structure and culture and the surge of interest in theories of language and culture comes the view that reality needs to be studied as a series of overlapping and sometimes competing discourses. If language does not merely represent but actually constitutes experience, then the linguistic context in which class is inscribed must be considered. It has often been pointed out that 'class' in its many usages does not always refer to the same phenomenon: 'class' can indicate a social description, a relation to production, a political self-definition or a cultural practice. This conclusion represents the reductive absolute of postmodern relativism, sacrificing the communal for the particularistic and shaping much current historiography into micro-study. More constructive revisionism emerges from detailed studies of early nineteenth-century use of the word 'class' and its modifiers, which argue that 'class' had little fixed currency in English, but was made significant by moral and occupational descriptors. Adjectives enlarged the 'leanness' of the British three-class model of society to accommodate groups such as 'liberal' professionals, 'respectable' artisans and the 'deserving' (or 'undeserving') poor.[36] If class is taken as an insignificant category there is little support for the notion of the power of social consciousness to define social being. At this point, even the bravest investigators in this direction hesitate and tend to withdraw to a conclusion that class is simply too useful a category to lose to ambiguity or arbitrariness. Despite the low profile of the middle class in (capital P) Politics, some current work concludes that (lower case) politics is the field in which to find the special choice of representations that characterizes the middle class as something distinctive as well as real.[37]

In the broadest sense, this is the realm of culture, where expressive practice makes the point even more effectively. The following chapters show that global Anglo society in the late eighteenth/early nineteenth-century period was suffused by values and behaviours which established distinctions that are most convincingly interpreted as class. In the light of the density of the studies mentioned above, the lament that the middle class is slippery to define might be thought entirely unnecessary. But despite the insights generated by social, feminist and postmodern histories and the various perspectives they cast on the growth of a distinctive class consciousness in the late eighteenth/early nineteenth-century period, it seems inevitable that discussion of the middle class continues to be required in terms of the classes above and below it. The sandwich structure of class is such that all its parts define the others. Hence analysis of the upper-class and working-class slices continues to be important in understanding the difference of the middle-class filling.

The hierarchy of class structure

At the top of English class structure before the twentieth century was a class defined by large, hereditary landholding. Despite some seventeenth-century efforts in the South, it was never successfully transplanted to America or to the Australian colonies. Nonetheless, the familiarity of the idea of an aristocracy shaped ideas about status and the structure of society in America and the Antipodes. Yet neither then nor now are these ideas incontestably clear.

The constituents of the upper segments of British society at the turn of the nineteenth century continue to divide historical sociology. Most clearly at the pinnacle of the hierarchy is the aristocracy and, immediately below it, the gentry, whose inclusion as aristocrats on either political or economic grounds is arguable. The topmost stratum – the nobility – was effectively inaccessible to any but those born into it; indeed, its hereditary nature sustained the group's mystique as well as its stable continuity of power. Pedigree was crucial to gentry status too, but its ambit was larger, looser and more capable of self-invention than the coherent, identifiable nexus of dukes, earls, counts and marquesses, who in 1830 numbered 355.[38] Beside lineage, the aristocracy was defined by the ownership of extensive landed property. Land was the major source of their considerable financial capacity, as well as the basis of their credibility; buying land increased family status, and selling land devalued family standing. So successful was this group that at the close of the eighteenth century it could be said that all the aristocracy were great landowners, though not all great landowners were noble.[39]

The English aristocracy had effectively controlled legal and governmental power since the Glorious Revolution of 1688. By the eighteenth century the habit of authority born among them found expression in an ethic of service which at the same time usefully secured their power; service was usually undertaken within the county community as unpaid law officers such as sheriff, quarter sessions magistrate, grand juror and institutional charity manager. Also under the rubric of service, aristocratic power extended via the House of Lords to the government of the state; property qualifications in the House of Commons, required until 1858, further put landholder aristocrats at an advantage. As noted above regarding the triumph or failure of the middle class, the presence of the aristocracy in the inner councils of power, as ministers and prime minister, was very marked until the early twentieth century, though there are revisionist assessments on the effect of the embourgeoisement of nobles in government.[40]

Fairly distinctly below the aristocracy was the gentry. The top rung of the gentry constituted the barony, the lowest level of hereditary title. Following the barons came the knights, the esquires and the gentlemen, feudal terms indicating the medieval origins of these ranks. The military attributes of knights and the rest had disappeared by the fifteenth century, but their gradations still contained particular meanings well into the late nineteenth century, even though never articulated in a written constitution. Like the aristocracy, land ownership was the critical identifier of gentry rank. Possession of land implied the ownership of wealth, though the translation of real estate into cash was not necessarily a possibility. The scale of land and money resources usually defined a family's position on the social ladder, a location that could move upwards or downwards over some generations. In practice, gentry life meant undertaking civic duties at a level appropriate to wealth, usually as a magistrate or justice of the peace.

But land and money were not sufficient conditions for gentry status. Genteel consciousness, behaviour and values comprised the other half of the requirement; indeed, rather than possession of land, it was the characteristic bundle of education, values and ideas that bound the gentry together.[41] For preference, gentry status was bolstered by a claim to ancient breeding, but the latter could be dolled up out of any more or less honourable history, or even manufactured outright and approved by the College of Heralds or Burke's *Landed Gentry*. Gentility, however, had to be learned, either at mother's knee or at school, and was therefore the mark of the true-born gentry or an attribute of the second generation of aspirant gentry. Birth and gentility without wealth could enable entry to gentry status, but rarely the other way round.

By the routes of education, riches and strategic marriage, the gentry was constantly replenished from both above and below. The English system of primogeniture meant that hereditary titles passed to only one male of each generation, and estates were almost always entailed to the title. This left a pool of younger sons to make their own way in the world, typically in the professions of arms, the Church, law or even business, where (possibly with a little family help or a prudent marriage) they could live as gentlemen. Their sisters became marriage partners at both levels. Thus the younger sons and the daughters of the aristocracy provided a reservoir of aristocratic family contacts which gave a real dimension of noble contact to the daily lives of the gentry. For those who sought admission to the gentry from below, the process could take two to three generations, making money, converting it to land, living the correct style and bequeathing it to children; over the same period, social movement could also occur in the opposite direction. The only indicator of success was acceptance by county society, mediated by the women who issued invitations and made matches.[42]

Aside from the requirements of birth and genteel manners, for most of the nineteenth century the English upper class – the aristocracy and the gentry – can be distinguished in blunt terms of land and money. The yardstick of membership of the aristocracy was the capacity to support both country and city mansions, plus their concomitant establishments. This has been calculated as requiring an annual income of at least £10,000; according to the same measures, the gentry level occupied the financial territory between £10,000 and £1000, subdivided in contemporary use into the greater gentry at £3000 to £10,000 p.a., and the squires at £1000 to £3000 p.a.[43] England's only land ownership survey since the count for the 1086 Domesday Book took place in 1873 and was popularly named the New Domesday Survey; by its calculation, the aristocracy as defined above owned nearly 25 per cent of England; the greater gentry owned about 17 per cent; and the squirearchy owned some 12.5 per cent.[44] The three groups numbered respectively about 350 families, 1000 families and 10,000 families.[45]

While there was considerable aristocratic investment in the American colonies before the Revolution, there was almost no emigration. The royal governors of Virginia did not stay on after their terms, and none of the noble lords who fronted colonial developments such as Maryland actually sailed to American shores, though occasional younger sons made appearances. Nonetheless, the local taste for English aristocracy persisted among more than the Loyalist constituency, for noble standards constituted the model of status honour and desirable lifestyle among Anglo transplants in America. In the absence of a ruling class sanctioned by tradition, the effective ruling class of the colonies, grounded in successful commerce and buttressed by land-holdings, became a truly functional aristocracy, capable of asserting its power via the politics of business and of proving its credentials to rule via displays of grandeur. Clearest in the South, where the scale of a plantation, slave labour force and splendid house visibly expressed power, similar devices (minus the slaves) characterized the elites of New England and even of the Quaker Commonwealth of Pennsylvania. Financial capital purchased the trappings of cultural capital, and if its charms were stretched in the manners of new wealth-makers, it sat easily on the second generation. In new lands where society was scarce, families managing to sustain intergenerational wealth could burnish the patina of established reputation with grandsons who became tycoons themselves and daughters born to live in high style. Thus grew the famous elites of the great cities of the United States, who, by whatever means, occupied the equivalent niche of the English aristocracy, or at least the gentry, in the social ecology of America, influencing government not only through business but in elective and appointed office.[46]

This upper class formed in three eras via distinctive economics: colonial period merchants; federal period merchants, manufacturers and bankers; and late nineteenth/early twentieth-century speculators and entrepreneurs. Edward Pessen's research shows that in all three eras, a generation which made a significant fortune was the most likely to produce further fortune-makers, and that rags-to-riches careers are almost apocryphal.[47] Most wealth was accumulated by the relatively small upper class and it stayed there, thanks to the usual mechanisms of intermarriage and family cooperation. Aside from the great city houses, country estates, gardens, libraries and collections that demonstrated the taste of the elite, the American rich were notable for their sense of *noblesse oblige* (alternatively known as 'richesse oblige') in giving funds to establish civic, educational and of course religious institutions.[48] As patrons of culture they speedily provided the apparatus of scholarship and art to colonial and then Federal society, thus creating themselves as cultivated as well as rich, combining the attributes of economic and cultural capital like born aristocrats. Like their English counterparts, they maintained a tightly controlled Society network, well-established even before it was encoded in the annual city *Social Registers*.[49]

The nature of the upper class in the Australian colonies presents a confusing set of circumstances. In New South Wales and Van Diemen's Land men with no noble claims held military and civil power and acquired large landholdings. They were promoted into positions of influence far beyond that they could have exercised in England; however, they did not own the traditional cultural apparatus of the ruling class. Investigation of the social origin of governors and senior civil servants by R. S. Neale shows that though a few had noble connections, they were mainly second-generation members of the stratum he called middling: their fathers were lesser clergy, military, professionals or businessmen. For the most part they had been educated privately or at minor public schools and many of them had been either to university or the Inns of Court for higher training. In general they had to make their own way in the world and they did so either as officers in the army or navy, as government agents in colonial service or through the law.[50] They came from the burgeoning middle class of early nineteenth-century Britain with few claims to high birth but every interest in gentility. Eighty per cent of them would have been unlikely to have personal knowledge of aristocratic circles in Britain but they were products of genteel upbringings, familiar with the practice of etiquette, the values of evangelical religion and domesticity and the ethic of consumerism. In Australia, they fulfilled an aristocracy-equivalent role as the powers of the land, the holders of patronage and the leaders of society.

As well as the oligarchy of the governor and other military and civil officers in each colony or outpost, membership of the so-called 'gentry' was generally held to include the wealthy free settlers, mainly those who arrived early and acquired land and labour at favourable rates, and thus established successful pastoral enterprises. A third segment of gentry was constituted by professionals and merchants, whose arrival from the 1820s onward heralded the overtaking of the penal settlements and the establishment of civil society. The small group of ex-convicts who made fortunes and lived like gentry was a contested fraction of society, for they explicitly challenged the relationship of economic to cultural capital in the gentility stakes. Yet in the long run of intergenerational success, riches almost always overrode accidents of genealogy; it became highly impolitic to enquire publicly into the origins of colonial citizenship, though private knowledge or rumour of convict ancestry haunted some circles into the 1970s.

An imprecise and historically contingent difference marks the division between the aristocrat/gentry elite and the next group down, the middle class. Here lurked the linguistic boundary between the enduring elements of the eighteenth-century society of rank and the new sector defined in the language of class of the early nineteenth century. Many who would have been called gentry in the old order of ranks and estates found or redefined themselves in the new order of classes as middle class, albeit the upper end. As already suggested, the defining circumstance of the middle class was the need to earn an income by the individual's own labour or wits, a condition that governed the non-rentier gentry as well. Two routes were available: entrepreneurship or investment, and the form of wage labour euphemistically called salaried employment. At the successful end of enterprise and the upper reaches of salaries, income and property ownership at the old gentry level were very common in Britain and the United States, and were indeed the springboard for rare, but occasional, admission to the aristocracy.

Commentators both contemporary and modern have defined the nineteenth-century British middle class via income levels usually between about £50 p.a. and £1500, a range suggesting the vast and various possibilities of lifestyles contained in the term.[51] One of the first household advice manuals specified budgets for no less than 18 income levels from £55 to £5000 p.a.[52] Thomas Webster, in his 1844 *Encyclopedia of Domestic Economy*, specified nine divisions according to income and the number of servants kept. In the top range was the nobleman of high rank and fortune, who would need twenty or more domestics, according to the number of personal maids or men required; the middle, fifth group, with an income of £1000–1200, would employ four servants; at the bottom was the 'establishment of the ninth rate' with an income of £150–200, which could afford but one maid of all work.[53] In 1867, the actual number of people within these classifications was estimated thus: 90,000 families, just under 1.5 per cent of the population of England, had an income between £300 and £1000; 510,000 families, just over 8 per cent of the population, had an income between £100 and £300.[54] In the United States, studies of wealth distribution show that, despite being counted regularly in visitors' accounts, the numbers of millionaires claimed in the nineteenth century are notoriously unreliable, though they were certainly large, and that the ranks of assets in the hundreds of thousands of dollars were even bigger.[55]

Income is a convenient quantification of middle classness, but, as shown by the calculations of domestic advisers, a preferred shorthand for Victorian contemporaries to identify status was the possession of one or more servants. Numerous analysts since have taken the employment of servants as the critical signifier of the levels within the middle class, and indeed its lower threshold.[56] The power of the indicator springs from the truth that the labour of servants was not only functional, but also semiotic. The relationship of master or mistress to servant was a contract that respectively gave power to and removed power from the individual in anachronistically feudal ways; such power over even one servant demarcated a critical boundary of class. Significantly, this arena of class power was located in the home and was principally enacted by middle-class women, though the grandeur of a *pater familias* was enlarged by having servants in the household, constituting additional bodies to be provided for and souls to be guarded.

A family wishing to live at a nice middle-class standard of comfort and cleanliness certainly required the physical assistance of servants, especially if there were young children or invalids to be cared for. In Victorian England, a minimum of three servants was considered requisite to maintain such standards.[57] Nonetheless, many would-be middle-class families made do with less, even sacrificing material goods to keep a maid. At the most basic level of household assistance was occasional or daily help, often of a laundress for the biggest, heaviest task of household management. The live-in labour of a female 'general' was a more realistic threshold of real and symbolic service, but considerably more expensive because of the costs of board and lodging (however plain a servant's conditions) as well as a wage. The usual priority of the middle-class need for servants was first, a general; second, a housemaid or nursery maid; third, a cook. Beyond this provision of services, the age and structure of the family would determine whether a general manservant might be kept, or a coachman to service the carriage, or another maid to undertake sewing and personal attention to the ladies. Besides their real tasks of service, additional servants were much more publicly visible than the 'downstairs' staff, and as such conspicuous evidence of the style and capacity of the employer.

The importance of servants as middle-class symbols had problematic ramifications in the United States and the colonies that did not trouble Victorian society in England. Few native-born white Americans willingly chose service. In a nation of equals, how did one acquire the right to demand the servility that defined a servant? The question indicates the deferential nature of service as something more than wage labour, even straightforwardly structured in an employer–employee relationship. Advice author, A Gentleman, tried to rationalize the situation, but had to conclude: 'there is something in the mind of every man which tells him he is humiliated in doing personal service to another.'[58] Service was a specially excruciating issue in a society where servility was the characteristic of slaves, despised for their race and therefore stigmatiz-ing their kind of work.[59] To avoid the connection, service was often re-defined as 'help' in the North. Similarly despised immigrant groups such as the Irish and the Chinese were often forced into service by necessity, but the master–servant relationship of service showed that, even among free women and men, political equality could be undermined by finan-cial inequality, a constant feature of federal and ante-bellum social rela-tions in America.[60]

In the Australian colonies, the servant problem was shaped by the long absence of a servant class other than convicts or ex-convicts, whose morality was definitionally suspect and whose social origins did not ready them for middle-class standards of service.[61] Colonial ladies were torn between their needs for functional assistance and semiotic power and the conditions of convictism, such as the risk to family morality of criminal associations and the truly primitive knowledge of housekeep-ing among Irish peasants and English workhouse girls. Even when free women emigrated, they were in high demand both as servants and wives, and rapidly left one position to enter into the other. This was also the case in America, and far from unknown in Britain as well. Middle-class women's letters and memoirs all over the world are filled with a jeremiad on the subject of servants, taking the conventional form of complaints about ignorant, flighty girls and describing the awful compromise of putting up with clumsy help for the sake of being in charge of it. In some circumstances, particularly on the frontier or in the bush, many a lady was reduced to undertaking her own housework, and a few concluded that it was worth it to have the job done satisfactorily. Despite the sense of achievement in such cases, dif-ficulties with servants amounted to a major hardship of women on the periphery, entailing not only worn, red hands but also a threatened sense of status.

In the light of such vulnerability, it could be useful to look to R. S. Neale's differentiations of class on the grounds of consciousness, turning on an attitude of deference among the upper ranks of the nineteenth-century middle class and of individual self-interest among its lower levels.[62] It is an attractive theory, for rather than identifying two distinct groupings, it better articulates the duality of attitudes within the one group, the push–pull tension of deference and confidence. The deference element is a function of the desire to move up to the next step; the confidence function asserts the integrity of the current step; but both are capable of simultaneous expression. Other historians have tried to separate out subsegments of the middle class, usually with lists of characteristics which, on consideration, are essentially unexclusive. Arno J. Mayer suggests that a handful of conditions stand out to mark the special character of the lower middle class: that it engages in work that is non-manual but not very literate; that it is neither upper nor lower class; that it is self-conscious and aspirant, but fearful of sinking.[63] The middle being contingently neither upper nor lower, the only item that stands out here as a substantial difference is the degree of literacy, for aspiration and nervousness haunted almost all within the middle class. There is certainly a zone of the middle class which accommodates Mayer's apt phrase, 'the up-and-down escalator par excellence of societies that are in motion', but it is a mechanism rather than a quality or character of middle classness. On the same hunt to distinguish the petty bourgeoisie, Geoffrey Crossick and Hans-Gerhard Haupt nominate the following conditions: a focus on the family, specially expressed in a concern for privacy for women and children; a taste for localism, interpreted as the reassurance of predictability in a familiar world; and an attachment to an enterprise 'conceived in moral as much as financial terms'.[64] But again, the same characters apply neither more nor less exclusively to the rest of the middle class. The consistency of the larger set of middle-class values and practices bolsters the claim that the upper and lower, great and petty, segments of the middle class were fundamentally unified by the same set of ideas.

The nature of work is often held to be the definitive mark of middle-class status in distinction to the working class; for all that work was a virtue among the Victorian bourgeoisie, the *kind* of work was all-important. The manual/non-manual work distinction is now commonly represented by the phrases 'blue collar' and 'white collar', which, while of twentieth-century American origin, demonstrate the continuing significance of work distinctions in social categorization. The colour blue has a long European history of attachment to the clothing of menials such as servants and charity beneficiaries. The significance of the colour white is its unstained purity, proving that one who wears white does not engage in dirty work, or if he does, that he can afford to have his clothes laundered. The apotheosis of the white collar as evidence of a non-manual worker's status (admittedly before the phrase found currency) was always a little undermined by inevitable body soiling, leading to the late nineteenth-century stratagem of the detachable collar. This enabled efficient use of a shirt while keeping up the freshest of collars with a clean one every day; it became a characteristic mark of the sensitivity of nervous middle classness. The status distinction between manual and non-manual labour is older than the class distinction, but its significance carried over to become shorthand for working class and middle class.

The importance of the distinction between manual and non-manual labour reflects shifts in the economies of both Britain and the United States in the early nineteenth century. Industrialization meant not only growth in waged jobs for labourers drawn from farmwork, but also an expanding need for technical, supervisory and managerial hands. Such employees had to be literate, numerate and respectable enough to engender trust in their judgement. They might come as bright young men with the middle-class cultural capital of education and the aspiration to make money, or from the ranks of self-improvers who studied at the Mechanics Institute; both were well situated to take advantage of the industrial and commercial opportunities which boomed (and sometimes bust) in Britain, America and the colonies in the 1830s and 1840s.

Among the threats to middle-class stability was working-class consciousness and activism. A foggy territory defined by the nature of work lay between the lower reaches of the middle class and the 'labour aristocracy' of skilled artisans; it was frequently negotiated via the traditional rungs of the trade ladder that could take a man from apprentice to small master. Manual labour marked the threshold of the working class, but the distinction between blue-collar manual workers and certain white-collar salaried workers could be clearer in manners than in money. In some aspects the labour aristocracy of skilled workers conforms to Neale's model of an upper-level group with deferential attitudes that discouraged assertive behaviour such as political action and encouraged emulative behaviour such as gentility, though in other aspects it maintained a pre-capitalist character of sturdy independence.[65] In the United States context, Paul Faler identifies traditionalists and modernists among the industrial working class, the former resisting the demand for temperance and punctuality, the latter adopting the middle-class ethic of self-control.[66] In both guises, a central tenet of class identity was the virtue of productive work, which separated the respectable working class from the rough, the petty criminals and casual labourers. Work was also critical to the honourable identity of working-class manhood, shared in importance with being the head of a family.[67]

The labour aristocracy was never a large proportion of the British working class, as shown by the reach of the 1832 Reform Act, which introduced the £10 income franchise to less than one in fifty workers.[68] Among this group can be traced the emergence of the male breadwinner as an ideal, expressed in the mid- and later-century struggle for a family wage, meaning pay sufficient for a man to support a wife and

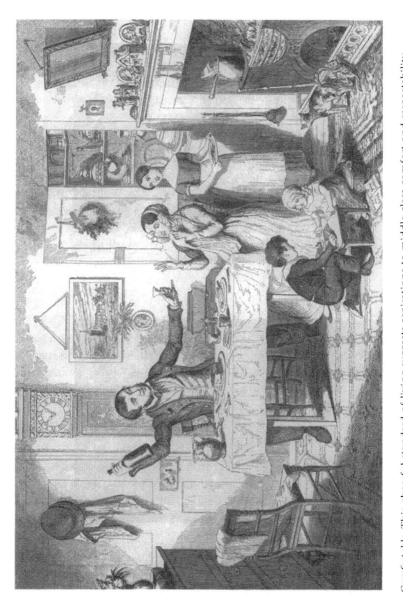

Comfortable: This cheerful standard of living suggests aspirations to middle-class comfort and respectability. George Cruikshank, 'The Bottle', pl. 1 (London: 1847).

children.[69] There was certainly an economic motive of survival in the campaign, for there are many cases of women and children competing for men's jobs with the threat of their traditionally lower wages. But the campaign for the family wage was constructed in the middle-class rhetoric of the essentially domestic nature of women and the abuse of that nature in having women at paid work. Thus alongside the ideal of the working-class male breadwinner emerged the ideal of the working-class female mother-and-housekeeper, 'regardless of her actual job commitments'.[70]

Such realities and fictions of working-class culture can be viewed as a species of gentility, here differentiated as 'respectability' (though the concept and term 'respectability' always remained a significant characteristic of middle-class gentility too).[71] Working-class respectability was characterized by attitudes about self and work grounded in the genteel value for self-respect and the dignity of productive labour; independence was its key quality, contrasted with the shame of dependence in the form of charity. Among the working class it was expressed in self-controlled behaviour, dedication to regular employment, and determined association with other respectables in spheres such as housing and leisure.

The values and practices of 'respectability' and 'gentility' are evidently similar; what then justifies distinguishing them? It is tempting to explain respectability as a trickle-down version of middle-class culture into the domain of the working class. Respectability in diluted form has sometimes been condemned as the duping of the successful working class into adopting middle-class values, a form of cultural colonization to promote ruling-class advantage.[72] However, the autonomy of working class culture vis-à-vis middle-class models can also be demonstrated, for example, in that the working-class value of independence was not the same thing as the middle-class value of individualism.[73] Subverting the whole issue are cases showing that working-class people could and did put on respectable performances if it was to their advantage.[74] There can be little doubt that respectability functioned effectively as a mechanism of class control, vividly evidenced in the contest between respectable and 'rowdy' working-class cultures, but it was also practised as a vehicle of personal confidence, group prestige and social advancement.

The presence of a mother at home became a key element of working-class respectability, increasingly important in mid to late Victorian Britain and the United States. Matched by an employed father, the practice of working-class respectability focused on the family and the home, expressed by the deployment of resources for a parlour, best clothes for Sunday, and decent (that is non-pauper) burial. The latter in particular represents the stress on economic independence in respectable working-class life, the central issue that distinguishes it from middle-class gentility. Other bourgeois values of domesticated family life may have been desired, but were subverted by the need, frequently unachievable, for a regular, sufficient income. Hence it was the most skilled, those who could rely on adequate wages, whose respectable practices constituted evidence of the aspirations to comfort and decency which made the labour aristocracy an influential vehicle of middle-class cultural penetration within the working class.[75]

Skilled workers who could command regular employment were in a promising situation to join the consumer revolution that enabled the introduction of elements of genteel living into the home. Nonetheless, most studies of working-class standards of living in both Britain and America indicate that there could have been little spare money for the trappings of gentility. In this regard, Ivy Pinchbeck shows that the wages of working women and children could make a crucial contribution to the family income, enabling a standard of living above the level of sheer survival.[76] The higher wages of factory work were available for better food and clothing, a point extended by Neil McKendrick in his observation that it was women who controlled such expenditure, and that they chose to improve their families' standard of living with goods such as cutlery, table china and bed linens, which expressed the material face of respectability.[77] Yet for all the comforts to be obtained through consumption, that other crux of middle-class status, the privatization of women into domesticity, was also sought after and often attained by working-class people, even at the cost of less consumption. As a compromise, piecework in the home (though notoriously underpaid) and taking in boarders became the means of satisfying the demand for the extra income required for genteel consumer goods while maintaining the image of respectable female domesticity. The effort to live respectably demanded a major commitment of spirit as well as resources, and the lengths to which people would go to fulfil it speak to the power of the ideal.

In the end, the only certain boundaries to middle-class status in Britain were the chance of birth that demarcated the aristocracy and the necessity of manual work that marked the working class. Only the latter existed in the United States, as long as one wasn't a slave; a free black man's aspiration to middle-class life was fundamentally constrained by the lightness of his skin colour.[78]

In between was a heterogeneous and endlessly subdivisible middle class not unified in any public sphere but sharing a body of ideas and behaviours, communicated through education, reading, the practice of religion, the practice of servant management and kinship connections. On both sides of the Atlantic, these characteristics joined together a great body of subjects and directed their action and experience in such common ways that it is feasible to call nineteenth-century Britain and the United States bourgeois-inspired societies led by the middle class.

Social mobility

The indeterminate boundaries both around and within the middle class enabled unprecedented, though not uncontrolled, social mobility. De Tocqueville marvelled over the utility of this indistinctness: '. . . everyone who drew near might think that he formed some part of it . . . and draw some distinction or profit from its power.'[79] A very few made the transition to the core of the aristocratic ruling class of England via an exclusive mechanism of mobility in the form of Society: 'a system of quasi-kinship relationships which was used to "place" mobile individuals during the period of structural differentiation fostered by industrialism and urbanisation.'[80] In response, Society enlarged and consolidated its influence as a community of status honour based on lifestyle. Older women within the status group permitted and encouraged promising individuals, invariably already wealthy, to join the old elite, thus acquiring access to networks of influence, political power and economic advantage. The genteel manners of such class-migrants were entirely adequate for their new status thanks to a shift of embourgeoisement among the ruling class in the early years of the nineteenth century. Strict morality was the essential nature of this change; its sources were liberal reform and evangelical revival. G. M. Young, one of the first historians of the Victorian era, wrote: 'by the beginning of the nineteenth century virtue was advancing on a broad, invincible front,' and by the 1830s, tolerance of aristocratic vice had disappeared among both middle-class and respectable workers.[81] The strategic need to be seen to accommodate the new morality altered patrician style: for instance, Queen Victoria adopted genteel values to separate herself from the degenerate aristocracy of her uncle's generation.[82]

Even though only a minuscule fraction of aspirants were thus promoted to the aristocracy, a huge number of middle-class people practised the same techniques, learning from etiquette books and living up to the maximum standard. In 1835, the Unitarian minister W. J. Fox preached on class and morality: 'In the middle classes we note an almost universal unfixedness of position. Every man is rising or falling, or hoping that he shall rise, or fearing that he shall sink.'[83] The field of the middle class was, in the late eighteenth/early nineteenth-century period, so much a construct of steps that it offered a huge range of possibilities for social mobility. The mechanics of the process can be suggested by extending Weber's concept of status stratification 'resting on usurpation'. In contemporary England, this meant a challenge to the aristocratic monopolization of status symbols through their appropriation by the middling order, which could and did take place in every conceivable stratum of the middle class.[84] The usurpation mechanisms of the British middle class were not violent or revolutionary but commercial and moral, which is why they were so translatable to American conditions. Status was gained by being rich enough and good enough according to certain standards, though neither strategy was sufficient in itself. The desire to become middle class, or more refined middle class, drove a vast effort of self-improvement among aspirants.

From its earliest manifestations among the middle class, the discourse of gentility contained a notion of facilitating mobility into superior society. The code claimed that genteel minds and actors could exist in any material circumstance, though in practice gentility required the resources to afford the distinctive kit of knowledge and goods with which to create the right environment and enable correct behaviour. It was a difficult project, for not only was elite refinement grounded in wealth large enough to permit leisure and luxurious consumption, but its aims and purposes were often strategically opposed to the interests of the aspiring classes. Contradictions in the appropriation of aristocratic values and practices were inevitable, and many problems remained embedded in the system of gentility throughout its long career. That they were negotiated with little damage to the integrity of the system indicates its flexibility and suitability to its constituency. Davidoff and Hall call gentility 'one of the most effective instruments for social control ever devised'.[85] This is true as an assessment of the tremendous influence of the genteel mentality among the middle class and segments of the working class, though perhaps no more true in the degree of its power than other influential social systems, especially those buttressed by religious practice.

The most outstanding expression of nineteenth-century social mobility through gentility occurred among the middle class via professionalism, sociologically described as 'a novel possibility of gaining status through work'.[86] The critical element of the professional claim to higher status was education, the site of considerable capital investment by the middle class on both sides of the Atlantic, and the source of its

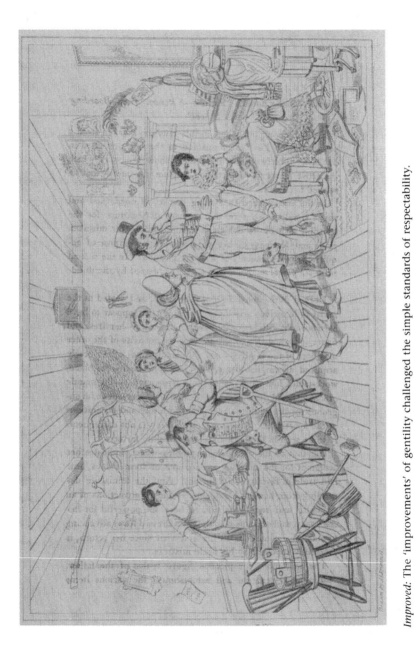

Improved: The 'improvements' of gentility challenged the simple standards of respectability.

J. L. Krimmel, 'Return from boarding school', *Analectic Magazine*, vol. 2 (Philadelphia: 1820).

professional income and authority. The original universities offered not the technical education necessary for successful mercantile or manufacturing practice, but the liberal education of a gentleman, which comprised the classics and certain branches of mathematics. Though designed for the upper classes who did not need to earn an income, a classical education contained the possibility of genteel transmogrification, thus accommodating the necessity to earn an income. Nonetheless, the kind of work which produced an income was consistently presented as acceptable only in so far as the professions could be regarded as moral callings in the service of mankind, requiring spiritual discipline and intellectual labour. Here is the root of the American history of university vocational, as opposed to classical, education, where degrees and academic titles proliferated as the means of distinguishing graduates within the classless nation.[87] Thus the gentlemanly standard grew to meet the needs of increasingly complex societies, not by dignifying the skills of 'trade' with a businessman ideal, but raising instead the professional ideal.[88] It was at this nexus of exclusive symbol and economic acquisition that the character of nineteenth-century gentility became distinctive: here the middle class actively appropriated genteel values and practices from the aristocracy to themselves, an enterprise of maintaining the outward forms of older institutions, but transforming their content.

In Britain, the natural occupations of the gentry had always been government and war, both of which required private resources and the exploitation of patronage, until the challenge of merit opened up entry by competitive examination in the 1850s.[89] Apart from these, the traditional limits of acceptable employment for genteel people had been divinity, medicine and the law. It was assumed that a classical education was sufficient guarantee of the competence to acquire the specialized techniques of these callings. Genuinely critical assessments of skill in the form of examinations (today seen as one of the marks of professional standing) were not enforced by the older professional bodies of physicians and barristers until the later part of the nineteenth century. However, examination came to play an important role in enlarging the field of genteel professions to include practitioners of the lower branches of acceptability such as surgeons and solicitors. Examination also validated the emergence of relatively new or transformed professions such as engineering and dentistry, and (with more difficulty) the arts, journalism and school-teaching. Slowly acknowledged as professions, guaranteed by examination as the moral equivalents of a classical education, the aura of genteel status spread to hitherto insignificant occupational groups. In the new British civic universities and in the United States, the objective standards implied by examinations were bolstered by increasingly rigorous student selection processes and teaching with regular textbooks, thus imposing external conditions over the privileges of birth as the prerequisite for professional accomplishment in society. In the new morality of work as the expression of the person, professional qualifications amounted to a public statement of the agent's talents, discipline and character.

The power of the professions depended on public interest in, and demand for, their expertise, but professional prestige still depended on the acquisition of wealth.[90] The new professionals established their status (and protected their turf) by self-consciously adopting both the values of gentility and its practices, in the form of ethics and etiquette combined into codes of professional conduct.[91] Codified professional credentials enabled the public to judge the integrity of practitioners, and simultaneously differentiated professionals from quacks to the business advantage of the former. Professional gentility offered palpable business advantages, an example of the nexus between the middle-class need to earn an income and middle-class status which was expressed in characteristic cultural practice. The nineteenth-century professionals constitute a unique case of middle-class advancement, adapting the learned nature of the older professionalism in line with the formation of new classes.

Other would-be middle-class agents had to make sufficient money to equip themselves with the goods which allowed them to practise the skills and manners they had to acquire from books or tutors. This was the lot of those who inhabited the dimmest borderlands of the new class structure, whom money and ambition could push upward or dash down according to circumstance and luck. Success in this sphere was mocked as the rise of 'the Gent', the small opportunist who seized the trappings and mannerisms of superior society, but whose 'futile aping of superiority inspires us with feelings of mingled contempt and amusement, when we contemplate his ridiculous pretensions to be considered "the thing." '[92] Yet at least such people had a chance to gentrify their condition. The same opportunity was held out to the working class in a play of democracy, which it is not too strong to call repressive tolerance. Since the 1830s the desire to get on in the world had been met with improving articles in the popular press, advising the cultivation of respectable moral qualities and hard-working habits. Often presented in the form of aphorisms in the almanac tradition, the advice thus offered took on the weight of common sense and religious sanction, though the values it contained were pure middle class-genteel. Addressed to the upper strata of the working class, it identified the sterling hallmarks of respectability as dignified work, reflected in steady employment; deference to superiors, indicated by knowing one's place; and self-control, specially evidenced in abstinence from alcohol.

The guru of the self-improvement movement was Samuel Smiles, author of *Self-Help*, the best-seller of nineteenth-century success literature with 250,000 copies printed in thirty years of British and international editions.[93] Smiles advocated a strategy of industry, perseverance, prudence and resolution as the route to respectability, and hence the way by which a determined man might realize a better, that is middle-class, life. His first steps in the self-improvement project had been as a gentleman-lecturer to aspiring working-class lads at their friendly society meetings in Leeds. By the time he cast his message into his famous volume of inspirational biographies and their lessons were drawn out into an explicit philosophy, the text had subtly shifted from exhortation to succeed, to a prescription for individual action to realize better conditions, an essential lesson in middle-class individualism. The promise of self-help was that the product of this programme of moral and intellectual development would be 'the true gentleman', whose qualifications depended 'not upon fashion or manners, but on moral worth, not on personal possessions, but on personal qualities.'[94] There was a genuine middle-class model for this aim: the gentleman of breeding (as opposed to birth), which allowed that learning could qualify a person in gentility. However, seen from the larger perspective of stratified society, self-made gentility was a hollow promise, for in practice morality was never a sufficient condition for genteel status. Several American studies trace the reality of working-class social mobility more as a record of 'surprising immobility' or at best 'isolated cases of spectacular success'.[95] The gap between aspiration and achievement therefore represents a considerable testament to determination and faith.

Investigating the uncertain nature of middle classness, G. S. R. Kitson Clark writes, 'the people who might be called middle class vary so widely in so many different ways that . . . any general statement . . . to include them all must be a fallacy . . . must be a delusion.' Nonetheless, he adds, 'Of course, the general expression "middle class" remained useful, as a name for a large section of society.'[96] This discussion indicates that it is more than possible to describe the middle class of the turn of the nineteenth century and its following hundred years; the writers on class cited in this chapter demonstrate a broad span in this project. What common structures or essences do they discover to define the allegedly elusive middle class? The major model has been socio-economic; Eric Hobsbawm sums up this style of analysis with the following characteristics of middle classness: no manual labour (except as recreation); possession of at least modest capital or property; employment of others, specially a servant, for wages; and not being employed for wages, except by the church or state.[97] It might be argued that these criteria merely constitute a post-hoc classification with no evidence that its categories contained lived meaning for its subjects, and to some extent this is correct. But the reduction of the social world to language, and of context to text, amounts to another form of abstraction that ultimately prohibits what Joyce Appleby and her co-critics call 'transhistorical and transcendent grounds for interpretation'.[98] Aiming to construct connections (while acknowledging differences) between meaning and experience, the model of cultural practice moves on from socio-economic reductionism while permitting ample contextualization of interpretive insight. By such means it is the objective of this book to offer a sustained analysis of middle-class formation and influence.

What it shows is that the individual characteristics identified as gentility spread wider than a middle class neatly demarcated by economics or politics, but that they still sustain a coherent identification as a measure of particular groupings. Thus middle-class gentility can be seen as distinct from aristocratic courtliness, even under some bourgeois influence, and distinct from working-class respectability. The constellation of values and behaviours that define middle-class gentility is the subject of the next chapter.

3
The Civilizing Process: the Morphology of Gentility

Prescriptions for gentility have been offered in Europe for more than five hundred years in manuals of advice, grounded in the principle of self-control, instructing the rude in the dos and don'ts of polite behaviour and the correct elements of refined living. Until the nineteenth century, specific changes in the nature of refinement were less than the degree to which refined standards came to be practised by increasing numbers of people. But though the outward forms of refinement remained the same, the internal structures of traditional courtesy were transformed in the fifty years around the turn of the nineteenth century by the processes of middle-class formation, which, riding a wave of religious revival, reformulated ideas about manliness and 'true womanhood' and generated a highly focused domestic ideology of separate spheres. The new scenarios arising from these intersections were practised in a surging environment of social contacts structured by prescriptive etiquette and by consumerist enthusiasm fuelled by rising levels of income and the new capacity for mass production. At this nexus, the Victorian middle class actively appropriated to themselves refined values and practices from the aristocracy, and established their own new and characteristic cultural system of gentility.

The individual products of the genteel system were gentlemen or gentlewomen (or ladies). The terms point back to the rank on the periphery of the English nobility which was the aspiration of those not born to it, but they also contain all the varieties of meaning encompassed by nineteenth-century use.[1] The 'gentle' root here referred to three basic forms. The first definition of a gentleman was the gentleman of birth, of noble blood, whose significance Thorstein Veblen analysed dryly as 'blood which has been ennobled by protracted contact with accumulated wealth or unbroken prerogative.'[2] The organic matter of genetic descent constituted the claim of the aristocracy to gentle status, but within even this constricted group existed a hierarchy of the origin of one's ennoblement, whether dating from the Conqueror or from a profligate like Charles II. The second character was the gentleman of wealth of his own making, always more suspect, for though he owned the key to social mobility, it did not automatically bring the knowledge to use it correctly as a gentleman. Nonetheless, riches usually guaranteed eventual acknowledgement of gentlemanly status, and truly enormous wealth tended to open access to the real aristocracy. Marking the centrality but also the ambiguity of riches, R. H. Tawney defined as a gentleman, 'a man who spends his money as a gentleman.'[3] The third type was the gentleman of good breeding: the learned, attainable status most accessible to middle-class advancement, and containing, as the following quote from the *Tatler* expresses, the slightly nervous assertion of the aspirant: 'The Appellation of Gentleman is never to be affixed to a Man's Circumstances but to his behaviour in them.'[4] The idea of the self-made gentleman of breeding contained a grain of truth, but also a grain of optimism, requiring measures of luck and good management to realize.

The French *gentil* meant 'noble' when it moved into English in the thirteenth century; it applied to the lesser classes of the aristocracy, those of gentle birth. The fully Anglicized spelling made a second migration at the end of the seventeenth century to describe the 'genteel' style of good manners. In both guises, it referred to upper-class, aristocratic values and behaviours. The English nobility was slow in adopting the new *civilité* of the Italian Renaissance, which focused on emotional and bodily control, deference to rank, and respect for and charity towards others, epitomized in Giovanni della Casa's guide of 1558, *Il Galateo*, thereafter much translated and reprinted.[5] The medieval code of chivalry as practised in England had embodied the values of deference and charity, which came to comprise the ideal of English courtly behaviour, but the polish and self-control of continental manners failed to find a receptive audience among the upper class until the Restoration period.[6] From the mid-seventeenth century the nobility began to practise continental manners and polite speech, and to express themselves in fashionable dress, comfortable furnishings and symmetrically planned houses: in short, to adopt the spectacle of refined taste. As eighteenth-century prosperity enriched the purses and minds of the gentry and the rising middle classes, they sought to emulate noble behaviour and style.[7] However, the particular circumstances of middle-class living transformed the inheritance of courtesy and *civilité* into the novel culture of Victorian gentility.

Given the elusive structure of bourgeois gentility and its class boundaries, E. P. Thompson's perspective on class as a relationship rather than a category suggests the connection between class and culture. Gentility is recognizable in its expressions among people, and from them it is possible to infer the distinctive class that practised genteel culture. For the purpose of this study, gentility is considered as grounded in self-controlled action in three spheres of life: the body, the self in society and the self in the material world. In each sphere, individual agency worked the mechanisms of etiquette and consumption to manufacture the distinctions which defined and identified the middle-class person. This chapter aims first to describe the characteristics of nineteenth-century gentility; next to consider the fields of its application in everyday life; and third, to observe the dynamics of nineteenth-century gentility in action.

Contradictions, compromises and consequences

A crucial strategy of middle-class formation was to distinguish itself from the working class below by emulating the aristocracy above. The aristocratic values and behaviours of *civilité* or courtesy were accessible to a degree determined by wealth. But they were limited by the definitive fact of middle classness: not owning the private resources to live like a lord, the middle class had to earn its own living. Despite the Biblical injunction to work by the sweat of the brow, the western tradition always contained a strand which devalued labour as evidence of poverty and powerlessness, whereas it treasured leisure as the mark of riches and power. The necessity of earning a living made it impossible to live the leisured life.

This contradiction was resolved (though never entirely comfortably) by the turn-of-the-nineteenth-century middle class via two strategies. The first was an ingenious turning on its head of traditional aristocratic values, so that work became an honourable calling and a moral necessity for the genteel person.[8] Where practice of the old courtesy required a leisured life funded from sources other than direct labour, now *not* to work became perceived as either decadent or shiftless, according to class. Among the landed aristocracy labour was despised as a sign of the absence of wealth, and so was the range of means of earning a living through business or trade (though it was always acceptable to make a fortune by almost any means). But to the new middle class, the daily grind of earning an income took on the valorized mantle of correct behaviour, conveniently integrating necessity and honour. Making a virtue of necessity, the emerging middle class ennobled work for its expression of duty, responsibility and right-mindedness: a fundamental act of class self-definition that had a major effect on the reshaping of traditional courtesy into bourgeois gentility. Work became the source of respectable identity, the measure of the man. Work had been ordained in the Old Testament as the lot of mankind, and the Biblical call to be productive was adopted into the middle-class ethic with enthusiasm. Productivity gave foundation to the new honour paid to the middle class as 'the wealth and intelligence of the country, the glory of the British name', and on the other side of the Atlantic, 'the most valuable class in any community'.[9]

The second strategy was a construction of lifestyle to counter the compromise of the first: the enabling of at least part of the family unit, in the form of a wife and children, to live a leisured life at home. A domestic wife demonstrated that the successful middle-class worker possessed the wealth to support a family of dependants, a smaller-scale echo of the conspicuous consumption of an aristocratic household equipped with a retinue of servants. But while the work ethic belonged to middle-class men, the carefully constructed leisure of middle-class women was suffused with yearning for the luxurious style of the nobility. To this end they engaged in ingenious fictions to pretend to the aristocratic life. They prohibited the topic of money-making work from conversation and attention as if it did not occupy a vital part of their lives, and they drew their own occupational exclusions among those who confessed that they (or rather their husbands) worked to make a living. The effort to live up to standards not entirely congruent with reality could induce anxieties about personal and social presentation that haunted some women's expression of the genteel habitus, imbuing it with self-doubt about doing the right thing.[10] In the field of consumption, middle-class women adopted into their lives cheaper versions of prestigious goods such as dinner services and suites of drawing room furniture. They were careful to select affordable but correct clothes with appropriate accessories, though the distinction between the fine, the fashionable and the flashy was made in the eyes of beholders as much as in the taste of the agent. The middle class met the problem of keeping up appearances bravely: they could not afford leisure on an aristocratic scale, but made it a virtue in microcosm.

This partial imitation of aristocratic living generated yet another characteristic expression of middle-class gentility, the gendered split between public and private life. Men worked in the world, women were supported in the home, and the separation of spheres underlaid the entire structure of middle-class life. The gendered division of labour had ancient roots, but in the late eighteenth/early nineteenth-century period it grew more powerful and dynamic than ever before.[11] Among its consequences, the construction of the leisured wife contained a bundle of knotty internal contradictions. Prime among them was the charge of female idleness. The professionalization of household management and child rearing into the 'science' of domestic economy resolved this problem to some extent.[12] Even the fancy handcrafts of middle-class Victorian women were named 'women's work', to dignify otherwise trivial pursuits with the honour of being work. At the same time, women undertook the representational or symbolic labour of negotiating the family's middle-class status, a project that had to remain hidden for its effects to seem natural and normal.[13] This project operated in the public sphere of social relations, where the apparent leisured butterfly represented the family name in the rituals of afternoon visiting, fashionable promenades and attendance at concerts and balls, the latter often the only events which men attended in company with their wives.

Within the private sphere of the home, middle-class women engaged a second contradiction in the shape of female frippery. Educated almost exclusively in the genteel arts of entertainment, bourgeois women were simultaneously held to be incapable of household management and excoriated for it. In the first half of the nineteenth century there is a substantial literature of conduct books directed, not at the niceties of etiquette, but at the daily business of living as a respectable woman, and there is yet another, much smaller, category detailing the hands-on how-to of housework.[14] The gap between the two types of advice book constitutes the unspeakable reality of the manual labour necessary to operate a household, the fundamental mechanism of the genteel home. The hands that laboured in the genteel cosmos belonged to a servant; the eyes that watched the servant belonged to a middle-class mistress. Precise knowledge of household tasks such as laundry and cleaning was dangerous to the genteel woman, because it contained the risk that she might know about it by the experience of necessity; yet she was regularly enjoined to understand the topics well in order to keep up effective surveillance of her servant's work. This uneasy relationship between technical knowledge and active effort was hidden from public notice, and household management was politely disregarded as the 'labour that is not labour'.[15] But it constructs the household as the site of a female form of power, apparently passive, yet crucial in establishing the discipline of serving that defined the class identity of the served.

The genteel domestic wife was situated at the fulcrum of the management of class power, her labour managerial in two senses. In the tradition of the good housekeeper, she managed economically but appropriately to the standing of her family, ensuring that servants did not steal and tradesmen delivered the correct quantity and quality of supplies. In an innovative sense, she managed servants by the discipline of surveillance to assert the new norms of middle-class dominance and working-class subservience. Here the nature of managerial knowledge had to find a balance between authority and familiarity. Newcomers to middle-class status and very young women were often nervous about taking on the authoritative role of mistress, so contrary to women's persona in other realms of experience. Further, middle-class women often had to manage workers who themselves were new to service, perhaps new to the city and new to genteel standards. In America and Australia, destinations of emigration by the desperate, Irish peasants and urban riffraff found themselves seeking employment as servants. In this context, the regular Victorian lament about the irresponsibility and untrustworthiness of servants indicates the incongruence of each party's expectations of the other. The hidden managerial work of middle-class women casts them as key agents of the symbolic capital with which the rising power of the class was consolidated, though at the cost of the pernicious myth of idle, incompetent women.

An idealized vision of female identity and purpose became influential at the same time, named in the American literature 'the cult of true womanhood', and recognizable throughout the Anglo genteelizing world. True womanhood comprised the characteristics of piety, purity, submissiveness and domesticity.[16] All were said to be inherent in female nature, an explanation which masks the degree of self-discipline contained in their expressive behaviours. Religious sensibility constructed the core of this feminine virtue, conveniently underpinning all the others, for it separated sexuality from maternity, validated female passivity and did not take women out of the home. In practice, religious faith offered women a mode of purposeful daily living, for it carried the crucial junction between godliness and the family. The ideal of spiritual love extended to family relations, and as the demarcation between men's and women's work reduced the bonds of shared business, family members connected themselves by intangible love (or by self-sacrifice or guilt). This development marked a major shift in emotional consciousness from patriarchal authority to domestic affection. It thrived on a new veneration of motherhood and gave women a concomitant power over men, expressed through intimate affection.[17] This was the substance of reformer Caroline Chisholm's prescription for the establishment of an ordered colony in New South Wales, to import 'God's police – wives and little children', proving the power of wifely goodness to inspire an environment of family life in which civic virtue might be cultivated.[18]

While true womanliness entailed social subordination, the dissenting churches promoted women to spiritual equality, a view that further raised female ethical status.[19] The gains came at the expense of increasing physical confinement and continuing subjection to male authority in almost all other spheres, but offered some women a platform, authorized by religion, for unprecedented independent action and authority. Some radical denominations permitted women to preach and minister; more commonly, the field of Christian charity offered opportunities for activities as diverse as raising money through fancywork bazaars, visiting the poor, undertaking 'fieldwork' in sinks of vice from theatres to brothels, and evangelizing in overseas missions. Middle-class women showed here that they were capable of developing complex enterprises, requiring the skills of organization, advocacy and management, and some certainly exploited the opportunity to assert a degree of power in the public world of men.[20] For most women, however, the canon of domesticity, reinforced by the ideology of true womanhood, effectively marginalized them onto pedestals whence the sexual division of labour was legitimated and genteel standards proclaimed. Overall, it seems that early nineteenth-century women capitalized on such activist opportunities as were permitted by the domestic and charitable ideals to only a small degree, but it is certain that the new ideology offered middle-class women an intellectual independence which in turn facilitated the claims to material emancipation that followed in the middle-to-late century.[21]

In a profound strategy to restructure family life and relations between the sexes, the ideology of true womanhood endowed women with an enlarged responsibility and even power and status within the 'natural' sphere of the home, whence their moral influence would spread out to the public world. New standards of privacy surrounding the family and its conduct resonated through social life in ever more constricted forms, asserting the special but highly controlled character of 'home'. Both Kant and Hegel gave philosophical formulation to the popular culture of virtuous private life, sourcing the growth of the individual to the safe garden of the private home.[22] The focus on home life developed into one of the keys to middle-class genteel identity; domesticity among women took on an influential moral character, as had work for men. In an intensification of previous practice, wife- and motherhood were affirmed to contain the essence of female godliness. The home and the activities which went on there absorbed sacred values, bolstering the ideological construction of worldly activity as crass and even sinful, of the home as a bastion of purity, and of both as firmly gender-linked. From the private haven of the home, women nurtured their children and succoured their men, who returned from the world's work weary and perhaps soiled. A morality inhabited the split between public and private life – men's and women's spheres – casting the one as tainted and the other as redeemingly pure. In the scheme of separate spheres, it required a strong soul to venture into the corruption of the world, and the ministrations of an 'angel in the house' (in the phrase of Coventry Patmore's poem) to refresh and cure it.[23] In this way the moralized home served the useful purpose of accommodating and palliating the strains of new work systems in the emergent capitalist economy.[24]

The ideals of domesticity shaped new life experiences for men, women and children by assigning them distinct and separate roles.[25] Domesticity introduced a new degree of female dependence on men by abolishing the household as the site of a cooperative work economy, and simultaneously excluding women from men's world of commercial or professional achievement. While domesticity shielded women from the risks and dangers of the world and gave them status within the sphere of home, church and polite society, it was at the cost of self-assertion in intellectual, economic and social life. Personal accounts of stultifying frustration are not uncommon, disclosing other manifestations of female repression such as 'hysteria', careers of bed-ridden illness and intense religious experience.[26] These expressions raise questions about the nature and degree of women's responsibility for the construction and application of the domestic ideal. It can be argued that women capitalized on the new kinds of moral power with which 'true womanhood' endowed them, in turn generating the sentimental culture described by Ann Douglas as the precursor of modern mass culture.[27] On the other hand is the view that the burdens of idealization imposed dire restrictions on women's capacity, that life on the pedestal of male esteem circumscribed the agency of women within thoroughly male-controlled dimensions.[28] It is clear from contemporary accounts that many middle-class women lived the domestic ideal whole-heartedly and that few critiques emerged until the 1963 publication of Betty Friedan's *The Feminine Mystique*.[29] In the long run, domesticity determined the exemplary model of female and family life for generations, well into the twentieth century and perhaps beyond. The seeds of domestic feminism grew into the issues of public feminism in the late nineteenth century, with its focus on child health and education, urban services and reform, social welfare and eugenics: soon recognized by politicians as 'women's issues'.

The family was the most crucial and intimate instrument of domesticity.[30] Marriage was the gateway to adult respectability, but by the end of the eighteenth century, its basis was transforming from strategic arrangement to a union based on romantic, sexual love, an ideal thoroughly consolidated into bourgeois ideology during the first quarter of the nineteenth century. The internal government of the family so formed was now ideally shaped by intimate affection, though consolidated by laws that abolished the concept of wifely existence on the grounds that the husband represented the interests (and assets) of both parties. Once married, the birth of children opened up the prime roles in the respectable scenario of middle-class life, fatherhood and motherhood. Becoming a father, a man took on the role of head of a family, drawing on his essential character of virility, a transformation described by Dr William Acton as linking sexual potency with social organization: '[Virility's] existence . . . seems necessary to give man that consciousness of his dignity, of his character as head and ruler, and of his importance, which is absolutely essential to the well being of the family, and through it, of society itself.'[31] The first subject in the hierarchy of the middle-class family was the wife, who, according to the ideals of married love, took on the subordinate position willingly and realized herself through maternity.

The children she produced received more focused attention for longer than ever before in history, nurtured as individuals living in an essentialist world of innocence and purity, literally defined as childlike. More or less excised from the puritan tradition of original sin, early nineteenth-century middle-class children were closely monitored by their parents to protect their innocence as they grew into right-minded adults. Self-control was the key structure of the new psyche, driven by precept, lesson, guilt and terror. The model of parental behaviour offered the surest transfer of middle-class cultural standards and practices, aided by formal instruction from teachers. The early nineteenth-century growth of schools, separate for girls and boys, equipped the child with a new distinction of knowledge. Classics and, later, literature, together with some foreign languages, defined this asset; it could be desirably extended with a certain quantity (short of academic specialization) of philosophy, history and botany. Such topics were famously useless in most practical senses, but they were functional within the system of gentility in providing a common resource of cultural refer-

MARRIED.

Loving: The domestication of ideal manhood introduced a new vision of family life.

Nathaniel Currier, 'Married', Currier & Ives (New York: *c.* 1840).

ences and a shared mode of thinking. More importantly in the struggle for class, they constituted a distinction which was very difficult to emulate without putting in the years of study it actually took to acquire. The availability of education further enabled the spread of polite manners and refined expectations. Whether a great public school inculcating a classical education, or a young ladies' academy of elegant embroidery and singing, or a Sunday school rehearsing Biblical texts, the academic guise of education functioned as the vehicle as much as the substance of cultural fluency.[32] Teachers have always been the agents of transmission of cultural capital – the leading values of a society and its modes of practising them. The production of ladies and gentlemen was a major, if not central, purpose of the entire range of Victorian education. Even among those who construed this aim as frivolous, such as the serious evangelicals, or unproductive, as many commercial men believed, the standards of gentility still constituted the dominant ethical character of education.

At the same time, a vast new advisory literature became available for parents and teachers to educate the young in correct behaviour. Religious prescription always maintained a disciplinary role, but the core technique of the middle-class moral education of children became the construction of a web of guilt-inducing self-consciousness grounded in the threat of the withdrawal of maternal love. This threat replaced some of the terrors of religion and transformed the nature of personal experience.[33] Thus the middle-class Victorian child grew into a self-regulated adult, internally equipped with the battery of standards and practices that comprised the cultural capital to enable capable autonomy.

Enclosed in the home and subject to the loving attention of a mother, children justified and fulfilled the prescriptive necessity of idealized domesticity. Children remained dependent on the family for unprecedentedly long periods, well into the liminal state of young adulthood, occupied by an extended, often costly, education. Dependence could last for some years thereafter, while young men began to establish the careers that would enable them to marry and young women took on a genteel apprentice-like relation to their mothers in household management, waiting for their own careers of marriage. The expense of rearing a family at middle-class standards was substantial. An income had to provide not only for family members but also for servants, including tutors and governesses, plus the equipment they all needed to express or carry out their duties. Apart from the necessities of food and accommodation, this included symbolic goods such as a piano, a carriage and travel for pleasure. When male children finished school, they required support at university or while training with a businessman or professional; young women required the costs of a social life to expose them on the marriage market. The rising number of people aspiring to live in middling decency on limited incomes learned to pare down expenditure, but the irreducible minimum required a servant and appropriate accommodation.[34] Such costs delayed marriage for men, though not necessarily for women. The expense of maintaining a family also appears to have induced the growth of birth control practices, knowledge of which spread through publications in the 1830s, though a middle-class decline in fertility did not become apparent until the 1860s.[35] Paradoxically, despite the new power of emotional tenderness in the family, the private life and personal growth of middle-class people was tightly controlled by conventional circumstances, and often managed by analogy with the effective investment of economic resources to produce quality products.

Equally influential on the large scale of middle-class ideology was the continuing vigour of the dissenting churches and the evangelical revival in England, and in America the Second Great Awakening, all of which shared many beliefs.[36] Here was the source of the moralization of the middle class. Leonore Davidoff and Catherine Hall identify three aspects of dissenting and fundamentalist religion that made it so appealing to the new class formation: it offered individual identity; it offered community; and it gave confidence to know right from wrong, how to behave.[37] These firm directions enabled the new middle class to negotiate the insecurities and risks of the shift to the city, the challenge of different kinds of jobs, and contact with unknown people. As they struggled to distinguish themselves from the working class in a niche that was still worthy vis-à-vis the aristocracy, the varieties of Protestantism that stressed patience, diligence and perseverance contained obvious attractions. Central to the theology of revivalism was the concept of individual responsibility, replacing the old piety with new convictions of personal morality expressed in adherence to discipline in all aspects of daily life. In general, evangelical belief focused on the need for redemption from original sin, seeing obedience as the route towards holiness and conversion as the critical act by which the broken contract between man and God could be restored.[38]

The life of those who followed these precepts was realized principally in the social structure of the family and in public commitment to philanthropy. Among the converted, fathers were empowered to reign as unchallenged heads of family conduct, with submissive wives, obedient children and humble servants, all of whose behaviour was strictly enjoined and monitored. Departures from acceptable standards were punished with guilt inspired by the loss of religious community. Parenthood was accepted as a mission to bring up God-fearing children, whose essential lessons in self-control were also promoted by recourse to the external disciplinary apparatus of religion and patriarchal authority.[39] The public responsibility of evangelicals was to take the Lord's word to the world, reforming the vicious, rescuing the fallen and converting the heathen, but in contrast to the dissenting churches, these activities were predominantly undertaken by men. For all its extremes, the evangelical 'serious' mode of life offered an ethic for the emerging middle class to cultivate the values of respectability, conformity and duty, ideas which occupied the high ground of Victorian ideology.

For men, this involved a redefinition of behaviour based less on honour and more on duty.[40] Still excluded from political power, commercial and professional men could find status in religious faith and the conviction that God's work is a man's work. The practice of religion gave middle-class men a sense of self-respect and respectability and the roles of *pater familias* and moral reformer enabled a satisfying personal authority. At the same time, the image of the submissive Christian rubbed uneasily with traditional modes of masculinity, for in addition to a positive value on celibacy (or at least continence), some of the more demanding expressions of faith came dangerously close to effeminacy. Here the chivalrous aspect of the concept of the gentleman offered a means of combining masculinity with morality, bolstered by the enormous popularity of Walter Scott's *Ivanhoe* novels and the personal prestige of Prince Albert, the practical but idealistic model of bourgeois chivalry. In the 1840s–50s a highly focused movement arose cultivating the concept of 'Christian Manliness' to connect spirituality and physical prowess via heroes such as Major General Havelock of the Indian Mutiny and Captain Hedley Vicars of Crimea.[41] The same ethos was presented in the novels of Charles Kingsley, in *Westward Ho!* and *The Water Babies*, and Thomas Hughes in *Tom Brown's School Days*, in which a vigorous, liberal Christianity expressed by manly enthusiasm was justified in the name of God. It engendered the late nineteenth-century phenomenon of 'muscular Christianity', inculcated among middle-class schoolboys through what grew into the cult of games. By the turn of the twentieth century, commitment to competitive sport had replaced the faith of religion, producing an entirely new kind of sports-loving manhood.[42]

Mind over body

Through the disciplines of self-control, whether voluntary, learned or imposed, came an ethic of self-improvement, regarded in moralizing terms as a journey out of wilfulness into civilization.[43] It was the socializing journey of the child into adulthood, but it was also the journey of the self-conscious counting house clerk or tradesman's wife into refined values and practice. It was grounded in asserting the mastery of mind over body.

Self-control touched a multitude of personal characteristics and behaviours, beginning with the body itself. The genteel demand for personal cleanliness spread throughout the nineteenth century from the visible body – face and hands – to the entire, though hidden, body, with the fastidious middle class forging the way.[44] Bathing demanded a whole new apparatus: at a minimum, a shallow tin bath and a sponge (soap was long thought too drying-out for regular use), or, moving up the scale of elaborate equipment, a full body bath or shower bath. All types necessitated labour to heat water, deliver it and dispose of it, deploying servant resources or requiring the installation of expensive fixed plumbing, itself based on a whole public infrastructure of water supply and drains. The discipline of cleanliness further identified particular bodily elements such as teeth and hair, which had long been treated with traditional remedies, but now generated new manufactures to service them in the form of toothbrushes and hairbrushes, dentifrices and hair creams. The clean body demanded to be dressed in clean clothes, facilitated by investment in large quantities of white cotton underclothes, changed and laundered regularly. A fresh white edge of cloth peeping out at neck, cuff or hem might contain an erotic message, but it also indicated the respectable self-control of cleanliness.

The self-controlled body was further subject to the disciplines of upright posture and graceful carriage. Self-improvement meant avoiding the stooped posture of the labourer as well as the lounging posture of the layabout.[45] A genteel person must stand and sit erect to demonstrate moral backbone as much as a naturally strong spine, which was in any case, assisted or even coerced by tight clothing and underclothing designed to show off the upright torso. Knobbly joints and nether limbs came to be well draped by the fashions of the 1830s and thereafter, when trousers replaced figure-hugging pantaloons and skirts billowed over multiple petticoats in contrast to the earlier slim, neoclassical style. Calm, highly controlled movement constituted the kinetic ideal for the genteel person. This was a specially difficult constraint on energetic children, for whom lessons in dancing were prescribed as an education in holding the body and moving it with grace, as well as training in the major social entertainment of the century. Advice books invariably noted that uncontrolled ticks, habitual repetitive gestures and abrupt movements were specially to be quelled. Into this class also fell sneezing, coughing and blowing the nose. If unfortunate necessity induced such an act, it must be accomplished as quietly and discreetly as possible, with the aid of a clean handkerchief.

Among the severest tests of bodily self-control was eating in public.[46] Native greedy tastes and the instinct to gobble have had to be educated out of every generation of children; the task was that much harder with self-improving adults, even when highly motivated. Nineteenth-century gentility generated an explosive growth in rules and equipment to govern manners whose high point to date had been the sixteenth-century invention of the fork to separate the diner from his food and the napkin to keep his lips and fingers clean. Far beyond these basics, the Victorian repertoire of table manners and its cast of cutlery simultaneously enabled and required diners to structure their eating into ever more discrete parcels and to ritualize it with many steps. Failure to meet the standards identified and condemned any ignorant imposter. Thus did dining create a hurdle of anxiety on a field of performance, where the tactic of nonchalance was to delay one's own action under cover of assisting the neighbouring diner until certain of the right thing to do.

Discipline of the emotions through concealment of feeling was integral to gentility: ideally, no passionate feeling should disturb the even tenor of social intercourse.[47] The topic that most concerned the writers of advisory literature was anger; hence they recommended that arguments and contentious topics should be avoided at all costs, for the loss of control expressed in anger constituted a loss of self-possession, failure in the test of genteel standards. Overt manifestations of affection and even laughter were likewise advised against, and the behavioural prescriptions for the genteel person came rapidly to be expressed in the language of calm dignity. Specially difficult for modern people to appreciate, the apparent coolness of many middle-class accounts of moments of extreme emotion such as risk or joy point up the high degree of self-consciousness required to be genteel. The rigorous control of emotion was not merely for polite show, but had strategic ends in always presenting the agent as calm and reliable, the kind of person whom one could trust and do business with. In a world of flux where old kin and social networks could no longer vouch for all with whom one came in contact, a self-assured and self-controlled manner amounted to a respectable middle-class credential. The weakness in this logic of appearances was the possibility of dissimulation, which offered the dramatic motive of many a nineteenth-century novel where a smooth young man turns out to be a cad.[48]

A further aspect of the regulated self was marked by acceptance of increased awareness of time measurement and the widening span of its applications. Beginning with the medieval ordering of religious practice, time, motion and human action grew more structured and disciplined until everyday life itself seemed naturally ordered.[49] The precision and responsibility of being in and on time suited the well-regulated psyche of the middle class for whom work was a virtue. It found a domestic niche in the discipline of domestic behaviour such as mealtimes and visiting hours, demonstrated in the growing presence of clocks in the hall, drawing room and kitchen. Both children and servants were inducted into middle-class habits through the control of time by clocks, whose daily or weekly winding was often practised by the Victorian husband as a ritual of family order. Possession of a tall clock was a sign of the a well-ordered home, and a pocket watch was a mark of respectability for both men and women. Besides, both were fairly expensive items, opening possibilities for the conspicuous display of wealth as well as gentility.

The well-mannered society

The high degree of self-consciously controlled behaviour that comprised Victorian etiquette was a stratagem of power through inclusion and exclusion. It worked because the moral economy of etiquette conducted its exchanges in the currency of learned culture and not in money. Confidence based on the individual's sense of superiority or inferiority made the practice of manners critical to personal identity, for the successful genteel performance constituted the evidence of his or her claim to recognition by peers. Here lay a crucial dilemma of middle-class gentility: the discourse of advice manuals and novels made it clear that gentility was a state of mind which had to be lived at every moment, had to be, in fact, one's natural self. The ideal contained one of the original formulations of polite character, the concept of *sprezzatura* – ease and nonchalance in every social situation – as described by Baldassare Castiglione in the 1528 courtesy book, *The Book of the Courtier*.[50] The easy style represented the opposite of pomposity; it reflected confidence and a degree of self-respect which could be deferential without being self-abasing. This kind of gentlemanly independence made gentility an attractive stance for self-made men and reached down the ranks to inspire working-class ambition, yet such smooth confidence could be hard to achieve. Pretending, by putting on manners for company, or turning it on or off in the form of dressing up for particular occasions, belied the claim to true gentility, and such behaviour was interpreted as insincerity and mocked or condemned.

The mastery of gentility was expressed in public performance, guided by internal rules as a complex system of manners. These became the substance of a tide of conduct and etiquette books from the late eighteenth century on, directed overwhelmingly to the rising middle class.[51] The major segment of genteel manners as expressed in nineteenth-century etiquette was the modern application of the ancient courtly values of deference to superior rank and polite but determined assertion to inferiors. Permeated by middle-class commitment to the Christian virtues of humility and kindness, they were translated into precisely focused behaviours such as reserve and tact, which governed social contact upwards, outwards and downwards on the social scale. These, at least, were the ideals presented in the prescriptive and advisory literature, whose limits in reality must be taken with the proverbial grain of salt. Nonetheless, they contain a stable core of ideas and behaviours that inscribe them as a particular discourse of genteel standards. Further, to have survived in a brimming market for self-improvement, the structures of genteel practice they outline must be assumed to have been fundamentally credible to the readers who aspired to their recommendations.

Nineteenth-century etiquette as codified in the advice literature was profoundly hierarchical. Adherence to the rank-ordered society of England was never challenged by the genteel middle classes, who in their contradictory desire for noble connections, expressed the essential non-nobility of their situation. The anxiety of mastering this delicate condition is exemplified by Jane Austen's character Sir William Lucas: formerly in trade, he was knighted while mayor of Meryton-town and having retired to enjoy his rank, he added courtly polish to his own 'inoffensive, friendly and obliging' nature. Yet 'in spite of having been at St James's', when meeting the great aristocrat, Lady Catherine de Bourgh, he 'was so completely awed by the grandeur surrounding him that he had just courage enough to make a very low bow and take his seat without saying a word'.[52] Despite detailed instructions, no etiquette book could strengthen a faint heart.[53]

Seemingly irrelevant, the English court standard was often referred to in American advice books as the touchstone of correctness. The question of whether there could or should be republican manners suitable for living in a democracy received little attention until the 1830s, fifty years after the Revolution that created the equality of all citizens before the law. Even then, the problem was dealt with either by assertion, as in the production of *The American Chesterfield*, which abstracted maxims from the original letters, or by brutal acknowledgement of incompatibility: 'None are excluded from the highest councils of the land, but it does not follow that all can enter into the highest ranks of society.'[54] Political equality could not connect the social distinctions of money or of cultural capital. C. Dallett Hemphill argues that in these circumstances Americans used manners as a polite charade to disguise their enthusiastic pursuit of economic opportunity.[55] Though the practice of etiquette was indeed a highly codified performance, the suggestion that it was entirely cynical fails to recognize the dynamic of habitus. The middle-class habitus, in all its fine divisions, evidently absorbed the concept of political equality without disturbing the distinctions formed by knowledge and money.

Nonetheless, the threshold of appropriate behaviour towards equals remained tricky in both England and America. The rhetoric of the status of gentility contained both a measure of self-approbation and a context in which the fellow genteel were equals, establishing a baseline of behaviour beyond which extra degrees of deference were the product of deliberate calculation. Lord Chesterfield had advised an easy frankness in company with equals, and indeed with superiors (when a relationship had been established) and even with inferiors whose goodwill could be useful. This was fine advice for a polished aristocrat to give to his son, but it did not necessarily satisfy the tense environment of middle-class contestation, where giving and receiving recognition was critical to social identity. Situations in which potentially deferential behaviour had to be negotiated focused on introductions, meeting in passing and being a guest: in each circumstance, who has precedence to speak, to pass, to proceed?

Establishing the genteel practitioner's perspective on whether to give or expect to receive deference in social encounters depended on a fast assessment of his or her own relative status. Outside the caste of titled persons, occupation or position offered some index of discrimination, often being a shorthand for wealth or influence; to denominate them more elegantly, some American advice books adopted the circumlocution 'persons of distinction' or 'those to whom you owe respect'.[56]

Beyond this calculated judgement to give or seek precedence, the polite standards of conduct among equals came to be constructed in relation to age and gender: the young should defer to the old, and men to women. The most difficult field in which to assess the right level of deference was vis-à-vis aspirants to middle-class status whose claims one did not want to admit in their entirety, or whose deference one sought to receive. In the system of genteel etiquette, this interaction marked acknowledgement by peers or subpeers, the acid test of status honour.

The tools to express deference were reserve and tact; the general strategy was reticence. Reserve protected one's own honour; tact protected the encountered. The motor of such caution was the maintenance of personal and others' privacy. Strangers were easy to deal with in this manner, though reserve practised to its logical conclusion produced the unfortunate effect of ignoring everyone with whom one did not have a formal acquaintance, creating the impression of snobbery or indifference that still taints English manners. To make and consolidate social contacts was more difficult. Every advice book recommended against pushing oneself into the attentions of the great, most on the grounds that the great do not like to be importuned, but some pointed out that grovelling represented little self-regard. Yet even the etiquette literature was inconclusive on the exact location of the polite line between desirable reserve and well-bred sociability.

Tact can be seen as a different form of reserve, a withholding of judgement based on standards of refinement and charity. Unlike reserve, tact contains a position of power, the power to withhold knowledge or opinion. Yet it is a sensitive power: the tactful person knows how to help others without implying inadequacy on the part of the helped, truly a charitable perspective. The ethic of charity is among the most ambivalent characters of Victorian gentility. An aspect of Christian duty requiring some quantum of self-sacrifice, charity was stiffened by a firm base of standards and duty, giving the practitioner the confidence of superiority in dispensing advice or goods. The innovative aspect of bourgeois genteel charity was that it should be delivered with kindness and, among the truly pious, with humility. The apparently contradictory qualities of superiority expressed with humility are presented in novelistic accounts of charity without any of the doubt or irony that colour modern readings. However, there are sufficient primary accounts of the humiliations of being on the receiving end of middle-class charity to be certain that the highest Christian standards did not always inform charitable acts.

The world of tasteful goods

Among the intangible products of an education in gentility was taste. Like the whole bundle of characteristics that were meant to be inherent and natural in the genteel person, taste is most obviously described as the sum of correct knowledge or cultural capital with which the genteel person distinguished himself or herself from people who did not have it.[57] The visible expressions of taste in clothes, furnishings, manners and so on were perceived as manifestations of the internal person's character; refined taste implied refined morality. Taste also contained a special dimension of aesthetic appreciation. Richard Bushman discovers in taste an entire cultural project, 'a mission for the refined population to beautify the world, beginning with their own persons and radiating to all they possessed and influenced.'[58] Situated within the romantic aesthetic that contrasted beauty to sublimity, this distinction speaks eloquently on the limits of gentility. Where the sublime was powerful and magnificent, even terrifying, the beautiful was soft, smooth and harmonious. These characters were used metaphorically to describe admired personalities, as well as to express material beauty. In this respect they can be felt as much as seen in the most valued personal artefacts of the practitioners of gentility: softness in fabrics and upholstery; smoothness in ceramics and plastered walls; harmony in colours and symmetry of house façades.

The material world was a critical element of genteel practice. Gentility stimulated the power of the Industrial Revolution, with its immense extension of goods to people who could not previously afford such items as individual china tablewares, fabrics for domestic use and decoration, and small metalwares like cutlery and jewellery. More goods were available, and in a range of qualities that made them affordable to a span of incomes in an age when new earnings empowered new populations to spend. Neil McKendrick describes the dynamic of the new consumerism: '. . . luxuries came to be seen as mere "decencies" and "decencies" came to be seen as "necessities." '[59] The effect on the standard of living was to make domestic life more comfortable, more attractive and more complex and differentiated. Such standards had long been available to the aristocracy; indeed Werner Sombart ascribes the sensuous drive to luxurious comfort beginning in the Middle Ages as the very motor of civilization.[60] Luxury goods in many registers of quality served as criteria of civilized gentility in the early nineteenth century: if one could not afford silver, then electroplate, Britannia metal or even lustreware china could still enable possession of a shining teapot and milk jug. Thus equipped, a person could participate in the central ritual of genteel Anglo sociability.

The question of the causality of the rise in consumerism in the late eighteenth/early nineteenth-century period bats between the instrumental and the ideological: between an idea that the increasing quantity of consumer goods produced by the might of industry created its own market, and an idea that social developments generated a demand for more goods which could be fulfilled by industrial production. Colin Campbell traces an elegant genealogy of middle-class consumerism grounded in the growth of the bourgeois taste for self-expression through owning and using luxury products, goods superfluous to basic survival needs. Beyond the semiotic purposes of such goods, Campbell sees them serving the novel goal of emotional satisfaction in producing imaginative pleasure through their meanings and associations. This strand of nineteenth-century action grows from a rejection of Calvinist predestinarianism and the development of a cult of benevolence, sentimentalism and romanticism; yet at the same time, it is twinned by the strand of the Protestant work ethic of rationality, industry and achievement. The present book takes up the vision of twin cultures in nineteenth-century middle-class expression, seeing them as an inversion of aristocratic ('hedonistic') culture, bifurcated by the separation of public and private spheres, and legitimated by the ethic of self-control. The appropriation of elements of aristocratic culture by bourgeois women was a project of daily labour which required the same degree of self-control as did men's money-making work. In this scenario, the consumption of goods is not driven by the urge to hedonism, though it undoubtedly contained elements of pleasure, but by the need to assert or maintain status honour. The vision nicely fits the gendered roles of nineteenth-century middle-class people, and enriches understanding of the social functions of taste and consumption.[61]

In practice, genteel consumption required ownership of both financial and cultural capital to acquire the right equipment and decorations, but the cornucopia of goods available for sale fuelled the expectation among some wealthy, would-be refined persons that gentility was a commodity like any other. The intersection of money and learning defines the field of taste and removes it from the popular meaning of either personal or universal aesthetic judgement, showing it instead as a cultural and mutable construct. The standards of middle-class taste, like the system of etiquette, functioned to describe and assert a different, separate and legitimate culture neither aristocratic nor proletarian. Its major criterion was a concern for art over richness, which

Tasteful: Neo-medieval style furnishings suggested both ancestral grandeur and up-to-date modernity for the genteel middle class.

'A drawing room in the Norman style', *Architectural Magazine,* vol. 1 (London: 1834).

usefully contrasted tastefulness as the opposite of extravagance; these became key poles of personal judgement in the discourse of gentility. The possession of tasteful goods evidenced genteel affiliation, connecting economic power and encultured learning in the practice of consumerism.[62] The domain of such consumption was unprecedentedly domestic, thus casting women as the prime practitioners of tasteful choice. Women became the vehicles of bringing tasteful goods into the home, whose effect on the family took on a morally determinative influence, named by Katherine Grier 'domestic environmentalism'.[63] In this way, the home as women's sphere was further differentiated from the sphere of men's productivity as the major site of the new consumerism.

The role of tasteful consumerism in establishing gentility appeared to offer a conveniently accessible means of adopting the genteel lifestyle simply by spending money on goods. In the uppermost reaches of wealth, this was to some degree the case, because much could be forgiven the extremely rich. However, most hopefuls stumbled over yet another dilemma in the construction of gentility by failing to understand that its essence was self-improvement. The outward signs of gentility had to represent the internal state of the mind and the soul. The refined mind sought improvement through reading English as well as classical literature, through subscribing to libraries, attending courses of lectures and participating in learned or philanthropic societies. The refined soul sought to spread the light of genteel morality throughout society, especially through charitable endeavour to preserve or rescue orphans, or the purity of women whose economic circumstances took them outside the enclave of domesticity into the risks of the world. These projects received the validation of the evangelical belief that salvation was attainable by anyone, thus giving an ethical foundation to the constant human dream of betterment. In this way the idea of middle-class gentility came to contain the notion that self-improvement would lead to elevation to loftier circles, in this world as well as the next.

The dynamics of gentility: etiquette and consumerism

As discussed, one of the enduring contradictions of the middle-class adoption of aristocratic culture was the gendered split between the virtue of work and the extravagance of leisure. To establish and maintain family honour, middle-class women's role shifted from productive labour to social representation and conspicuous consumption. Yet a trace of the older morality that valued labour always remained to colour the new practices of etiquette and consumerism with the brush of worldliness. It soon attached to feminine practice, interpreting aristocratic social activity and consumption as the taste for luxury for which women have long been condemned in the Christian tradition. It generated new stereotypes of the idle woman and the voracious shopper.[64] Carrying out the family mission of gentility, women became social radars and influential consumers for the first time, and were condemned for the frivolity of it all.

Yet elegant manners and conspicuous consumption were necessary evidence of gentility, not in mere quantity to flaunt wealth, but in the quality and combination of practices and goods, which demonstrated the correct taste of the family representative and therefore the family's status. Manners and goods were the vehicles of expressing genteel competence. Of course, in asserting correctness, all but the highest aristocracy were at some risk of being judged inadequate or incorrect, and suffering judgement and exclusion in consequence. The performance of rituals such as visiting, tea-taking and dancing, plus the assembly of personal or domestic genteel equipment, thus became the litmus of 'true' gentility, swinging between the Scylla of showy excess, and the Charybdis of inappropriate conjunctions. More and more people faced choice for the first time, and they needed new social guides and norms to enable them to do it. Knowledge, or cultural capital, offered the only certainty of getting it right; this explains the wave of advice books on etiquette, conduct, interior arrangement and home decoration which broke into a torrent in the early to middle nineteenth century.

The power of etiquette to express personal and family gentility achieved high moral character from evangelical religious practice, and managed to maintain the sacred reputation while actually easing its demands into more calculating and deliberately graceful habits which made good manners more visible to others. Similarly, the reach of consumerism depended on the productivity of the Industrial Revolution, conditioned by demand for differentiating goods which also prompted new manufactures, as exemplified in the history of the import to Britain of Indian calicoes in the early eighteenth century.[65] In having available manners and goods in such tremendous variety, a vast new vocabulary became available for the expression of choice, for drawing distinctions, for asserting differences. The nuances of etiquette, the precise inflection of an assemblage of furnishings: both spoke volumes for the individual taste, and therefore the character, of the chooser. Manners needed to be correct but not cold, pleasing without self-abnegation, noticeable and yet not insincere. Goods had to be rich and stylish but not flashy, modest but not old or cheap, comfortable and not overbearing, personal and yet in the mainstream of conventional practice. The middle-class fear of impinging on courtly splendour introduced an exceptionally tricky requirement to avoid grandiosity while maintaining sufficient style to indicate easy familiarity with aristocratic standards. Expenditure had to be commensurate with income to be truly genteel, neither above nor below one's station, thus expressing exquisite consciousness of self in society. In sum, the practice of gentility required active, informed and constant performance.

The system of gentility was complicated and contradictory; to understand it requires that the entire bundle of its expressions be grasped. As a way of life, the outward forms of gentility belonged to the aristocracy who could afford to live in leisure and mock the necessity of labour, yet it was desired and imitated by most other classes even when it undermined their entrepreneurial instincts and collective interests. The conflation of gentility and morality, grounded in religious egalitarianism, was claimed to offer everyone the possibility of self-improvement, but in practice functioned as much to exclude as to improve. While gentility offered women major new status and influence on social life, it constrained them tightly within the domestic sphere, which subsequently developed into the oppressive model that survives well into modern times. These essentially middle-class conditions of life were inspired by the culture of the aristocracy which, via radical bricolage in an unprecedented environment of opportunity, created a sufficient dynamic to become the cultural paradigm of the nineteenth century. Having reformulated its aristocratic origins, gentility became central to nineteenth-century culture, as a code of behaviour, a material world and a model of morality.

The psychic internalization of genteel values, their total adoption within private family life and their influence in larger world events from religion to consumerism show that gentility achieved a remarkable degree of naturalization as the normative middle-class way of life. Genteel values and behaviours have a long but diverse history. A core of characteristics remains identifiably coherent from the Middle Ages to our own day, but further qualities in different proportions have attached to the essence over time, generating distinct forms of practice. It is awkward enough to separate stages in modern ideas about gentility from those of the past; and then there are those of the past.[66] Among them, the nineteenth-century variety of gentility was outstandingly vigorous, wide-reaching and influential. It appears not merely as a mentality contingent upon a conjunction of small conditions, but as a complex cultural system that long governed personal and social life. On the scale of the individual, it was most powerfully manifested in self-disciplined performance and consumption; within Anglo society, both metropolitan and colonial, the ethic of betterment in the name of civilization reformulated not only social relations but also the material world.

4
Under Control: the Genteel Body

Self-control was the fundamental principle of the courtesy traditions that preceded the genteel revolution. Regulation of the body and its appetites, desires, effluvia and excrescences constituted the first step in the civilizing process, located in both the individual and society. Freud depicts resolution of the struggle between self-control and instinct as the repressive compromise between 'civilisation and its discontents', a phrase with special resonance in the discourse of gentility. In his own psychoanalytic terms, Freud traces self-control as the individual's bio-logically grounded passage from infantile libidinous drive to adult estab-lishment of the superego, expressed as a conscience, a sense of guilt and the capacity for remorse.[1] This vision of natural stages of psychic growth frames the view that social development occurs at the expense of indi-vidual desire. Elias refers to Freud's interpretation, but inverts it by his-toricizing the regulation of the body within the social order defined by different expressions of state power. The hypothesis that external power shapes the individual psyche according to evolving techniques of power is illustrated by the history of increasingly self-managed controls over the body.[2] Both theories illuminate the growth of human cultivation as the sublimation of animal instincts by order presented in rules imposed by the authority of kings, parents or teachers and naturalized as civil, adult behaviour. Upright posture and restraint of hands and feet; clean-liness of person and clothing; control of nose-blowing and excretion; control of emotions and desires: these were the basic conditions of medieval gentle manners as codified in the earliest courtesy books, but they had to be inculcated anew in every generation, directing the animal infant into the correct channels of self-possession. They remained the central elements of bodily control within the genteel code of the nineteenth century. Unsaid, because unsayable as much in the fifteenth century as the nineteenth, was the control of sexuality. Despite public silence, the repression of sexual desire underpinned the entire apparatus of self-control. The engine of genteel presentation, self-control, became self-perpetuating, as cited by an anonymous adviser in 1839:

> Long *self-control* has such composure wrought,
> That *self-control* becomes a thing
> Of which there is no need.[3]

The taste for cleanliness

Bodily cleanliness has almost always had strong positive associations, analogous to mental and spiritual purity. Exceptions were certain early Fathers of the Church who suggested that bathing could be too sensuous to be godly, a view summed up by St Francis of Assisi that, despite the virtue of Sister Water, dirtiness was among the badges of holiness. The renunciation of cleanliness was a sacrifice akin to the monastic pledges of poverty and chastity, in itself evidence of the worldly desirability of living cleanly. Cleanliness was, however, a relative condition, dependent on standards, technology and wealth. Clean hands and face were widely advocated throughout the Middle Ages, first for communities of religious, for whom elaborate washing facilities were built into refectories, and soon for communities of style, such as the court, where servant labour was available to heat, transport and remove the necessary water.[4] Courtly standards and technologies established the ideal of personal cleanliness subsequently aspired to and codified in courtesy books.

Historians note a decline in cleanly self-presentation in the sixteenth and seventeenth centuries, despite the continuing production of courtesy books advising the contrary.[5] It made conspicuous the notable rise in clean standards by the turn of the nineteenth century, when a taste for personal cleanliness picked up and began to spread down the social scale in line with new aspirations to live the civilized life. Cleanliness in person and clothes was constantly enjoined in the conduct books of the late eighteenth/early nineteenth century, such that by the 1830s, personal cleanliness was so much a baseline standard of the middle class and its aspirants that it no longer needed to be specified within instructions for gentility. The periodical *Chambers Information for the People* opened its entry on 'cleanliness' with the assertion: 'This is not a mere matter of decency.'[6] Degrees of cleanliness were now conceived as a distinction, a measure by which to recognize kindred spirits and exclude undesirable company.

It is impossible to quantify the extent and frequency of body washing. There is little reliable information on how often or how extensively people washed, though in 1841 Catharine Beecher opined of Americans that 'to wash the face, feet, hands and neck is the extent of the ablutions practised by perhaps the majority of our people.'[7] Advice books stress the necessity of a further degree of personal cleanliness but rarely stipulate frequency of washing. Mrs Copley, for instance, urged 'not merely the face, neck and hands should be subjected, but the whole body, either by plunging or the shower bath, or at least by means of a large sponge'.[8] Anonymous author, A Lady of Distinction, advocated that every lady should possess a bath, but offered no more detailed advice on its use. The school mistress Mrs Emily Thornwell recommended standards she seems to acknowledge were unlikely to be lived up to, proposing 'the necessity of all persons (ladies especially) passing a wet sponge over the whole surface of the body every morning and evening, or, at any rate, every morning.' Advice for men taking exercise suggested that the whole body should be washed 'at least once a week' in warm water with moderate use of soap, followed by a cold splash.[9] All these sources are prescriptive, advocating standards that were evidently not commonly practised even among the segment of society dedicated to genteel living. Beecher's assessment is unique in aiming to assess real practice. In the light of her context, it may be taken that she describes Anglo practice, in which case it may be not unreasonable to apply her judgement to the transnational Anglo dimension.

The basic tools of this degree of cleanliness were a small basin and a jug, politely named a ewer, which had been the principal tools of cleanliness at table since the Middle Ages, when a servant would pour warm water over the diner's hands held above the basin. The development and spread of forks in the sixteenth/seventeenth-century period obviated the need for washing at table, and by the mid-eighteenth century the basin and ewer were moved into the genteel bedroom for private washing to meet the newly discovered taste for personal cleanliness. From this time the basin stand was remade as a dedicated piece of furniture, explicitly named the wash-hand stand. Its new career began by continuing its medieval size and elements. Early examples appeared in furniture catalogues of the 1790s, when George Hepplewhite presented simple little table-like stands, and Thomas Sheraton designed elegant neoclassical versions in fashionable wood veneers.[10]

In the first decades of the new century, the wash-hand stand was enlarged to small table size with a larger basin standing on, or perched in a hole in, the surface, which was made waterproof with a marble top and low splash-back or wash-board; the body of the table was constructed of polished or painted wood and increasingly mass produced.[11] More complex views of the extent of personal cleanliness required additional pieces of washing equipment, now named a chamber set or toilet set: a basin, ewer, soap dish, sponge bowl, toothbrush jar, slop pail for dirty water and perhaps a footbath. Matching sets of these pieces were mass produced in the potteries of Staffordshire in a huge range of styles and prices, from the utilitarian white to the lavishly decorated. Ornamentation followed no special theme of cleanliness, but was as pretty and fashionable as table china, embellished with the same moulding and gilding. Elaborate beyond necessity, the correctly chosen toilet set demonstrated the individual's determination to observe specialized standards of cleanliness. In larger houses, the wash-hand stand occupied the dressing room; in smaller houses, the bedroom. In a shared bedroom, wealth and taste determined whether the occupants also shared a washstand, had two washstands, or had a double basin washstand complete with double toilet set; all these types were illustrated in furniture catalogues of the 1850s.[12] Evidence of the extent of take-up of these useful articles is indicated by the fact that wash-hand stands were present in all of a sample of insolvent Scottish businessmen in the later 1830s, almost every one of a sample of citizens of Delaware who died in the 1850s–60s and all of a sample of middle-class Sydney households auctioning their contents in the 1840s.[13] A basin stand, wash-hand stand or washstand in the bedroom was essential to daily cleanliness in the middle-class Anglo world.

The two- or three-bar towel stand accompanied the washstand as the furniture of people dedicated to clean self-presentation; probably of medieval origin, towel stands became part of the standard suite of bedroom furniture during the first half of the nineteenth century.[14] The traditional towel had been a hand towel, a piece of textured linen, later cotton, in various qualities according to who would use it, often embroidered for specially honoured guests. The much larger towels that came to be used for drying the body after washing were named bath sheets. The looped pile cotton textile now known as terry towelling was invented in the 1840s, first in silk and wool, then cotton; it appears to have become used in body bathing only towards the end of the nineteenth century.[15]

Most personal washing employed water only, for common soap was so caustic that it dried out the natural oils in the skin. Making soap has an ancient history as a home-craft, one of the housewife's occasional

Cleanly: The 'bason stand' or wash-hand stand in the bedroom enabled washing as part of intimate everyday life.

Sheraton, *The Cabinet-Maker and Upholsterer's Drawing Book* (London: 1793), pl. 42; Loudon, *Encyclopedia of Cottage, Villa and Farm Architecture* (London: 1833), p. 1086; Webster, *Encyclopedia of Domestic Economy* (London: 1844), p. 276.

tasks; composed of rendered animal fat and alkaline lye derived from ash, it was chiefly for use in laundering household linen and clothing. Offering less risk to the skin were elegant soaps for personal use, made with olive oil and, later, palm oil, mixed with the alkaline barilla [soda] plant.[16] Both ingredients and readymade soap were available from apothecaries, imported from France, Italy and Spain; a particular attraction of manufactured soaps was their fine, hard-milled texture, which retarded sliminess, the besetting sin of the home-made version. Standards for commercially made soaps were established in Britain in 1712, along with a tax, which by 1815 had risen to 100 per cent of the retail price, and double for imported soaps. Soap duties were halved in 1833 and repealed in 1853, indicating the steady transition of soap from status as a luxury to a decency to a necessity.[17]

One piece of cleanly furniture was dedicated to the special use of ladies in early nineteenth-century England: the bidet. Originating in courtly France a century before, Sheraton described it in detail as a novelty: 'a small stool with four legs . . . contains a pan made of tin and japanned, or of earthenware, made for the purpose.'[18] The stool was rectangular for convenient straddling; the pan elongated and waisted; and the whole concealed, either under a polished cabinet lid or folded into a dressing table. Frank acknowledgement of such an article offended polite ideas of propriety, but the increasing presence of a bidet in middle-class bedrooms suggests that women might now prefer to compromise with the indelicacy of the thing in exchange for the improved cleanliness it enabled.[19] Bidets were present in nearly half the main bedrooms in middle-class colonial Sydney in the 1840s; however, less than 10 per cent of Scottish businessmen's households contained a bidet.[20]

The revival of interest in bodily cleanliness in the late eighteenth century was to some degree a function of the capacity to hire servants to fetch and carry water, and therefore confined to a certain level of wealth – but functionalism does not explain the whole phenomenon. In fact, the taste for washing can be shown to precede the technology which seems in retrospect to have enabled it, in the form of middling householders who went to great lengths to install bathing facilities at home before the urban infrastructure of reticulated water was in place.[21] This is evidence of a powerful social impulse towards cleanliness, increasingly expressed as a positive pleasure in contemporary polemic: 'Bathing possesses great claims upon our attention, not only as a source of great purity of person, but as a refined enjoyment, a delightful recreation . . .'[22]

Household inventories of the early nineteenth century show baths and shower baths increasingly common in middle-class households from the 1830s. Domestic economist Miss Leslie noted that 'In some families, it is the custom to have in each chamber a small deep tub painted white; and a large stone[ware] pitcher of warm water is left every morning at the room door.'[23] The nineteenth-century bath tub was a mobile piece of furniture, usually taken out of storage in the kitchen or an outhouse to the bedroom of the bather. Tubs took many forms: the sponge bath was a wide, shallow, metal dish upon which the bather stood to pour or sponge water over the body; equally common was the hip bath, round or oval with a high back and lugs at the sides to rest the arms, soap or sponge. Moving along the scale from dabbing the body to total immersion, the full bath, a long, deep tub of modern dimensions, was demanding to fill and empty, but still portable. The

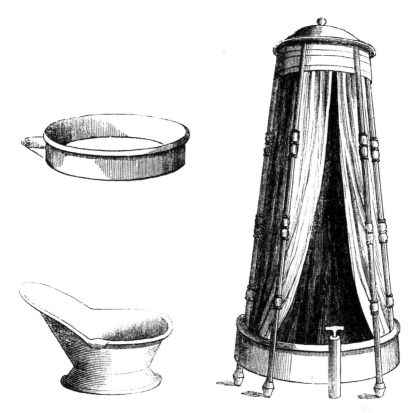

Hygienic: The sponge bath was the minimalist item of whole-body washing, followed by the hip bath, and topped by the shower bath.

Webster, *Encyclopedia of Domestic Economy* (London: 1844), pp. 1221–2.

slipper bath was a more snug and convenient variation, a boot-shaped metal capsule enclosing the body in a sitting position; the bather was wrapped in a sheet to avoid contact with hot metal surfaces. Baths were sometimes made of copper, more usually of steel with a round rolled rim, and often marbled with a paint finish to suggest grander things. All were portable, reflecting the scarcity of indoor plumbing.[24]

The developing taste for whole-body cleanliness was connected to a rising interest in the healthy effects of water, taken as a drink, a shower, a steam bath or a plunge in a mineral spa, indoors or even outdoors.[25] The elaborate nature of immersion bathing made it seem specially efficacious as a therapeutic treatment, though the aim was not so much cleanliness as an invigorating effect upon the whole body. The act of bathing or showering, whether in cold or hot water, plunged the patient into a foreign element and challenged his or her condition; it was the shock of the bath, not the incidental cleanliness, that motivated the connection of bathing with health. All-over washing contained an aura of specially vigorous healthiness which made it particularly attractive to men, and by the same token, offered an excuse to put bathing beyond the delicate constitution of women other than enthusiasts. Nonetheless Mrs Thornwell recommended to ladies that 'a warm bath, with friction for a quarter of an hour with a soft flesh-brush, after being thoroughly dried' is very good for the skin.[26] This kind of advice, and the availability of special brushes, demonstrate the growing scientific understanding of skin physiology, often cited (sometimes less than correctly) in advice books.

Showers were claimed to be particularly effective for good health: 'The shock from the shower-bath is, in general, felt to be greater than that from simple immersion,' advised Thomas Webster.[27] Therapeutic showers tended to be elaborate mechanisms or high pressure jets whose undomestic nature bolstered the authority of the treatment; simpler devices were adopted into the home in the 1840s. The domestic form in England and the United States, also in the Australian colonies, comprised a tent-like frame attached to the tub, supporting a small tank which was filled by a handpump via pipes in the frame uprights, the whole swathed in a shower curtain. The bather stepped into the tub, pulled the tank plug above via a chain and received a shower of water; 'he should then be briskly rubbed with cloths, and dress with all dispatch.'[28] Both showers and baths were scarce in middle-class Scottish and Delaware households in the late 1830s. Antipodean hot weather perhaps explains why Australian inventories number nearly three times as many shower baths as bath tubs in middle-class homes of the 1840s.[29]

The growth of interest in whole-body bathing is evident in building and architectural textbooks. Prior to the 1840s they rarely present plumbed-in baths, but from about 1840, bath, bathroom and plumbing references multiply.[30] Fitted baths plumbed into dedicated bathrooms appear in wealthier houses in Britain and America in the 1830s–40s, but while fixed plumbing flourished in America, it remained scarce in Britain until late in the century.[31] They were filled from private cisterns fed by springs, or, in the city, connected to privately piped water services; depending on the level of local urban infrastructure, baths might be drained into public drain systems or simply into the streets. Bathrooms of this era were large and grandly fitted, in keeping with other massive bedroom and dressing room furniture; the bath was set permanently into a cabinet of polished wood, and might have a shower apparatus mounted above. Merchant Alexander Reid's lavish bathroom in suburban Edinburgh was one of these: carpeted with velvet pile, lit by gas, screened by crimson curtains with a mahogany cornice, the furniture was mahogany and the wet areas were faced with white marble.[32] Careful house design located the bathroom close to or above the kitchen, for access to the source of hot water. The rational wash-house of Catherine Beecher's *Treatise on Domestic Economy* was labour-saving and multipurpose, drawing hot water from the backroom boiler for kitchen and laundry as well as bath.[33] But like many rational schemes, pure efficiency failed to capture the spirit driving the new taste: the ideal of personal cleanliness was anti-industrial and private, requiring installation close to the bedroom. By the turn of the twentieth century, the rational arrangement of laundry-cum-bathroom came to be common for servant use, but those who could afford a purpose-built bathroom preferred it upstairs.[34]

The take-up of whole-body washing in both Britain and the United States correlates most significantly with the availability of reticulated water. The surge of nineteenth-century city development made it almost impossible for piped water services to keep up with urban growth, and since water and sewage lines were laid according to who could pay for them, the geographical spread of fixed baths was uneven.[35] The situation in England in 1845 was revealed in a survey of 51 towns, of which only 6 had a good water supply, 13 an indifferent supply and 32, 'very bad systems indeed.'[36] In the United States, the number of municipal waterworks increased steadily, from about fifty in 1840, to 68 in 1850, to 132 in 1860.[37] The introduction of iron water pipes, beginning in some parts of urban England in the 1780s, and of filtration systems, beginning in the 1820s, improved the availability of water for domestic use. Water consumption multiplied wherever a reliable system was installed: as soon as mains water became available, more and more was used. But it must be remembered that the early dates cited represent rare examples and that widespread access to reticulated water spanned more than a hundred years beyond the first efforts, especially in the poorest quarters. The history of working-class cleanliness is a further story.

Associated with bodily cleanliness came a rise in standards of grooming the teeth and hair, established through the internalized discipline of daily practice. Lost or rotten teeth, once a fact of life, came to be perceived as a mark of shoddy personal standards and low class. The conventional method of cleaning the mouth and teeth was to gargle with clean water and rub the teeth with a sponge or cloth, possibly dipped in toothpowder;[38] to clean between the teeth, a sliver of wood, a bird quill or a knife (criticized in advice books) was used as a toothpick. A rustic toothbrush could be made by chewing on a twig to produce a fibrous, brushy end, as suggested by Mrs Thornwell: 'bruised and bitten at the end, till with a little use it will become the softest and best brush for this purpose.'[39] A more elaborate method was advertised with an aristocratic provenance: 'Lady Morgan's tooth brush' comprised dried roots of marsh mallow, six inches long and as thick as a cane, gently bruised for half an inch at the end with a mallet to form a brush, and then steeped in gum and dried again.[40] The twig toothbrush was convenient and effective, and is still used in some parts of the world.

Small manufactured brushes were adapted to the teeth about the late eighteenth century, made by craftsman brushmakers on the same principles as painting and cleaning brushes. As with handmade industrial brushes, the handle or stock was shaped of wood or bone, in which pig bristles were set by looping the bristles with wire through holes in the base and setting them with pitch.[41] The London Comb Warehouse in Edinburgh, bankrupted in 1839, sold bone handled toothbrushes for 2/6 a dozen; ivory handles cost 10/1 a dozen.[42] In this essentially modern form, the toothbrush received the royal imprimatur, beginning with the appointment of an official toothbrush maker to George IV (1820–30). Toothbrushes have been located in middle-class archaeological deposits at Annapolis dating from 1766, with a steady rise in frequency between the 1820s and 1860s, suggesting mass production and widespread use by a large segment of society.[43] Brushes were used with dentifrice or tooth powder, an abrasive powder purchased from the apothecary and often advertised as having miraculous advantages for the teeth and gums. Cheap alternatives to tooth powder were powdered charcoal or gunpowder.[44] Nonetheless, the foul breath of decayed teeth was an unpleasant constant of the social environment, managed by polite distance or quick fixes such as chewing on a Florentine onion root or gargling with fennel water.[45]

Washing the hair remained uncommon throughout the nineteenth century, promoted by fear of catching cold. The difficulty of drying long hair has since been met by the fashion for short hair and by hair dryers, and the difference in attitudes towards hair is telling. In the nineteenth century, luxurious tresses – woman's traditional crowning glory – did not have to be washed clean to be beautiful, though hair had to be cared for and well dressed, a need met by a new cult of brushing the hair. The modern style of hairbrush was an innovation of the early nineteenth century, appearing in growing numbers on richer women's dressing tables from the 1830s; until then, combs had been the standard hairdressing device for all classes. The London Comb Warehouse stocked five types of hairbrush: from those with cheap white wood handles to 'inlaid' and 'Venetian' handles, as well as children's brushes.[46] Mrs Thornwell advised a morning brushing of half an hour, or three-quarters of an hour for long hair, plus five to ten minutes before dinner and the same before bed.[47] Hair was dressed with perfumed oils and creams generically known as pomades, combed through to give body and lustre. Men were offered particularly masculine pomades, with a special focus on so-called beargrease.

In any case, throughout the first half of the nineteenth century, adult women's hair was conventionally hidden under a cap for indoor use and a bonnet for outdoors. Caps were substantial fitted headgear, usually of light fabric for daywear and rich, decorated materials for evening; bonnets or outdoor hats of the time were predominantly fitted to the whole head, with a wide brim framing the face. Charmingly feminine as they were, caps constituted a contemporary nineteenth-century expression of ancient patriarchal control of female sexuality, a condition much older than class or gentility, and mandated by numerous religious groups. Worn by married women and unmarried women of a certain age, the cap suppressed the sexual suggestiveness of hair. The all-class respectable wearing of caps persisted in England and America in real practice until the 1850s. Conservatives maintained the habit, but in fashionably conscious society caps declined into symbolic forms as decorative trifles perched on the head. The cap was now an accessory, though it remained a badge of submission for female servants. The old decency of wearing a widow's cap with its characteristic long streamers at the back was extended beyond other cap fashions by Queen Victoria's widowhood in 1861; at the time when many women abandoned the necessary respectability of caps, Victoria in a starched white widow's cap continued to project a powerful image of traditional wifely virtue.

The whiteness of items of clothing such as caps introduces the genteel standard for clean clothes. The metaphoric relation of clothing to self as the outward sign of the inward person demonstrates the genteel necessity not only of bodily polish but also of clean clothes, which were the object of John Wesley's famous aphorism that 'cleanliness is next to godliness.'[48] The new requirement was facilitated by the increasing availability of multiple clothes for ordinary people. Thanks to the revolution in English cotton production and Indian cotton imports in the mid-eighteenth century, cloth became lighter and cheaper, and cotton

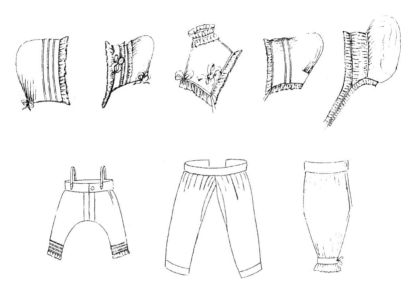

Modest: Ladies covered their hair with modest caps, so pretty that they came to define femininity, and equipped themselves and their families with respectable white cotton drawers.

The Work Woman's Guide (London: 1838), pl. 7, 15.

replaced wool as the major fabric for everyday clothing and under-clothing.[49] Printed cottons and glazed cotton chintzes changed the style of women's fashion, but plain white cotton had more profound conse-quences for Anglo taste throughout the world. White cotton undergar-ments came to intervene between the skin and the outer clothes. Their cheapness made it possible for middling people to own enough for regular changing, while their washability enabled body soiling to be laundered away, keeping outer clothing fresh.[50] The critical item was the undergarment in contact with the skin: for women, the shift (which took the elegant French name, chemise, about 1800) and the shirt for men. Both came to be owned in increasing quantities, with three as a baseline requirement and dozens not uncommon among middle-class people, as shown in the inventories of domestic and personal posses-sions of petty bourgeois insolvents from Scotland to Australia in the 1840s.[51]

At the very beginning of the nineteenth century, upper-class women embarked on a radical innovation in underclothing as a vehicle of clean-liness by wearing white cotton drawers. Royal patronage by Princess

Charlotte gave respectability to women's use of what were essentially men's breeches, an appropriation treated with suspicion by modest ladies. However, drawers came to be worn by more and more women, and gradually men also, throughout the nineteenth century.[52] As items of special dedication to personal cleanliness and delicacy, drawers amounted to 'a garment of class distinction' among the newly self-conscious middle class.[53]

Clean clothes came to be taken as a personal distinction by the fashionable and the rustic. George 'Beau' Brummell, the masculine style arbiter of the Regency, required of a gentleman, 'no perfumes . . . but very fine linen, plenty of it, and country washing.'[54] Even an old radical like William Cobbett wrote in 1829 in his *Advice to Young Men* that they should judge a potential wife (among other criteria) by the state of her chemise: 'if the white be a sort of yellow, cleanly hands would have been at work to prevent that . . . a sloven in one thing is a sloven in all things.'[55] Keeping clothes clean represented transcendence not only of the body but of a manual labouring environment; considered in another light, it indicated possession of a laundress. The absence of the grubby consequences of manual work demonstrated basic middle-class status, and so did the presence of a servant to maintain the clean evidence. Middle-class children's clothing specially challenged both cleanliness and washerwomen, for infants and children were commonly dressed in white cotton dresses or pinafores to demonstrate the purity of innocent childhood. Although white cotton was sturdily washable, such standards imposed heavy work on laundresses. If a washerwoman was unavailable (as on the frontier or in the bush), a middle-class or aspirant woman had to do the job herself, as Louisa Clifton decided to in Western Australia in 1841: 'I passed a great part of the morning in making my noviciate in washing, an employment I expect often to be engaged in.'[56] A family in dirty clothing was self-condemnation to exile, not only from familiar circumstances but from the genteel world.

The entire complex of clean practices constitutes an increasing emphasis on individual presentation, a development with contradictory consequences for the genteel person. Consciousness of individual presence and genteel performance placed a new value on the socially acceptable body. But the sin of vanity haunted individual interest in appearance in households where Biblical reminders of the inherent evilness of the body were influential. The inner struggle between beauty and piety was fierce, for the belief that facial features revealed character constructed a powerful reason to seek the conventional signs of beauty. At the same time, face paint was regarded as the proof of immorality, exemplified by Jezebel, the wicked woman of the Bible.[57] Nonetheless, advisory books, while stressing that fresh-faced innocence was the ideal state, invariably added recipes for cosmetics for both men and women to whiten the skin, redden the lips and cheeks and make the hair glossy and thick. The serious purpose of making oneself beautiful was materialized in the increasing presence of the dressing table or toilet table, a small stage at which the central actor watched herself or himself in the mirror, to see the self as others saw it. Rationally and elegantly reshaped from rococo grandeur by Hepplewhite and Sheraton in the last decades of the eighteenth century, the dressing table became a central element of the Victorian bedroom.[58] Dressing tables appear as standard equipment in Scottish, Australian and Delaware bedrooms in studies of the 1830s–40s.[59] A masculine version, the shaving table, made an appearance at the same time, but appears to have been usurped by the wash-hand stand, and never achieved a lasting place in the bedroom or bathroom. Mediating the use of cosmetics, a new rationale developed for bodily attention, stressing the health-giving effects of 'pure' treatments and downplaying any sensual pleasure in comfort and beauty. Its most extreme expressions emerged in 'sanitary' cults such as hydropathy, in which cold water treatments and rigorous abstinence from inflammatory substances and experience ensured that cleanliness was perceived as a moral way of life.[60]

'Personal cleanliness is valued by all nations in proportion to their advance in civilisation,' asserted the *Encyclopedia Britannica* in 1853, suggesting that Britain compared well in the international clean and civilized stakes.[61] In truth, the advanced state of Anglo genteel cleanliness of the person depended on highly internalized standards of middle classness. Expenditure on private furniture and equipment for the bedroom and elaborate apparatus designed for whole body washing indicates people with a determined commitment to cleanly ways and a mindset convinced that the end deserved specialized means. Their adoption of cleanly standards committed them to new sensitivities in social contact, exhibiting no offensive odours or evidence of dirty work.

Control of bodily substances

The polite control and disguise of the excretion of bodily substances has a long history in courtesy literature. The mid-sixteenth-century Italian conduct book *Il Galateo*, one of the most frequently copied sources in advice literature thereafter, instructed that things which disgust should not be performed in the presence of others, or even be mentioned or referred to: 'No polite person will prepare himself for the relief of nature while others are looking on.'[62] Elias cites such comments dating before and after *Galateo*, yet their very persistence indicates continuous resistance to the sense of propriety that the rules sought to inculcate.[63] Anatomical arrangement and material conditions have always made it easy and convenient for men to urinate in public places, and the decision to be discreet about it, or not, may contain an element of deliberate animal assertion of precisely the kind that genteel rules sought to suppress. There were always degrees of publicity in defecating in public, generating distinct differences in acceptability between doing it in a nominated place, in a convenient dark corner, or anywhere public but unpopulated; these are still to be seen in some cultures. Women were historically less likely to offend in the same way due to the controls of traditional modesty; throughout history, a woman excreting in public proclaimed herself of the lowest class of morals and manners. Female comfort has usually suffered in consequence.

By the turn of the nineteenth century, self-control of excretion was effectively motivated by the value system that labelled natural functions so disgusting they must be hidden absolutely. Language was reformulated to describe excretion and its apparatus with a vocabulary of euphemisms that supplanted the vocabulary of slang. Some such words survive today, emphasizing that the topic remains unacceptable for adults, in private as well as in public.

In the late eighteenth century most urban people in England, America and their settlements stepped outdoors to a privy perched over a cesspit during the day; for convenience at night, a pot was slipped under the bed. The rising threshold of distaste for excretion was expressed by making both the product and the vehicle invisible, via a lid on the pot, and the pot in a cupboard, drawer or chair. The latter drew on the late seventeenth-century aristocratic practice of hiding the pot in a decorative close stool, further disguised by euphemisms such as 'necessary stool' or 'night stool'.[64] The new taste for cleanliness promoted the device into middle-class use at the turn of the nineteenth century in the guise of a chair, under the name 'night chair'.[65] Pots were also hidden in bedside cupboards, another late eighteenth-century invention for the purpose, made, as Sheraton slyly put it, 'in a style a little elevated above their use'.[66] A set of bedsteps, described as 'fitted' or 'furnished', indicated a pot in a drawer in the middle step. John Claudius Loudon, the encyclopedist of genteel housing, described and illustrated a set of fitted bed steps, 'with two of the steps arranged as cupboards. The tread of the top step is hinged and lifts up; the middle step pulls

Discreet: Furniture forms in middle-class bedrooms were adapted to facilitate, but hide, excretion.

Loudon, *Encyclopedia of Cottage, Villa and Farm Architecture* (London: 1833), pp. 322, 1082; Sheraton, *The Cabinet-Maker and Upholsterer's Drawing Book* (London: 1793), pl. 75; Webster, *Encyclopedia of Domestic Economy* (London: 1844), p. 277.

forward; and when drawn out its lid lifts up, and shows a space for a bidet or other convenience.'[67] Not many Scots insolvents of the late 1830s owned night stools as such, but from one inventory listing a 'chipped pan' in the bedsteps, it seems likely that as many as a third of households enjoyed such comfort.[68] By contrast, almost all the citizens of Wilmington, Delaware, and neighbouring towns, seem to have done without either bedsteps or night chairs, though their probate inventories list numerous 'stands' which may have included bedside chamber-pot cupboards. Nearly half the Sydney middle-class sample of the 1840s owned a night chair or close chair, invariably to be found in the main bedroom, with other members of the family, and the less well-off in general, continuing to make do with their pots under the bed. A further quarter who did not have a night chair possessed bedsteps, and though it is not certain they were fitted steps, it is clear that the colonial bourgeoisie desired modern standards of personal cleanliness and comfort and that practising such standards was a distinctive mark of their refinement.[69]

The development of the water closet, designed to remove human wastes cleanly and efficiently, is a story of isolated attempts over several centuries. Its modern history dates from the patented S-bend feature invented by watchmaker Alexander Cummings in 1775 and improved by inventor Joseph Bramah in 1778; this became the most satisfactory flushing toilet for nearly a hundred years, Bramah claiming that more than six thousand of his valved design had been sold by 1797. Further refinements are recorded in numerous patents issued in the UK and the USA, the work of practical plumbers and sanitary reformers. Still, water closets could not be truly useful until the construction of effective sewerage systems; in London this began in 1858.[70] But all this time, the topic of excretion was far too indelicate for discussion other than by reformist sanitary engineers. All that can be said is inference from the evident willingness of middle-class people, as well as aristocrats, to adopt the new technology despite its relative expense and the difficulties of connecting to a reliable water supply. Water closets were often the first, and specially in Britain, for a long time the only, item of fixed plumbing in middle-class houses; the reformer Loudon asserted, 'A WC or privy ought to be attached to every human dwelling.'[71] It is clear that genteel people sought to make their bodily functions as clean and inconspicuous as possible and that they consumed an array of specialized furnishings to help them do so.

Even the tiny excretion of blowing the nose took on the same polite invisibility as its bigger simulacrum. Controlling the noise and product of the act had been a regular topic of the old courtesy literature, and though nineteenth-century standards were polite enough not to need instructions about the undesirability of wiping the nose on the tablecloth or coat sleeve, there remained the necessity of achieving a compromise between manners and necessity. 'When thou blowest thy nose, let thy handkerchief be used, and make not a noise in so doing,' prescribed *The School of Good Manners*, a manual of French origin, translated into English in 1595, adapted by Boston schoolmaster Eleazar Moody about 1700 and published in at least 34 editions between 1715 and 1846.[72]

The eighteenth-century handkerchief worn as a neckcloth always had a practical application in workers' clothing, handy for absorbing sweat or cleaning grime or even wiping the nose. But like many accessories, handkerchiefs took on a decorative, fashionable character as a fresh white frame for both the manly and the feminine bosom and neck, no more to be exposed to mopping up than a lacy apron or silk cravat. The modern handkerchief dedicated to blowing the nose is difficult to date, for its function could be fulfilled by any scrap of fabric, and probably was from ancient times. However, handkerchiefs smaller than neckerchiefs, made of fine fabric and edged with deep flounces of lace, came to be used as delicate props by ladies and dandies, having trickled from courtly use to middle-class drawing rooms with the rise of nineteenth-century gentility.[73]

The problem of dealing with the need to blow the nose was met among the genteel less with handkerchiefs than with behavioural proscription: if a nose was so unseemly as to require frequent blowing, it was not fit for company. Nonetheless, so-called 'morning handkerchiefs' are mentioned in mid-nineteenth century fashion journals, apparently for operational purposes; plain, with hemmed or rolled edge, they became smaller throughout the century.[74] There was some leeway in the nose-blowing rules for gentlemen, or men in their own company, who could sneeze or blow openly in certain relaxed circumstances away from the presence of ladies. Indeed, a large handkerchief was a part of the apparatus of taking snuff, and by extension, a gentleman could express a sneeze with a handkerchief and no loss of face. But ladies were constrained by the ideal of female refinement constructed by contrast with men and the world. Ideally, there was no nose-blowing in the genteel world of the nineteenth-century middle class.

The uprightness of the body

Polite self-presentation required mastery of the body in space and in motion, for a person's external image constituted evidence of his or her internal spirit and was essential proof of gentility. Upright carriage was enjoined as representing strong moral fibre, while slouching connoted the opposite. Calm control of the limbs and facial expressions evidenced an untroubled soul in command of all faculties, one who could be trusted. Graceful posture in sitting and walking demonstrated that the practitioner's refinement was innate and natural. These outward signs were summed up by Lord Chesterfield, the courteous but cynical diplomat, as essential evidence of 'good breeding'. It was the goal towards which his *Letters to His Son* were constantly directed, and which, after publication in 1775, established the behavioural standards of nineteenth-century gentility, plus vital new moral ideals. Good breeding, Chesterfield wrote, requires 'a genteel and easy manner and carriage, wholly free from those odd ticks, ill habits, and awkwardnesses, which even many worthy and sensible people have in their behaviour.'[75] The same ideal principles applied to men as to women, but like many standards, more so for women. While men could relax in private, whether at home or in male company, women had standards to uphold even in the home, and especially in the arena of the drawing room where genteel values were performed for family and visitors.

'All natural motion is graceful,' claimed a popular Scottish journal in 1835.[76] The assertion that genteel deportment was the natural human mode of carriage was a major physical discrepancy that expressed the desire to project the culture of gentility as unaffected and normal.[77] Reality demonstrates the contrary, via the extensive advice literature showing that children had to be trained for years into disciplining their movements before they could become well-presented adults. Much the same standards of good posture had been urged on the young since the Middle Ages: 'Stand not wriggling with thy body hither and thither, but steady and upright.'[78] To achieve the central signs of dignified bearing, children were drilled, punished and dressed in apparatus to pull the shoulders back and mould the spine upright. 'When you sew, write, draw, or practise the harp or piano, you should be careful not to bend over, or hold your figure in a constrained position,' instructed the principal of a ladies' college in Maryland, demanding highly disciplined rigidity in ordinary parlour circumstances.[79] Genteel people controlled their hands, feet and mouths by avoiding extravagant gestures, clumsiness, gobbling and gabbling. As if to reduce the presence of these physical appurtenances and their capacity to get out of control, an aesthetic of idealized smallness in women and children developed, visible in Victorian illustrations and admiring references to tiny hands, fairy feet and rosebud mouths.[80]

To learn this degree of bodily control with graceful expression, children were sent to dancing lessons. The dancing master was something of a figure of mockery, for he represented the critical process of transforming the rough dolt into the polished beau or belle; thus he knew how artificial were the habits of grace he inculcated. Nonetheless, dancing was agreed to be the most effective vehicle of learning good comportment, since much of the repertoire of graceful body language derived from the French court ballet of the seventeenth and eighteenth centuries. Here the rituals of social intercourse had been stylized into conventional moves and counter-moves which came to govern even the robust traditional country dances of England, staple of balls before the introduction of the seductive waltz in 1812. Dancing instilled the discipline of set movements, the dexterity of quick, neat steps, and the courtesy of accommodating a partner within a social ritual. It could also be a pleasure, an expression of physicality that had few other outlets.

As such, dancing inherently risked the boundaries of self-control in the company of the opposite sex, making it a suspect activity and forbidden by some religious groups such as Calvinists. Even among the respectable who countenanced dancing, conduct at balls and assemblies was monitored closely by older women and the intimate body contact of waltzing was eschewed.

Uprightness in the body was aided and even mandated by styles of clothing and furniture. Women's bodies had long been shaped by corsetry to fulfil changing ideals of beauty, and different ideals followed each other throughout the eighteenth/nineteenth-century period. An erect back was central to good posture, so corsets always stiffened the upper body and usually smoothed the lower body, though the tight-lacing bemoaned by authorities was practised mainly by the young and fashionable. The focus of bodily control in the first half of the nineteenth century was on the upper body. Even the neoclassical fashion for light, loose clothing in the 1790s–1820s required most women to wear short stays, shaped with innovative cup-gussets to emphasize the bosom.[81] When fashion reverted to more traditional fabrics, colours and styles about 1830, the upper body remained under control with tightly fitted, short-waisted gowns billowing into skirts that hid the legs and their sins. Hemlines were usually low, but in the 1830s rose from the ground to above the ankles, exposing the feet for further instruction and control. A wishful taste for tiny feet emerged in idealized images in both fashion and fiction, aided by narrow, slipper-style shoes to mask reality.

Men's clothing also fitted the torso closely, directing the body into straight posture, though only extreme fashionables took on the additional discipline of corsets.[82] Epitomized by Beau Brummell, the early nineteenth century witnessed the birth of the standard of inconspicuous consumption that came to characterize men's clothing thereafter, relying for distinction on refined taste rather than sheer splendour. From the beginning of the century, male legs began to be concealed in long, loose trousers, where they had been previously conspicuously displayed by tight knee breeches and a brief fashion for tight pantaloons. The top hat grew taller towards the mid-century, exaggerating the verticality of correct stance and the presence of the gentleman who wore it. But where men could slough their tight-fitting coats and tall hats to relax in intimate and exclusive environments such as smoking rooms and private clubs, ladies' posture and clothing could be relaxed only in the privacy of undress at home.

The private domains of middle-class men became the seedbeds of the modern relaxed style. To lounge with the spine curved, legs crossed and feet up, and to enable such posture by tilting on the back legs of a chair, was to adopt the stance of the common man. Chesterfield advised that good breeding demanded one to stand straight or lean gracefully, never to loll: the classic behaviour of assertive dominance.[83] Nineteenth-century conduct manuals concurred, imbuing leaning or lounging with moral implications of slackness and social overtones of working-class idleness. In public, such behaviour would demean the character by implying unrigorous standards. Kenneth Ames makes an argument that masculine relaxation in a tilted chair expressed mythic republican Americanism, explicitly rejecting the controlled formality of aristocratically inspired uprightness.[84] It is a nice case, pointing to the inspiration of all genteel standards, but it could apply only in a democracy. By this argument, the English or colonial gentleman should never sit any way but upright in public: so when a subject of the Queen tilted comfortably backwards in his chair at home or in the club, was he expressing a democratic consciousness, or simply slumming for comfort?

The two standards – upright and relaxed – were facilitated by specific furniture styles and forms.[85] The public furniture of the drawing room and dining room remained resolutely vertical throughout the nineteenth century, indicating family hierarchy by the presence and size of chair arms; by contrast, small children were often encouraged to improve their posture by being seated on benches or stools without any back at all. The degree of comfort in seating furniture was less significant to the practice of gentility than the observance of appropriate forms, such as possession of a matching suite. Buttoned upholstered chairs, named easy chairs, were the prerogative of the ill and the frail in the late eighteenth century, coming into general use only in the 1830s, when they too were marked with arms according to the status of the occupant: elbow-height arms for the head of the household, low wings for the lady of the house, no arms for padded chairs used by family or visitors. The uprightness of furniture was most radically challenged by the invention of the rocking chair, requiring recourse to other elements of the genteel habitus to justify its loose, relaxed rhythm. Rocking chairs appear to have developed concurrently in Britain and the United States in the late eighteenth century, by adding rockers to cottage ladder-back or Windsor-style chairs.[86] In America they became a national icon of relaxed comfort by the end of the nineteenth century, but in 1840 the domestic adviser Miss Eliza Leslie warned, 'Swaying backwards and forwards in a parlour rocking chair is a most ungraceful recreation, particularly for a lady . . .'[87] However, the ease and utility of

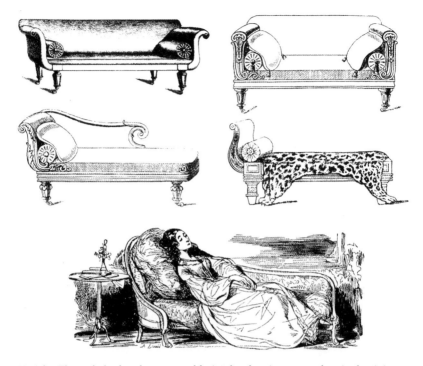

Upright: The sofa had to be respectable in the drawing room, but its lascivious bed-like characteristics were irresistible to illustrators.

Loudon, *Encyclopedia of Cottage, Villa and Farm Architecture* (London: 1833), p. 324; Webster, *Encyclopedia of Domestic Economy* (London: 1844), p. 212; Punch, vol. 2 (London: 1842), p. 59.

a rocker for nursing a child enabled the piece to take on an aura of cosy maternal comfort, justifying its inclusion in bedroom suites.[88] Rocking chairs took on gendered significance, testifying to relaxed democratic spirit in a man and fragile but nurturing domesticity in a woman.

Genteel culture in the early nineteenth century was not without reclining furniture such as the settee or sofa, and its use exhibits a counterbalance to the general principle of uprightness. The medieval ancestors of the sofa were the settle, the couch and the day bed, all essentially chairs with an elongated seat and a back of various heights.[89] This posture indicates two sources for the reclining pose: the invalid and the languid woman. Invalids, not well enough to sit up but not so ill as to be confined to bed, were a large class before the invention of modern therapies, and were treated with special concern for their physical comfort and diet. A variety of ingeniously bent furniture was devised to accommodate invalids in the drawing room, many recorded in patents and household advisory literature, where they may have resided forever while average households put up their invalids on more conventional sofas.[90] Nonetheless, patent apparatus constituted the inspiration of the reclining chair in the later nineteenth century, when relaxed comfort had become a much more powerful standard than in the early years of the century. The second source, the languid woman, expresses distinctly erotic values, severely criticized in advice books, and demonstrates the difficulty of maintaining the utmost self-control in posture all the time. For a respectable person to throw herself on the sofa, exhausted or bored, was possible, if not exactly permissible, only within the privacy of the family; it appears from novels to be a behaviour confined to young women. Nonetheless, the image of relaxation, buttressed by the lounging of men, prepared an acceptance of more casual posture towards the end of the nineteenth century.

The history of the sofa and the lounge chair show that the taste for comfort in furnishings, as likewise in clothing, is historically formed to different standards: respectability governed the satisfaction of individuals in the early nineteenth century to sit upright and wear corsets. The pleasures of relaxed posture and easy dress were not sought in the public domain, and if regretted, were compensated for by the sense of self-controlled propriety springing from adherence to the right standards.[91]

Checking emotions and taming desires

'Self-possession is the first requisite to good manners,' advised A Lady in 1837; 'Your whole deportment should give the idea that your person, your voice, and your mind are entirely under your own control.'[92] This advice restates the principle that restraint of somatic impulses indicated the correct character of the genteel person. Laughter was as inappropriate as crying, for though middle-class people could feel happiness, it must be managed in terms of rationality; 'rational happiness' meant a considered decision that circumstances enabled one to be in a state of contentment. Grief, on the other hand, was correctly managed by recourse to the consolations of religion. The calculated control of emotions both happy and sad is difficult for moderns to understand, and has often been taken to represent Victorian heartlessness or shallowness. On the contrary, as shown, for instance, in Elizabeth Bennet's suppression, as soon as other people come to the door, of her extreme agitation in response to Mr Darcy's proposal in *Pride and Prejudice*; it proves her a genteel person that when she finds she cannot contain her feelings decently, her flight upstairs is explained by a headache and her friends continue their appointed rounds.[93] This reaction witnesses the other side of the coin of emotional control: that others should restrain their responses to a subject's emotions. In the context of the novelist's craft, this episode also constructs Elizabeth as a person of feeling, a heroine sufficiently weak in human faults to generate sympathy among her readers, who sometimes also failed to manage their feelings at the official standard.

For the position that the ideal of gentility required total composure was an end easier to preach than to practise. It is relatively straightforward to train oneself to hold the hands still or to keep the feet together, but the suppression of autonomic reactions to external events is only achieved by Zen masters. Emotions ranging from surprise to fear were supposed to be met with composure, as described in the silver fork novel, *Granby*: 'She dexterously subdued her demonstrations of surprise, and contrived (which in such a case was of all things the most difficult) to look neither pleased nor mortified at the meeting, but to mould her features into an expression of civil indifference.'[94]

Many nineteenth-century middle-class people found such a demanding level of restraint was impossible to manage in all situations. Anger was the topic most addressed by the advisory literature, which recommended avoiding contentious topics as the safest technique to avoid argument. This may have been viable advice within social situations where people gathered to perform the genteel rituals of their status. In everyday life with its complement of frustrations caused by circumstances beyond the individual's control, the need to express anger could find a domestic outlet in rage towards inferiors such as servants, children or women. To express rage would be a major infringement of civilized standards, but its reality demonstrates that Victorian self-control was certainly not absolute in practice, and was also distinctly engendered. 'A man in a furious passion is terrible to his enemies; but a woman in a passion is disgusting to her friends,' wrote Mrs Ellis, commentator on English women's roles.[95] On the other hand, women were permitted more latitude than men in expressing love and grief (though excessive shows of either were considered ungenteel), and in weathering the trials of life, women enjoyed the emotional support of intimate networks of female friends and family.[96]

Masculine passions were particularly tested for resistance to the pleasures of losing control in gambling, drink and sex. An American book of sermons on dangerous amusements constructed the central issue thus: 'Can I not control myself? . . . Have I no power over my appetites and feelings?'[97] The writer's answer comprised a series of anecdotes about men who thought they could control themselves but were still corrupted by the insidious attractions of vice, inevitably ending in sordid death. In this scenario, the only guarantee to self-control in the face of the temptations of gambling and drinking was abstinence. Such scare tactics were a relic of hellfire religion, on the wane but still influential, towards the mid-century, when self-control was increasingly inculcated into the middle-class child via an internalized sense of shame or guilt.[98] Religion was one source of the standards of shame, but so were family and peer pressure, accomplished by informal group surveillance of its members by themselves.

Of the fields of self-discipline, sexual temptation was beyond the pale of conduct advice, but gambling and drinking successively constituted the poles of moral panic among the middle class in the nineteenth century. The public risk of gambling was the loss of gentlemanly trust, essential for business relations where the means of checking probity were few beyond family or church networks; the private risk was financial ruin, often affecting women and children. The risks were real, for gambling on sporting competitions and card games was deeply rooted in the traditions of English popular culture, into which many upper-class men dipped for a taste of the low life. Silver fork novels depict villains gambling in aristocratic settings as characteristic evidence of their evil nature; worse, they ensnare upright young men (often old school fellows) either to stand surety for a new victim or to become gamblers themselves.[99] The popular press records a much more diverse range of betting on any type of competition: horse races, football matches, cock fights, prize fights. Not even noble patronage of horse racing could make it entirely respectable in genteel circles, though the racehorse-owning lobby in the Houses of Parliament always protected the industry's legitimacy. In liminal societies such as the American and colonial frontiers, gambling became a focus for control campaigns by religious and sometimes government authorities.[100] In England, the evangelical campaign against gambling secured the banning of lotteries in 1826 and of public gaming houses in 1846, diverting gambling into private clubs and mobile bookie operations, respectively serving the aristocracy and the working class.[101]

The middle-class fear of gambling was overtaken in the mid-century by a new devil, drink. From roots in a campaign by evangelical and dissenting men, women seized a larger part in the temperance movement

Out of control: Drink has corrupted respectability and is set to destroy the comfortable home. Cruikshank became a temperance advocate in 1847, when this series of eight illustrations was made. Compare illustration on p. 59.

George Cruikshank, 'The Bottle', pl. II (London: 1847).

by the 1860s, coming to control it via separatist organizations such as the Women's Christian Temperance Union in the 1890s.[102] Alcohol had long contained the anti-authoritarian risk of public disorder, but it further came to be seen as immoral for its capacity to undermine character, religion, the work ethic and family responsibility – the basis for women's intervention and activism in the decades after 1840. Many subsets of opposition to alcohol inhabited the temperance movement: a view, especially in the 1820s and 1830s, that beer was harmless but spirits were deadly; the environmentalist perspective that public drinking was undesirable but that wine in the home was acceptable; and the crescendo of teetotal abstinence. The impulse to one or another position was driven more by religious commitment than class perspective, and genteel advice manuals generally approved moderate drinking by men and the occasional glass of wine for women. Throughout most of the nineteenth century, taking the pledge of abstinence implied either strict evangelical morals or born-again renunciation, though by the 1890s, signed-up temperance commitment grew ever more mainstream middle class.

Sexual restraint was a topic discussed in medical texts rather than popular conduct literature. It expressed a new (though not unanimous) view of women as asexual beings: in Dr William Acton's words, 'The majority of women (happily for society) are not very much troubled with sexual feelings of any kind . . . Love of home, of children, and of domestic duties are the only passions they feel.'[103] Thus scientific authority reinforced the construction of middle-class women's character as pure and spiritual, tipping the ancient image of the temptress of carnal desire onto working-class women. The reputation for sexual purity gave middle-class women a powerful moral advantage over men, and in some circumstances probably enabled them to control sexual relations.[104] At the same time, the pure woman was defined by her counterpart, the fallen woman, very often a servant, whose class powerlessness was preyed upon by middle-class men. The extended dependence of young adult men and the ideology that men's sexual desires were 'naturally' lustful sustained the underworld of prostitution that characterized the Victorian double standard of sexual morality. Nonetheless, most middle-class reformers, and seemingly most women, did not reject sex completely; they accepted sex in marriage, not only for procreation but increasingly for the expression of intimacy and love between partners.[105]

The key issue in male sexual self-control was less with whom he had sexual relations than whether and how he conserved the sexual energy represented by semen. The view that to ejaculate sperm outside the purposes of marriage was a waste of vital energy is an ancient theory, popularly known via the Biblical exemplar, Onan. Masturbation was medicalized as a problem of health in the eighteenth century, when it was attributed as the cause of general debility, digestive disorders, blindness and consumption; in the early nineteenth century, physicians focused increasingly on its alleged effects on the mind, ranging from nervous disorders to madness.[106] Within this context, the management of masturbation required the utmost self-control, augmented, especially for children, by restraint devices and the sense of guilt for failures of self-control. Many of the same effects of masturbation were identified among girls and young women, but the shape of their risk was conceived as precocious sexual awakening rather than vital exhaustion. Both forms of fear turn on the vision of childhood purity, and indicate that sex was viewed by the Victorian middle class as something for adults – that is, the married – only.

Once married, the pleasures of sexual relations were frequently haunted by the consequences of pregnancy. Despite active religious prohibition of techniques to avoid conception, there is evidence enough to be certain that many couples practised abstinence and coitus interruptus as fertility control measures, both methods relying fundamentally on self-control.[107] Specific information about these contraceptive techniques was published in the radical literature on the problems of pauperism and over-population among the working class of the late eighteenth/early nineteenth-century period. By the 1830s new books emerged with advice on contraceptives such as the vaginal sponge and vaginal douche, advocating fertility control also for the sake of enjoyment of sexuality without the fear of another child. *Moral Physiology*, by Robert Dale Owen, and *The Fruits of Philosophy, or the Private Companion of Young Married People*, by Robert Knowlton, were both first published in the United States and immediately reprinted in England, remaining in circulation until at least the 1870s. It is not clear whether this literature, ostensibly directed towards the working class, had any noticeable effect among its intended audience, but it seems to have been taken up by the educated middle class by the middle of the nineteenth century.[108] While the technological power of sexual self-control began to shift to women, it was so opposite to the maternal ideal of pure womanhood that contraception remained a conflicted resource until well into the mid-twentieth century. The ideology of self-control continued to grip the construction of the genteel person.

As shown by the many references above to the courtesy literature of the Renaissance, control of bodily function and physical action was a central element of upper-class socialization – of the cultural capital of gentle pedigree. Nineteenth-century aspiration to the conditions of gentility hugely enlarged the practice of these values and established them as the parameters of a distinctive habitus. The discourse of self-possession took on lived meaning to unprecedented numbers of people; cleanliness, uprightness and dispassion became watchwords of middle-class existence. They identified the select who could fulfil such conditions and counter-defined the character of the working class as dirty, slothful and self-indulgent. Thus a bigger and bigger middle class was called into existence by knowledge of the correct standards plus consumption of the right equipment.

5
Best Behaviour:
Public Relationships

The genteel code of etiquette was dedicated to the control of the self in society, a subset of manners for use in particular circumstances among particular people. A key dimension of the cultural capital of gentility was therefore knowledge of etiquette and the confidence to use it easily. Etiquette was a dynamic, evolving, yet prescriptive, discourse, manipulated by the fluent to identify their like and exclude outsiders. Its forms were acknowledged, but never conclusively explained, notwithstanding the claims of the extensive etiquette literature. In this way, knowledge of correct etiquette defined the shifting borders of gentility. The critic T. C. Morgan wrote in 1838: 'Etiquette . . . in its modern acceptation, refers to some line of conduct which has been *ticketed* with the approbation of the great leaders of society.'[1] The ticket analogy draws on the word's French etymology, but its implication of a pass/fail approval process suggests more certainty than existed in practice, as does the common descriptor of etiquette as a code. Certainty was what those outside the magic circle of middle-class gentility craved. For those within, *un*certainty blurred access to genteel exclusivity and protected their privileged knowledge; they could ascribe their own capacity to inherent good breeding.

Good breeding was the ineffable atmosphere of the genteel habitus, enabling its product, refinement. Both were difficult to detail, but throughout the nineteenth century, in Britain, America and the colonies, people looked back to the presentation by Lord Chesterfield in the letters he wrote in the 1740s to his (illegitimate) son, published by his son's widow in 1775 and remaining in print ever since.[2] Chesterfield called good breeding the goal of the programme of his son's education, nicely eliding the apparent meaning of 'breeding' as both pedigree and learning: 'As to good breeding, you cannot attend to it too soon or too much; it must be acquired while young, or it is never quite easy; and if acquired young, will always be easy and habitual.'[3] He had earlier described good breeding as the polish to more substantial qualities, introducing what came to be perceived as the moral dilemma of genteel substance versus appearances. 'I have often told you . . . parts and learning can alone make you admired and celebrated . . . but that the possession of lesser talents was most absolutely necessary, towards making you liked, beloved, and sought after in private life. Of these lesser talents, good breeding is the principal and most necessary one . . . it adds great lustre to the more solid advantages both of the heart and the mind.'[4] The gist of Chesterfield's advice for obtaining the lustre of good breeding was to be attentive to others and restrained in projecting one's self in social encounters, requiring a constant degree of self-consciousness and self-control. His examples are clear and elegant, but ultimately dedicated to self-serving ends that undermine the moral qualities of his advice with a calculating edge that makes them cynical. The sincerity of morality in manners was to emerge as one of the defining issues in the development of Victorian genteel culture.

Chesterfield's programmatic outline of good breeding indicates the importance of education as the key to establishing the practices of gentility in the hearts and minds of its successful practitioners. The ever-broader availability of education in the wake of the Enlightenment enabled the spread of polite manners and refined expectations as much as book-learning. Whether at mother's knee, or a great public school offering the classics, or a young ladies' academy of elegant accomplishments, the practised performance of gentility constituted the dominant character of education. There were those who considered this aim frivolous, such as the serious evangelicals, or unproductive, as many commercial men argued; here lies one of the nubs of the thesis of the subversion or 'failure' of the middle class.[5] Yet despite being contrary to the class interests of serious businessmen, genteel refinement continued to define the aims of child and youth education, and of subsequent programmes of self-improvement for adults.

The practice of etiquette demonstrates both its structuring and structured effects in the cultural practice of the middle class. Ideally, etiquette was encultured within the family. The 'heritability' of etiquette in these circumstances constituted a quantum of cultural capital that could be even more valuable to its heir than money, for while a fortune could be made by anyone, the ingrained practices of etiquette were difficult (though not impossible) to acquire by other means. 'Refined manners are like refined style, which Cicero compares to the colour of the cheeks, which is not acquired by sudden or violent exposure to heat, but by continual walking in the sun,' tuts A Gentleman in *The Laws of Etiquette*.[6] Thanks to the efforts of parents and teachers, a critical attribute of middle classness was naturalized into a function of birth. But this mechanism of class identification, so neatly paralleling the exclusivity of the hereditary aristocracy, created its own barrier to the expansion of middle-class definition, with problematic consequences for would-be entrants. How could one acquire the necessary polish without childhood training?

Here occurred another turning point of accommodation in the embourgeoisement of aristocratic practice: the validation of the concept of the gentleman of learning, the gentleman by education, the well-bred gentleman. That is to say, appropriate learning and successful practice of the polite arts became inexplicitly acknowledged as sufficient qualification for acceptance into middle-class society. Thus the barrier to insider privilege was made permeable, and camouflaged (since it was impossible to regulate) through a polite pretence that such translations never happened. By allowing that self-education in manners was equivalent to genteel upbringing, persons who behaved genteelly could be assumed into the magic circle as though they had never been outside it. The transition was knowable only by the acceptance of peers, and a collusive myth followed that, since gentility was a function of inborn nature, the acknowledged candidate must have always been so. At the same time, the polite pretence contained room for a degree of suspicion of any new acquaintance, adding a stressful undertone to many social encounters.

To maintain the purity of genteel society meant controlling its membership by excluding undesirables from the outside and monitoring the standards of those within; resisting the impure, as Mary Douglas describes the anthropology of social pollution, requires action on many fronts.[7] The contest for middle-class status was specially tense at its lower margin, where definitive pollution had to be repelled. Here could be seen the existential struggle by which the morals and practices of gentility became distinct through opposition to those of the lower orders, whose lack of deference, knowledge and taste cast them as the Other. However, the absence of an absolute boundary permitted a liminal zone where some crossover was tolerated and, in the process, a degree of uncertainty about status was condoned which could make less-than-confident individuals extremely anxious about their place in the order of things. Hence further protective action operated within this foggy margin to exclude unacceptable contenders. Of course, the marginal had nothing to lose and much to win by attempting to assert genteel status. It was possible to try because the fiction of genteel values as a guarantee of gentle birth was a gamble whose risk marginally middle-class people understood but had to pretend to ignore in order to protect their own integrity. People asserting their superiority could not afford to expose chinks whereby they could be exposed by others. Even within the secure territory of gentility it was important to keep the population under surveillance and to punish transgressions. Internalized self-control fulfilled much of this function, but the society of peers also maintained vigilant watch over personal behaviour. The system of etiquette provided a framework with which to make judgements in all these circumstances and offered techniques to enact the judgements via inclusion in and exclusion from social life.

The origins and nature of etiquette

Etiquette derived from the courtly practice of seventeenth-century France, where the Bourbon kings controlled the nobility with a centripetal network of highly ritualized ceremonies in which the monarch's favour transferred power to successful subordinates.[8] The English monarchy never attained this degree of control over the British aristocracy, though many French forms of princely courtesy gradually translated to the Court of St James, and the courts of the late seventeenth century were the most ceremonious ever known in the United Kingdom.[9]

Both the Anglicized meaning and the message of etiquette as a standard of behaviour among gentle people were introduced to England by Chesterfield's *Letters to his Son*. The first English dictionary reference to the term has been traced to the 1791 *Critical Pronouncing Dictionary*, where etiquette is defined as 'the polite form or manner of doing anything; the ceremonial of good manners.' John Walker, editor of the dictionary, noted: 'This word crept into use some years after Johnson wrote his Dictionary, nor have I found it in any other I have consulted. I have ventured, however, to insert it here, as it seems to be established; and as it is more specific than "ceremonial", it is certainly of use.'[10] The late eighteenth-century meaning of the term was clearly somewhat different from its French origins. Elias draws a precise distinction, seeing etiquette as a rational behaviour where court society compelled participation in the struggle for status, but arguing that it was irrelevant to bourgeois society, in which economic interest compelled professional behaviour.[11] This view is blinkered due to Elias's focus on the sociology of absolutism, obscuring the reality of status competition among the nineteenth-century middle class, where his functionalist analysis of etiquette can be read as convincingly as it does in the original exemplar, the court of Versailles.

The concept of etiquette as a system of manners as opposed to court ceremony marks a major shift in focus from behaviour imposed by the king's will to an individually internalized standard of social relations; thus it connects to the large phenomenon of Anglo middle-class formation and cultural articulation. Historians of etiquette have noted a shift in the character of English etiquette in the 1830s, a transformation of the continental tradition of manners initiated by Chesterfield into something distinctly middle class.[12] The change has been further analysed as a turning point between the influence of evangelical-inspired moralism and a more cynical approach to social mobility, disengaging morals from polite practice in the interest of middle-class advancement, but inventing a new blend of etiquette and ethics in the form of professional credentials of authority and codes of behaviour.[13] In the United States, the first locally-written etiquette guides appeared in the 1820s, when the evangelical fires of the Second Great Awakening were still strong; as Christina Dallett Hemphill observes, the substance of these books was almost precisely the same as the British etiquette literature.[14] Nonetheless, on both sides of the Atlantic, the standard of conduct grounded in religion had contended with the self-serving role of manners as confessed by Chesterfield for at least a hundred years before the early nineteenth-century accommodations of etiquette. This struggle is a field that can be dissected in Elias's terms, where membership of genteel society constituted the foundation of personal identification and social existence.[15]

The touchstone of genteel etiquette, even in the United States and the British colonies, was always aristocratic life – or rather, an idealized vision of aristocratic life. It was a conventional claim that the nobility was simple and unassuming, though quite evidently untrue in the light of contemporary diaries and memoirs, which show the usual range of venal and obnoxious human behaviours among the great. In one of his fashionable novels, Benjamin Disraeli describes the fictional Duke of Beaumanoir, for instance, as:

> munificent, tender and bounteous to the poor . . . A keen sportsman, he was not untinctured by letters, and had indeed a cultivated taste for the fine arts . . . there ran through his demeanour a vein of native simplicity that was full of charm, his manner was finished . . . His good breeding, indeed, sprang from the only sure source of gentle manners – a kind heart.[16]

The purpose of novelists and advice writers in asserting such oleaginous naivety was to demonstrate ways in which middle-class people could be the same as the aristocracy. There was some reality in the rhetoric, in that while the middle class sought aristocratic standards, the aristocracy was simultaneously seeking a less overtly splendid status and sliding into line with new bourgeois standards of gentility. Nonetheless, adherence to the rank-ordered society of England was never challenged by the genteel middle classes, who in their contradictory desire for noble connections, expressed the fundamental non-nobility of their situation even as they fawned: 'refinement, fashion, etiquette and what is called Ton, emanates from the palace...'[17] Even in America some etiquette books asserted that the royal court of St James was the model of the best manners.[18]

In the upper reaches of the middle class, where acquaintance with great or titled persons was a social possibility, the struggle between traditional deference and appropriate self-regard was often acute. Hence the study of the ranking of titles, honours and occupational status was taken seriously and regarded as the very pinnacle of correct social knowledge and behaviour. For instance, the order of precedence of guests at dinner was a regular inclusion in advice books, detailing how the wife of a younger son of an earl had precedence over the wife of an heir to a baronet – an intricate corpus, flatteringly implying that its reader would have such guests and therefore require the knowledge to resolve arrangements of precedence.[19] This kind of highly directed advice represents both a market-driven response to the fantasy of moving in the topmost circles, and a real lesson in polite procedures that may have been extremely useful for the socially mobile. Though superior status is usually couched in terms of rank, it could also function as a shorthand for anyone whom one wanted to impress by acknowledging precedence; in this way the rules of etiquette were as relevant to American citizens and colonials who lived in the absence of a hereditary peerage. The transition of aristocratic etiquette from the old world to the new was occasionally explained in the preface of advice books:

> The author believes that in America, there is to be found a society as well bred, graceful, and polished, as can be met with in Europe; but as the masses of people, so continually rising in the New World, can scarcely be expected successfully to emulate the manners and habits of those whose position has so long been defined, assuredly it can hurt noone, but benefit many, for them to compare the usages of

For the Servant's Guide.

Titled: The frontispiece to the 1832 *Servants' Guide* depicts the ranks of coronets, mitres and helmets of the English aristocracy. The book advises that 'a knowledge of their distinctions will be useful to the reader'.

The Servants' Guide and Family Manual (London: 1832).

polished nations with those of their own; and to consider whether a common sense application of the ordinary observances of good society, as practised in older countries, cannot materially elevate in the social scale, the aspiring and the successful.[20]

Putting the aristocratic ideal into daily practice, the individual's sense of superiority or inferiority in social circumstances made etiquette critical to personal identity, for the successful genteel performance constituted the outward and visible sign of the quality of the inner person. The expectation of transparency contained one of the central contradictions of middle-class gentility: advice manuals and novels made it clear that gentility was a state of mind which had to be lived at every moment, had to be, in fact, one's natural self. The notion of correct but relaxed manners was central to the Renaissance courtesy literature; it flowered again in the ideals of Victorian gentility. The easy style represented the opposite of pomposity; it reflected confidence and a degree of self-respect which could be deferential without being self-abasing. This kind of gentlemanly independence made gentility an attractive stance for self-made men and reached down the ranks to inspire working-class ambition, yet such smooth confidence could be hard to achieve. Pretending, by putting on manners for company, or turning them off for other occasions, belied the claim to true gentility; if discovered, such behaviour was interpreted as insincerity and mocked or reprimanded, as by Asteios ('man about town'): 'A man never becomes so ridiculous by the qualities which he has, as by those which he affects to have.'[21] Nonetheless, people were aware of the performative aspects of their 'natural' manners, a conflation that had been recommended years before by Lord Chesterfield: 'the well-bred man . . . observes, with care, the manners and ways of the people most esteemed at that place, and conforms to them with complaisance. Instead of finding fault . . . he commends their dress, their houses and their manners, a little more, it may be, than he really thinks they deserve.'[22] The rational frankness of this mid-eighteenth-century advice was out of tune with the spirit of early Victorian gentility, though it remained sound strategy for calculating aspirants. As a prolific advice-writer, the Rev. Dr John Trusler, observed, 'Though Lord Chesterfield has been condemned for recommending simulation among men, there is no getting on peaceably without it.'[23]

Parallel to the construction of the self through the performance of etiquette, its rules also governed internal relations within the middle class. Etiquette provided a semiotic system of minute but meaningful differences with which like could be united and others shunned. The manipulation of difference generated signs legible to just some within the multitude of status groups that comprised the generic middle class. Like insects flashing luminous signals to attract mates of the right breed, segments of the middle class recognized each other and constructed a society, 'sliced and sliced again to extremely thin status layers, subtly separated from each other by the infinitely resistant lines of snobbery.'[24] This was a more rarefied contest than the relatively clumsy act of gatekeeping. Its entire code was never expressly documented, despite the claims of the advice manuals. Here lurks the source of the angst that plagued the consciousness of all but the most assured genteel performers: how can we be sure we do it correctly? And on the other side of the social footlights, among those on the receiving end of the genteel performance, how can we be sure that this person, apparently acting correctly, is indeed one of us? The answers were always relative, introducing an element of amoral judgement about plausibility and conviction rather than self-evident guarantee.

The implication that etiquette could be sincere or superficial therefore raised questions about its moral basis. Good manners were an expression of gentility, but fashionable manners could merely satisfy the forms of etiquette and an insincere performer could skate by on appearances. This duality informed a suspicion among some of manners unassociated with religion; however, the evangelical strand in middle-class development was not universal and arguably was overtaken by the growth of class society by the 1830s. Still, when lapses in genteel standards between performance and morality were discovered, they were seized upon as evidence of distinction, justifying the status of the observer and complementarily condemning the observed. Thus a distinguishing characteristic of secure Victorian gentility was its moral dimension, to which Christian kindness and charity were integral. The conventional trope of such elision appears in many an advice book, typically: 'Good manners and good morals are founded on the same eternal principles of right, and are only different expressions of the same truths.'[25] Morality undergirded genteel practice and informed good manners, but was not intrinsically an element of etiquette: it could be said that while genteel substance was always expressed by genteel form, genteel form was not necessarily evidence of genteel substance. Constituted as a body of rules, publicly genteel behaviour was open to imitation and cynical misuse. Hence constant lookout activity was conducted by all genteel people; to be at either end of the microscope required the essential self-control of the middle class and its aspirant spirit.

Women were the critical agents of etiquette, like the larger culture of gentility. It applied to men, though only in the social sphere of elegant or aspiring society: 'Professional gentlemen are excused from many of those strict observances of etiquette, which might interfere with more important duties.'[26] For middle-class women, however, the steps and poses of etiquette amounted to their daily work and lifetime career, fully equivalent to the money-making work of men. Elias compares this circumstance of investing in and monitoring stock in personal opinion to a stock market whose currency is delicate shades of behaviour.[27] In Bourdieu's terms, the equivalence may also be measured in terms of capital, the one product earning symbolic income in the form of family prestige, and the other bringing in money, but both being exchangeable in the economy of social relations.[28] This insight into the necessity of middle-class women's etiquette-work indicates why its reality was so deeply suppressed by contemporary ideology that it was said that ladies worked not at all; commentator Mrs Ellis uttered a rare explicit statement when she wrote: 'Society is often to the daughters of a family, what business or a profession is to the sons.'[29] Correctly refined women demonstrated the cultural propriety of their (and their families') status or claim to status. The limits of an aspirant woman's capacity to be recognized by virtue of her accomplishment constitutes the self-deluding drama of Emma Woodhouse's project to improve Harriet Smith in the novel *Emma*; it also recounts the pain and embarrassment created by the denial of recognition.[30] But in some circumstances, especially where business deals were involved, women's skill in the social graces could make or break contacts with powerful connections. Nonetheless, across the spectrum of the middle class, the fiction of the idle domestic woman masked the representational activity of women as the vehicles of establishing, monitoring and maintaining class difference through the rituals of etiquette.

Etiquette books

Advice on courteous behaviour and self-cultivation had been published in English since the sixteenth century, often translations or adaptations of a handful of European progenitors such as Castiglione's *Book of the Courtier* (1528) and della Casa's *Il Galateo* (1558).[31] The arena of such advice was the princely court, replaced in the eighteenth century by fashionable London society as the focus of refinement. Evidence of the rise of the new middle class around the cusp of the nineteenth century, a surge of new instruction books on etiquette appeared. They systematized the rules of conduct in public, though small differences between them indicate that the real nature of etiquette was more subtle, depending on fine understandings of each other by both performer and audience. Advice books were regularly denounced by the genteel establishment but the demand appeared insatiable, evidence of massive popular faith in self-improvement, in the possibilities of *becoming* well-bred: 'It is very possible for a person to attend to etiquette without being well-bred, but no person can be well-bred who does not attend to etiquette.'[32] Where the previous several hundred years of courtesy books had focused on a substance of ideal moral conduct, the pursuit of worthy goals and the cultivation of civilized practices in everyday life, the new etiquette manuals stressed the style of manners and their conventional forms. An anonymous etiquette-writer advised in 1839: 'There are certain arbitrary peculiarities of manner, speech, language, taste &c. which mark the high-born and high-bred. These should be observed and had. They are the signs-manual of good-breeding, by which gentlemen recognise each other wherever they meet.'[33] But maintaining the mystery, the writer did not disclose what the precise forms were.

Most etiquette books were written for a specific demographic distinguished by age, sex, and sometimes class. The genre's tradition was overwhelmingly directed to the young in the form of prescriptions. Here it is important to distinguish the objective to cultivate self-controlled manners from works directed towards pure moral improvement expressed in right conduct, an even older tradition renewed via the evangelical revival of the late eighteenth century and producing a large literature in the early nineteenth century. The traditional recipe for instruction in behaviour that was nice as well as good is exemplified by the history of Eleazar Moody's *The School of Good Manners*. This immensely popular work derived from *L'A, B, C, ou instruction pour les petits enfants* of 1564, translated into English in 1595 and published at least four times as *ABC or, The First School of Good Manners*. It was adapted by Moody at the turn of the eighteenth century in New England and reprinted there in at least 34 editions between 1715 and 1846.[34] It returned to Britain under Moody's name and in adaptations such as the anonymous *A Manual of Manners, or, a Child's Book of Etiquette*, published in Glasgow in 1838 – a fine demonstration of the continuity and international spread of genteel precepts.[35] Older children on the threshold of adulthood constituted a further market for etiquette guides which, recognizing the forthcoming bifurcation of the ways of men and women, was almost always differentiated by gender, as in *Advice to a Young Gentleman on Entering Society* and *The Young Lady's*

Friend. Books for young women acknowledged the in-between status of girls out of the schoolroom but yet unmarried, addressing both the need for useful work, usually depicted as assisting mother in household tasks such as pouring tea, and the desire to shine in company, recognized with recipes for cosmetics. Young adults were further targeted at the milestones of independent life, as in *The Bride's Book* and *Model Men*.[36]

Hereafter, etiquette books addressed a general audience, predominantly in a voice that generously assumes a readership already genteel and needing only a little polish under the guidance of the (frequently anonymous) author, who is reliably A Lady or A Gentleman. The most popular nineteenth-century book was *Hints on Etiquette and the Usages of Society with a Glance at Bad Habits* by Agogos ('teacher'), selling 12,000 copies in its first three years.[37] In the same way as *The School of Good Manners*, *Hints* became the source of many further advice books, some directly plagiarized, some more subtly inspired and augmented, as in the 26th edition, 'Revised (with Additions) by A Lady of Rank.'[38] In the United States *Hints* was pirated in several editions, some under the fictitious name Count Alfred D'Orsay. William Charles Day, the original author, eventually published an edition under his own name specifically for the American market, *The American Ladies' and Gentlemen's Manual of Elegance, Fashion and True Politeness*.[39] Testament to the belief in its improving qualities, an edition of *Hints* was printed in the convict colony of Van Diemen's Land (Tasmania) in 1838, with the preface: 'If the pen which produced this useful little work has stood the test of metropolitan criticism "at home," no apology can be required from the present publisher . . .'[40]

Etiquette books were rarely directed to working-class improvement other than as better-behaved servants. Unusually, *Hints* contains a section of 'Advice to Tradespeople' and its earliest editions begin with the terse epigraph, 'To make a silk purse out of a sow's ear.' This was evidently *too* blunt; it disappeared from later editions. Nonetheless, *Hints* expressed conflicting positions on the realistic outcomes of its instruction. On the one hand, Agogos admonished his readers: 'remember that people are respectable in their own sphere only, and that when they attempt to step out of it they cease to be so.' Yet he concluded the book with the familiar assurance that 'Gentility is neither in birth, manner, nor fashion – but in the MIND.'[41] The two views framed the struggle to become genteel.

As well as advice books, the topic of etiquette was presented to the would-be genteel in the 'silver fork' school of fashionable novels, popular from about 1810 to 1840.[42] (The silver fork referred to an iconic item of genteel panoply, the emblem of respectable manners, style and income.) Tales of wealthy, fashionable life by authors such as T. H. Lister, Benjamin Disraeli and Mrs Catherine Gore offered readers both vicarious pleasure and models of refined behaviour, for which there was a voracious market. Silver fork author Edward Bulwer reflected on their popularity towards the end of their period of influence: 'In proportion as the aristocracy had become social, and fashion allowed the members of the more mediocre classes a hope to outstep the boundaries of fortune, and be quasi-aristocrats themselves, people eagerly sought for representations of the manners which they aspired to imitate, and the circle to which it was not impossible to belong.'[43] Explicitly acknowledging the aspirational frame of the genre, Mrs Gore, one of the most prolific silver fork writers, contrasted her field to Jane Austen's work as 'an attempt to transfer the familiar narrative of Miss Austin [sic] to a higher sphere of society.'[44] Critics disapproved of both their aim and product, castigating their narrow superficiality as encouraging, in the essayist William Hazlitt's words, 'admiration of the folly, caprice, insolence and affectation of a certain class.'[45]

The claim of etiquette books to tutor those not born to genteel society in the practice of etiquette manifested the worst fears of those who doubted the sincerity of codified manners. Hence the spate of advice books occupied an uneasy place in the economy of manners. The manuals appeared to commodify the cultural capital of the middle class and were therefore reviled by the already genteel. Two strategies can be traced in the process of camouflaging the codes spelled out in the books. First was a jeremiad against the upstarts who sought to penetrate middle-class society; they were condemned for even thinking about it. The second strategy of denial assured aspirants of the impossibility that they might or could learn anything that would assist their ambitions. Reviewing a rash of etiquette guides in 1837, the critic Abraham Hayward pronounced against 'the demand for this sort of trash [which] betokened an unworthy and degrading eagerness on the part of a large part of the community to learn how lords and ladies ate, drank, dressed and coquetted.'[46] As a last resort, mockery always stood ready to cut pretension:

> In Tenby Miss Jinks asks the loan of
> The book from the innkeeper's wife;
> And she reads till she dreams she is one of
> The leaders of elegant life.[47]

Yet for all the resistance drawn by the etiquette manuals, it is clear that, with some limitations, they described real practice. They do not reflect immediate historical events, despite the claims of many to have been written (or at least guided) by an aristocrat, but they helped to produce reality through their discursive presentations of practice. Hayward himself, otherwise thoroughly dismissive, acknowledged, 'it is undeniable there is a great deal of good sense, with many valuable suggestions regarding manners and conduct, in these books.'[48] Yet the inherent limits of codification meant the fine distinctions established in social contact could be recorded and published only to a degree: a manual is a finite piece of reporting on a dynamic process of communication. Writing it down and thus nailing it immediately establishes a canon which can be avoided by the empowered, as they re-establish boundaries to protect their exclusive interests, even as out-groups vie to fulfil its precepts. Hence authorial knowledge was challenged by reviewers, for example: 'The author of *Hints on Etiquette* is brief on the subject of Visiting, and is far from perfectly at home in it;' and shortcomings such as contradictions were gleefully pointed out.[49] But criticism never dampened the market for advice.

The ferocity of the campaign against published guides to etiquette suggests their power. Despite the tenor of the times and the numbers who evidently aspired and must have succeeded to some degree, genteel culture contained no positive regard for aspiration or self-improvement among any but the elect. Books regularly opined that it would be 'highly desirable that the agrémens of society should be more generally diffused among the middle class,' but critics consistently condemned status achieved by work instead of birth.[50] Popular explanations for their determined opposition include envy of parvenu success, the strength of aristocratic exclusiveness and a subversion of middle-class ideals. A blunter solution views the phenomenon as a sustained action to protect the status honour of the already genteel.

In the end, the concept of a 'guide' to etiquette was fundamentally impossible. To believe the premise of good breeding demanded the conviction that correct behaviour was inherent. But to compile etiquette advice between two covers or to buy an etiquette guide acknowledged that a segment of the corpus of genteel knowledge could be commodified and consumed. Agogos addressed the contradiction with a uniquely pessimistic view of class relations: 'Many will say, "We are just as good as they are, and as respectable". SO YOU ARE, but yet not fit companions for each other. Society is divided into various orders, each class having its own views, its peculiar education, habits, and tastes . . .'[51] This conclusion is entirely reactionary in its view of a rank-ordered society circumscribed by immutable barriers. It manifests all the ancient prejudice of the aristocracy against trade, against making money by commerce, which the rising middle class was accommodating through its positive moralization of work. Even in the world's first mass democracy, the shadow of class-embedded exclusions shaped the possibilities of social advancement. What does this say for the credibility of the readers of etiquette advice? Were they gullible fools, or punters playing calculated odds? Given the tremendous demand for advice books it might be expected that readers had a fair expectation, perhaps based on models of their acquaintance, that it was indeed possible to pick up the knowledge of values and behaviour that would enable admission to middle-class status. The influence and power of the self-help movement and its promise of social notice for virtuous hard work is evidence of a widespread conviction that individual agency could breach privilege and become middle class.

Public performances

The conduct of etiquette was concerned exclusively with public, social contact. Private relations among family and friends, and collegial relations such as in men's clubs and women's 'world of love and ritual', were assumed to be informed by affection and common interest not requiring prescription. Thus the Biblical injunction to honour parents was frequently reiterated in the class of moralizing conduct books of the first decades of the century and in advice books directed towards young women throughout the century, but it was not a function of etiquette; it was owed out of filial love and Christian duty. Nonetheless, to be truly genteel, polite performances had to be sincere. Hence the advice books criticized shyness, forwardness and awkwardness, advocating that one's correct manner should be entirely natural. If naturalness didn't come naturally, it must be learned. The circularity of this view highlights the risks to sincerity entailed by systematized etiquette, and demonstrates the advantage of the person inculcated since infancy with the knowledge and self-discipline necessary to deliver correct behaviour. (The process didn't always work, exemplified by the failure of Lord Chesterfield's son, Philip Stanhope, to respond to his father's careful programme to train him from boyhood to be a charming but self-possessed international diplomat. The young Stanhope never became a fine public gentleman, and died aged 34, 'a common bookworm'.)[52]

In the field of effective social relations the first step of etiquette was unwritten: to gauge one's own status and to identify the relative standing of others as superiors, equals or inferiors, in order to assess how to address or be addressed by them. Experts advised reserve on the part of the agent in this circumstance, even though reserve subverted the sincere ideology of gentility. Reserve encompassed two distinct parts: the suppression of emotional expression, and the maintenance of personal and others' privacy. Carried to excess, such behaviour amounted to coldness, and etiquette literature was inconclusive on the exact location of the polite line between desirable reserve and exclusive formality. The crucial characteristic protected by reserve was self-respect, whether one's own or others', and the genteel person was always aware of it, whatever his or her status. Thus A Lady of Distinction advised, 'To her equals, [a lady's] manner must never lose sight of a dignity sufficient to remind them that she expects respect . . .'[53] But the public expression of an individual's self-confidence, as constructed on a proper regard for the integrity and value of the middle-class person, was a condition easier to prescribe than to engage. The account in *Pride and Prejudice* of the relationship between the haughty Lady Catherine de Bourgh and the grovelling Reverend Mr Collins describes the worst expressions of assertion and deference, displaying both characters as ungenteel despite their respective aristocratic and clerical dignities.[54] At the opposite, aspirational end of the scale, the odiously ''umble' clerk Uriah Heep, in *David Copperfield*, presents as so ungentlemanlike that his subsequent perfidy is a foregone conclusion.[55]

Whether reserved or sincere, the technique of assessing others was small talk, the apparently trivial chat that establishes antecedents, wealth and social claims through 'incidental' references to family connections and property in the course of polite conversation. Small talk was specially an item of women's 'labour that is not labour'. Its investigatory purposes were so contrary to the ideals of genteel sincerity that it had to be condemned publicly as idle and frivolous. No etiquette manual commented on small talk other than in terms of warning against it and offering more suitable topics for conversation. Likewise, small talk barely appears in silver fork novels because their protagonists are far too genteel to indulge. It required the eye of a Jane Austen for permanent record, as in Lady Catherine de Bourgh's quizzing of Miss Elizabeth Bennet: 'She asked her at different times, how many sisters she had, whether they were older or younger than herself, whether any of them were likely to be married, whether they were handsome, where they had been educated, what carriage her father kept, and what had been her mother's maiden name?'[56] Austen presents this exchange to characterize the arrogant and unmannerly noblewoman, but its substance is a forensic investigation of the crucial elements of status. Small talk was dirty work, but it had to be done if a family were to live correctly and strategically, even at the cost of a female reputation for triviality or snobbishness.

The vital sphere of small talk was the ritual occasion of ladies visiting each other at home. Visiting, making calls and leaving calling cards was the special (though not exclusive) task of women, whereby relationships were assessed, monitored and maintained to generate the products of prestige and respectability endowed by the right contacts. 'Visits are a very important part of Etiquette . . . they enter into almost all the acts of life,' urged an anonymous author, though she did not articulate their special mystery.[57] It required a high level of self-control, a timed regimen of formal visits, so short that bonnets and shawls were not taken off, or, in the absence of the visitee, of leaving a calling card to indicate the visitor's intention. The aim was to establish acquaintanceship, not friendship; intimate friends were not controlled by etiquette. Visits were always referred to as 'morning' calls, even though taking place well after midday, a relic of the eighteenth-century habit of considering the time before dinner as morning. Agogos instructs that calls should take place between two and four p.m., for earlier may interrupt a lady's household business, and later could prevent her from driving out herself.[58] Visits should not last long enough to require taking off the outer garments, i.e., 10 to 15 minutes, a small window of opportunity to establish the right connections. Conversation was officially constrained to conventional topics: suitable topics were said to be 'subjects of universal interest' such as natural scenery and beauty, literature and the fine arts, which proved the cultural capital of the conversant, and enabled evidence of each participant's acquaintance with the right people, places and goods.[59] Novels often present the ideal vision of visiting: 'We found her at home, busily employed upon domestic duties [needlework and children] . . . A pianoforte stood open, and there were several books in the room, affording a tolerable earnest of the sort of conversation likely to await us.'[60] While observing the injunction that 'all conversations about one's household affairs should be studiously avoided,' judicious name-dropping and fashionable references enabled polite conversation to transmit the vital indicators, exemplified by Austen characters such as the elder Miss Elliott's ever-so-incidental mentions of 'our cousins, the [titled] Dalrymples.'[61] But the real strain of such performances made visiting a tedious task, as recorded in private

Polite: The ritual of a 'morning' visit required upright attention for a short period of time, indicated by the two visitors not removing their hats: their hostess (facing the fireplace) and an invalid (seated at right) wear their indoor caps.

Cecil-Elizabeth Drummond, 'Scene at Scotsbridge', Drummond family album, *c.* 1830.

diaries: 'Everybody seemed exhausted with the civil things they were obliged to utter, after cudgelling their brains for something new.'[62]

The purpose of the etiquette of visiting was to manage the cycle of ceremonious reciprocal obligations that constituted the social dynamic of class integrity. The precise rules of timing, conversation and bearing enabled the conventions to be fulfilled; the rituals of leaving calling cards extended it in a vicarious way to save time, fulfil obligations to the absent, or formally to commence or cease an acquaintance. 'These usages vary in different places, but it is easy to ascertain what they are, and then, by conforming to them, you are sure to do the right thing,' breezed A Lady, while yet following up with a rare, detailed list of rules.[63] Apparently empty of meaningful content, visiting has ever since been mocked and dismissed as the most trivial aspect of genteel women's lives, coming to represent later accusations of Victorian hypocrisy. The criticism that making calls and leaving cards was sheer form is true, but it is incorrect to infer that it therefore contained no meaning or amounted to no work. Visiting was a major apparatus for the structuring of genteel society and was ruled by particularly complex and changeable rules of etiquette. As Leonore Davidoff points out, the whole process was a parade of honour, an assertion of social territory, a representation of status conducted by women on behalf of their families.[64]

Having established the relative status of company through small talk, the right demeanour towards each category varied from deference to frankness to kindness – except for American democrats. In the aristocratic tradition of manners, Chesterfield recommended to his son that his manner should be 'respectfully open and cheerful with your superiors, warm and animated with your equals, hearty and free with your inferiors,' advice that lived on in nineteenth-century etiquette manuals.[65] American reformer Catharine Beecher, by contrast, spoke for the Christian and democratic idea of the equality of all, urging that 'the same courtesy which we accord to our own circle, shall be extended to every class and condition.'[66] Democracy was the official political stance of the United States, but it was regarded as a radical horror by most of the middle class in Britain; while Christianity advocated admirable principles, practising them democratically – as opposed to charitably – was beyond the call of well-bred manners. The critical perspective for the genteel person was a sense of his or her own worth, the principle that produces 'self-respect, and confidence, and an independent spirit.'[67] Understanding one's own status enabled correct and appropriate attitudes to others, neither arrogant nor servile. This high degree of self-consciously controlled calculation was the critical stratagem of power through inclusion and exclusion. It worked because the moral economy of etiquette conducted its exchanges in the currency of learned culture and not in money.[68]

Advice for social encounters with superiors occupied the leading segment of most etiquette books, for social advancement was the major object of the self-improvement project represented by etiquette instruction. Aspirants had to adopt perfectly self-controlled, correct deference to superiors, a key element of the genteel psyche. Among the confidently genteel it was matched by kindness to inferiors, but advice literature aimed upwards in social rank and rarely touched on the concept of managing social relations downwards, with some exceptions for dealing with servants. Referring obliquely to the critique of social climbing, some writers address the possibilities of moving with the elite as a risk requiring micro-managed self-presentation: 'To mix with our superiors is undoubtedly very desirable ... if we have a sufficient command ... to keep our wishes and desires within the proper bounds of prudence and discretion.'[69] Agogos' advice on dealing with noblemen is laden with canny strategy as much as correct prescription; his essential counsel: 'Do not *strain* after great people – for, although they like the homage, inasmuch as it flatters their vanity, yet they despise the dispenser of it.'[70] This scenario acutely describes the aspirant's conundrum of self-respect versus deference, ever mystified in popular self-help literature with the wishful assurance that good manners will ensure recognition as a genuine gentleman. Allegedly to help out but actually presenting the crunch of power relations, Agogos added a simple instruction: 'As a general rule – it is the place of the superior in rank to speak first to the inferior'.[71]

The chivalrous traditions of gentility constructed women as the moral superiors of men, and hence the code of etiquette cast 'ladies' with courtesy status and precedence: ladies first, assisted and protected by the supervision of gentlemen. The dignity of ladyhood enabled aspirant middle-class women to shape nicer lives than merely respectable working women, but it loaded their daughters with a new lifetime burden of constrained behaviour. The manners their mothers prized became normative and then repressive for subsequent middle-class generations. In time, the ripples of reformist politics engendered more inclusive social attitudes towards women, noted by Hemphill in the United States in the period 1820–60, though yet to be documented in Britain and the colonies.[72]

The most testing events in the arena of middle-class social contact were informal meetings in public places such as streets and assembly rooms, since organized social encounters such as visiting, dinners and balls were internally structured with their own etiquette. Acknowledging the power of reserve, the central concept of meeting people, especially in public, was privacy, expressed in the control of personal access. Agogos attributes the entire corpus of etiquette to the protection of the genteel individual: 'it is a shield against the intrusion of the impertinent, the improper, the vulgar – a guard against those obtuse persons, who having neither talent nor delicacy, would be continually thrusting themselves into the society of men to whom their presence might (from the difference of feeling and habit) be offensive, and even insupportable.'[73] Access, in the form of acquaintance, depended on the ceremony of introduction, which therefore constituted the initial practical chapter of nearly every book on etiquette. Measuring the legitimacy of an introduction, a superior had the right to permit or deny acquaintance; an inferior was instructed not to assert his or her claim to recognition but to wait for a sign, and if it was not given, not to press the point. Introductions were fundamental because they represented the achievement of acknowledgement, of admission to the circle. Having recognized a properly introduced acquaintance, both parties took on the obligations of civility. Choosing not to recognize a legitimate acquaintance amounted to a calculated dismissal, an insult to the pride and self-esteem of the outcast, as when the Misses Bingley declined to meet Jane Bennet in London in *Pride and Prejudice*.[74] The 'cut', in the vernacular, constituted the ultimate sanction in the struggle for identity through inclusion, its symbolic character felt as acutely as if it had been a physical slash to the person. Hence the confidence to assert a public greeting and risk a cut represented the currency of one's status.

Dinners and balls were the major public events at which husbands and wives jointly engaged in social communication, asserting their family presence among the ranks of the respectable. The courtly ideal imagined graceful relations between the sexes, and this remained a constant expectation of genteel social intercourse. Nonetheless, there are sufficient reminders in the etiquette literature that men owed polite duty to women at dances and, simultaneously, enough acknowledgements that men would always tend to drift off to drink and play cards leaving ladies unpartnered in the ballroom to indicate that after the age when biology impels interest in the opposite sex, a de facto gender apartheid operated on many social occasions. Such behaviour was incorrect, ungenteel and advocated by no one, but many a nineteenth-century novel recounts the frustrations of men disappearing as dance partners.[75] Perhaps t'was ever thus.

The critical goal of etiquette at such events was the ceremony of public identification with one's peers: for balls, arriving, being announced and greeting the host and hostess; for dinners, moving from the reception room to the dining room in an order of precedence determined by convention and the hostess. Here was the acid test of status as assumed knowledge: 'Among persons of real distinction, this marshalling of the company is unnecessary, every woman and every man present knows his rank and precedence.'[76] Aspirants could find their ambitions dampened, if not thwarted, by the monumentality of tabulated precedence as listed in every second etiquette book and conclusively listed in the numerous publications of the Debrett imprint.[77] Invariably commencing with the Queen, the panoply of English rank was laid out, starkly relegating the un-noble to the very end. The detail of the rules was unstable over both place and time, making local knowledge a further valuable item for confident performance. Governor of the colony of Van Diemen's Land, Sir William Denison, discovered several distinct local dinner practices he hadn't anticipated, and was consequently clumsy at a major engagement. Dining with the Chief Justice in 1847, he was first startled to be greeted by his host at the door, 'which took me so much by surprise, that I was very near taking him for a servant'. Second, Sir John waited for the Governor to lead the hostess in to dinner, instead of leading himself with Lady Denison, creating an awkward battle of deference. Third, the ladies having withdrawn after dinner and the gentlemen having finished their port, Denison failed to realize that his host expected *him* to lead the way out to the drawing room; again, the entire dinner party waited longer than comfortable to finally make the transition.[78] A Governor could afford to make the occasional mistake in local etiquette (he could always take revenge on ignorant colonials in his memoirs), but the way was thorny for the aspirant middle class whose social antennae were not yet sufficiently developed or not informed by a strategically placed wife or daughter, ready to observe and model the current best manners.

Eating in public was a more acute and unavoidable test of gentility; as Agogos wrote: 'Nothing indicates a well-bred man more than a proper mode of eating his dinner. A man may pass muster by *dressing well*, and may sustain himself tolerably well in conversation; but if he be not perfectly "au fait", *dinner* will betray him.'[79] The risks of exposure in responding to physical needs such as feeding had been a major topic in courtesy literature from the Middle Ages onwards; it was always one of the large achievements of self-control that the appetite could be civilized to a slow, ceremonious event of dining.[80] In fact, so antithetical is it to fundamental instinct that the self-discipline of the table needs to be learned by every generation which aspires to, or is socialized into, genteel eating. Hence the same prescriptions can be found in advice books of the fifteenth century, particularly those dedicated to training the well-bred child. For example, *The School of Good Manners* sets forth the standard rules of four hundred years of polite table manners:

> Eat not too fast, or with greedy behaviour.
> Eat not too much, but moderately.
> Eat not so slow as to make others wait for thee.
> Make not a noise with thy tongue, mouth or breath, in eating or drinking.[81]

By the nineteenth century such rules were made to apply to hugely more people than they had in the Renaissance, as unwilling children or willing adults struggled to learn to be nice.

Having mastered the bodily control aspects of genteel eating, there remained the confidence to manipulate the implements of dining correctly. As discussed further in Chapter 6, forks and serviettes were still new tools to many in the early nineteenth century, the meal having previously been eaten with hands, a knife and a hunk of bread from a common trencher. Individual table settings rapidly became one of the most significant markers of civilized dining. The essentially medieval style of presenting several courses of many dishes all on the table simultaneously constructed the major step of polite dining behaviour as the self-control to wait for the host to carve the meat and other guests to pass the many dishes. This show of generous plenty was overtaken among the stylish in the 1820s by service *à la Russe*, in which plated meals were presented by servants, thus displaying the host as a lord of men as well as provider of food. Nonetheless, older customs persisted in households of different degrees of fashion, enabling the more genteel to squirm in their diaries as they recounted the oafish behaviour of others.

Etiquette in new societies

The huge market for etiquette books was in part a product of the great population movements to urban centres and, indeed, to entirely new regions or colonies. New wealth underwrote middle-class development. The city now formed the frame of many more people's lives than ever before, in both Britain and the United States. People moved to the city to improve their chances in life with new kinds of opportunities and incomes that, especially for the new middle class, contained enough to enable discretionary spending above the mere necessities of life. Within the city, fields of work changed and grew, requiring men who were enterprising, literate, numerate and motivated, who by their scarcity could command steadily rising salaries.[82] The new urbanites aspired to live well, fuelling the urge to be genteel by spending their incomes on it, in order to be recognized as different and better. Emigrants to the western frontier of the United States or the imperial colonies of Britain hoped for the same: 'Few emigrate who enjoy prosperity at home,' wrote a transplant in 1839.[83] Making good or better in either the city, the frontier or the colonies provided new financial means, and the successful sought social advancement through investment in the cultural capital of gentility.

The problem of how to present well in new circumstances provoked doubt even among the confident for whom it offered new opportunities; for the shy or cautious, it could be pure torture, while for the opportunistic and the plausible, new possibilities opened up. Life in a new place meant the loss of face-to-face culture within a known community, and, simultaneously, the removal of know-all surveillance. Life elsewhere required the confidence to define oneself and to discriminate among strangers to establish the kind of circle necessary for improved living, to join the cast of 'the people we know.'[84] In a culture where physiognomy and style were prime evidence of the character within, appearances were crucial proof of morality, and so 'gentleman-like' or 'lady-like' demeanour became specially desirable qualities. The possibility that imposters could pass as genteel challenged the very basis of society's recognition of its own members. This risk contained dangerous implications for the stability of the new middle class, giving rise to the threatening figures identified by Karen Halttunen as 'confidence men and painted women'.[85] These demons abused the genteel conventions of sincerity with precisely the fine edge of calculation that Victorian gentility condemned in eighteenth-century manners. Lord Chesterfield was too clever for the sincere ethic with his casuistical definition: 'It is *simulation* that is false, mean and criminal . . . dissimulation is only to hide our own cards, whereas simulation is put on, in order to look into other people's.'[86] Both were only too possible in new environments.

Although settlers and emigrants departed (whether from Britain to the outreaches of empire or from east coast America to the west) with a history and a status, on arrival the genteel persona had to be

Snobbish: The worst fears of colonial barbarity are realized in a genteel London drawing room. The irony of this Australian cartoon is that the hirsute bushman would cause consternation in any middle-class environment in the world.

Samuel Calvert, 'Brother Harry returns from Australia – great sensation in Baker Street' *Melbourne Punch*, vol. 1 (Melbourne: 1855).

recreated in the new context of frontier or colonial society. This varied according to the state of the new settlement, whether still a pioneering environment or already an embryonic town.[87] Studies of settlement on the western frontiers in the 1820s–40s show the tremendous effort to recreate genteel society, from the microcosm of the correctly furnished home to the establishment of social circles in brand new towns. The arrival of women in the ever-expanding frontier settlements shifted the initial masculine culture of adventurous pioneers towards the domestic ideal via serial migration of family members, religious associations and, suggests Annette Kolodny, gardens planted in the 'wilderness'.[88] Establishing the relationships that defined middle-class status called forth all the resources available to the individual or family: evidence of sufficient wealth to live respectably, drawing on patronage or family connections to show good antecedents and giving a correct performance of genteel standards through refined behaviour in social encounters. Given the possibility that all of these could be fabricated or imitated and that the only proof was thousands of miles and many months away, the problem of recognizing individuals in the new society provoked considerable anxiety. Halttunen writes of the American case: '. . . in an urban social world where many of the people you met face-to-face each day were strangers, the question "Who are you *really*?" assumed even greater significance.'[89]

In the tiny middle-class environment of the Australian colonies, etiquette was an ambivalent resource, evidence of genteel status but possibly dubious evidence. Van Diemen's Land, as exemplar of the colonies, was a social cauldron of arrivals from many corners of the globe. Recognizing the correct kind of people with whom to associate, whether as a transient or a resident, was a critical step in social positioning. The only certain way of not being duped by an unknown into an undesirable relationship was to rely on an introduction via a mutually trusted umpire such as a friend, relative or patron. Some of these validating connections could grow attenuated – say, the friend of a friend's friend – but on the other side of the earth from 'home', even a distant claim to acquaintanceship would be preferable to none. In these circumstances, middle-class emigrants often carried letters of introduction; some were preceded by them, as in the case of Elizabeth Prinsep and her husband Augustus, taking a voyage for the sake of health broken in India: 'I was expected – nay, welcomed – letters had arrived before.'[90]

The growth of gentility was specially fraught in the Australian colonies, accentuated by the dubious associations of emigration for other than a tour of duty or for business. Emigration was for odd people:

the ambitious, the failed, the black sheep – none of them obvious can-didates for genteel society. When the destination was a penal colony, inhabited by convicts who were immoral by definition, there was even less assurance of acceptable society. Further, the population of the Australian colonies was small and people were thrown together first by the long voyage and later by the circumstances of employment and residence in limited communities, creating intimacies that would not have been countenanced at home. The special risk to gentility in colonial Australia was the threat of the polluting convict presence. To the surprise of many, a circle of genteel society was well grown in Hobart by 1830: 'the tone of society here is very superior to what I had expected to find – indeed I was fully prepared to be without any that I could mingle in', recorded the wife of a retired Indian Army officer in her journal.[91] Yet inevitably, former convicts aspired to and achieved middle-class status – some must have acquired the Hobart edition of *Hints on Etiquette*. To accommodate or exclude, different etiquettes came to apply in different quarters. Some 'pure Merinos' (the source of colo-nial wealth before the gold rushes) boycotted balls if even the children of convicts were among the guests; at the same time, some Governors were prepared to receive 'emancipists' (time-expired convicts) at Government House. Convicts were overwhelmingly of plebeian origins, but they were the brawn and sometimes the brain of the colonies and as they fulfilled their sentences and regained civil status, they added an unusual strain to colonial middle-class society.

The growth of genteel etiquette in the United States encompassed one important condition that did not apply in Britain or its colonies: democ-racy. How could a system of manners grounded in class distinction have a place in a republic of equal citizens? The question troubled some con-temporary writers of etiquette advice, excited many foreign commen-tators and has confused historians ever since. An increasing proportion of American conduct books acknowledged the issue, but few proposed any specific democratic recommendations and, as noted, several main-tained the primary standards of the English court as the measure of real gentility. Even among authors claiming to be 'truly American and Republican', the majority of advice is, as Hemphill writes, 'shockingly similar' to the original English product; in fact, it is virtually identi-cal.[92] Overtly democratic Americans were disturbingly eager to practise refined ways that would distinguish them from their compatriots. One author presented a blunt view that 'society remained unrepublican': 'There is perfect freedom of political privilege . . . but this equality does not extend to the drawing room. None are excluded from the highest councils of the nation, but it does not follow that all can enter into the highest ranks of society.'[93] Another acknowledged the essentially discriminatory consequences of democracy for genteel manners: 'True republicanism requires that every man shall have an equal chance – that every man shall be free to become as unequal as he can.'[94] Republican individualist values reinforced the possibilities of self-improvement and social advancement open to all, shaped in Jeffersonian terms as the natural aristocracy of virtue and talent which would make its deserved way to success. In this trope, travellers such as Harriet Martineau noted plenty of 'natural' ladies and gentlemen, whom she distinguished from the wealthy urban elite.[95] Likewise but less confident about praxis, Alexis de Tocqueville desired to commend the decorous consequences of democracy, but recognized that American manners were not really *comme il faut*: 'In democracies manners are never so refined as among aristocracies, but they are also never so coarse.'[96] Contemporaries could not put their fingers on the nub of the problem of democratic gentility.

Nor have historians of social conditions in the United States, though noting the inherent contradiction. Some follow de Tocqueville's optimistic view of a democratization of high standards, as in Arthur Schlesinger's line that 'The passion for equality . . . found expression in the view that all could become gentlemen, not that gentlemen should cease to be.'[97] Others see the culture of etiquette and gentility as relic of pre-Revolutionary culture, preserved by elites for their own aggrandizement: Richard Bushman observes gentility as a 'vocabulary of honour', a vehicle of distinction that employed the forms of the old regime within the mass society of democracy. He suggests it became somewhat democratized via the idea of the virtuous rural or, in the context of the expanding frontier, pioneer, life of republican purity as opposed to ungenteel urban degeneracy.[98] According to Hemphill, the impact of capitalism on the American economy was more important than political equality. Suggesting that American etiquette books of the ante-bellum period enabled polite people to deal with the contrary forces of democracy and commerce by providing a framework of manners that disguised the real calculation of business encounters, she concludes that under the cover of genteel manners, Americans did not practise the equality they preached.[99] All interpretations can be resolved more simply by the view that in practising the rules of etiquette, Americans sought middle classness more than aristocracy.

The self-made, self-improving culture of the United States and the British colonies constituted sufficient evidence for English genteel society to abhor such peripheral places, but it was an empty snobbery. American and colonial standards were not just derivative; they were transplanted. Their behaviours were not merely imitative, they were the same, granted that local fashions generated occasional idiosyncrasies in practice, just as happened 'at home'. The originality and integrity of genteel culture and its common preconditions demonstrate the truly transnational identity of bourgeois interests.

6
Correct Taste: the Material Conditions of Gentility

The genteel habitus required the right kind of environment in which to live, shaped by a battery of material goods to enable management of the self-controlled body and presentation of the self-conscious social person. Considered as performances both in private and in public, material goods constructed the stages on, and the props with which, to conduct the genteel life. To produce effective performances, the material appurtenances had to be the right kind, defined as correct taste, 'the material counterpart of influence'.[1] The precise calibration of setting, equipment and decoration could prove or disprove the middle-class person's possession of the cultural capital of gentility. The assemblage of goods possessed presented messages about the actor to the audience, enabling others to classify the agent's exact stratum within the possibilities that composed the nineteenth-century middle class.

The choice of goods was a demonstration not only of the agent's knowledge of standards but also of his or her capacity to realize them; it was a material insight into character as well as a visible proof of means. The economic necessities which determined the selection of goods in a particular price range were intelligible to others because degrees of wealth were objictified in the clothing, furnishings and other items that adorned the person and environment of each individual. Despite the sincere rhetoric of learned gentility, gradations of middle-class standing depended upon such readings of wealth and its material expressions, as manifested by the lowly position of the genteel poor and the accommodations sometimes made for (as the phrase still has it) 'filthy' rich aspirants. The aristocratic disdain for explicit riches translated into the bourgeois sentimental pretence that money didn't matter: 'We none of us spoke of money, because that subject savoured of commerce and trade, and though some might be poor, we were all aristocratic.'[2] Mrs Gaskell's gently ironic picture of the ladies of Cranford village is self-evidently untrue, but it represents the position conventionally maintained in polite public discourse. This standard masked a deep respect for the power of money embedded in capitalist culture; only the heroines of moralizing stories ever found money an ambivalent resource. But suppressing the admiration of wealth supported the illusion that manners and other forms of genteel knowledge put one on a par with other genteel people who might be very rich indeed, which could be a very sustaining thought. Happily for the convenience of sizing up self and others, the richness of material possessions indicated the financial status of all without requiring overt acknowledgement.

The gendering of responsibility for the genteel habitus is clear: financial capital was the legitimate domain of men. Money and the business that generated it were managed by men in the masculine world, separate from women, among whom it needed to be disguised as private gossip: 'Poor dear Launceston . . . never suffered me to talk about his pecuniary concerns,' confides the fictional Lady Launceston to her sister.[3] The consequences for women when their men died or disappeared could be dire, and often frame memoirs and novels. For either sex to possess high cultural capital in the absence of money was a desperate situation. Whether a younger son, an orphaned daughter or a widow, the problem could be really resolved only by marriage to a wealthy spouse. The fate of the governess, the archetype of the disjunction between financial and cultural capital, became a metaphor for cruel chance in art, literature and popular culture.

Aspirants to middle-class status needed to learn how to consume the decencies and luxuries which new values taught them to desire and new incomes could sustain. Certain pieces of equipment actively enabled new behaviours; others decorated the person or the environment in conventional but exclusive ways. Both kinds of goods were more than merely symbolic or representative of the distinction sought by the would-be genteel. Owning and using items such as a bath or visiting cards instrumentalized the transformation into genteel status. The individual who washed his body every day had adopted the mental set of valuing a high degree of personal cleanliness; it separated him from the great unwashed and connected him to the refined body of gentility. The person who distributed visiting cards in the card receivers of selected people's halls possessed self-respect and a vision of the middle-class society; if her cards were accepted, she belonged to this society. Without a bath or the pieces of engraved pasteboard, aspirants remained unable to participate in genteel culture. At the same time, possession of the goods without the knowledge to use them correctly constituted not just the absence of gentility but a definition of nouveau riche ignorance: 'the blunder of confusing *fashion* with *taste*,' as it was named by Andrew Jackson Downing, advocate of domestic taste.[4] Exposing oneself to classification by what one consumed could therefore be an anxious step for the inexperienced. The benefit of being brought up with the right standards was large; so was the challenge of learning them through advice and observation.

Like the other varieties of genteel knowledge, the stock of knowing what goods are correct in various circumstances was bolstered by learned experience within the family, conditioned by a fine awareness of fashion. The later eighteenth century had encompassed the transformation of many domestic and social goods, which became increasingly available in the early nineteenth century due to mass production. Consequently, intergenerational experience with the new material culture offered a significant advantage in fluent knowledge of its use. Childhood familiarity meant that improvements in goods arrived with a known context of use which advantaged the competent consumer, exemplified by the nightmare of sitting down to unintelligibly complex table settings. Would-be middle-class people could also learn about correct genteel behaviour in other spheres of life. Adolescent job training such as for commerce or the law involved a long period of apprenticeship which, besides the necessary literacy and numeracy, now included aspects of self-controlled cleanliness, manners and ceremony; the young man who emerged from his articles was well positioned to make use of his salary to buy the right goods that would polish him up. Young women might acquire knowledge of gentility in school or even in service, readying them to consume correctly if and when money was available. Adult aspirants had the incentive of high motivation, but needed to acquire both the equipment and the knowledge to put it to use, as well as dedicate time to becoming experienced.

The trap for genteel aspirants was that wealth had to be consumed with taste, the mechanism of applying cultural capital to the material world. This view draws on Bourdieu's analysis of tastes as the product of ideas and values shaped by material conditions; there may be a range of inflections of taste, but they are sufficiently homogeneous to distinguish affinity and habitus. The genteel taste was an expression of adherence to middle-class values; it was not, as the modern meaning has it, a style of individual choice. The fundamental value of genteel taste was restraint exercised by self-control. In the material world, cleanliness was essential and neatness demonstrated control of the situation. Restraint applied to all the characteristics of goods: colour, texture, ornament, size, materials and manufacture. This is not to say that middle-class taste was plain and cheap, because correct taste was further qualified by being appropriate to its circumstances. Ostentatious consumption belied taste, yet modesty of expenditure where more could be afforded showed insufficient respect for middle-class propriety. The opposite side of the coin condemned expensive tastes where incomes were known to be insufficient and implied scrimping on other elements of the habitus that were hidden from the observer. Advice books stressed that spending on goods should be appropriate to the agent's financial resources, neither excessive nor mean. The level of public exposure often determined the degree of appropriate finery in clothing and furnishings, though age, status and riches modified differences. Restraint was further invoked to justify the economy of good quality, a judgement that underwrote the new middle-class standard of expensive simplicity. By renouncing conspicuous opulence, the traditional signifier of power and wealth, the middle class yet again inverted the aristocratic model of lifestyle. The practised genteel eye could read degrees of taste, noting its propriety and quality in each context, and thus classify self and others. With these standards, parvenu incorrectness could be condemned: 'The furniture, new, gaudy, and expensive, glittered with gold and silver, silk and damask. Ormolu branches, china, alabaster vases, buhl clocks, marquetry cabinets, and plate-glass screens, were crowded one upon the other, with all the profusion of Mr Jarman's shop, but without a particle of his taste.'[5] Such observation was one of the central functions of the continuous mutual surveillance that guarded the integrity of the middle class.

The clash between the traditional aristocratic politics of display and the novelty of bourgeois restrained taste reverses Veblen's analysis of conspicuous consumption as a means of asserting social standing.[6] Inconspicuous consumption appears a contradiction in terms. In practice, it was a diversion, relying on redefining the nature of expressive goods away from the showy towards the specialized. Honourable living now required *particular* goods, in highly differentiated forms to separate aspects of lifestyle, such as clothes for particular events and times of day, and furniture for specific rooms and functions. Such goods could be very expensive, as well as being available in cheaper registers, but the degree of financial investment was evident only to spectators who understood the code. The power of the idea was buttressed by the morality of modesty, especially in the Protestant traditions, exemplified by wealthy Quakers who, though maintaining plain styles, spent comfortably on personal and household goods, 'of the best Sort but Plain', as a

Philadelphia merchant described his new cupboards.[7] The inconspicuous ideal mystified common expectations of status in its contrary expressions. Some genteel advocates presented a radical vision of invisibility: 'There is a large class of excellent female characters, who, on account of that very excellence, are little known, because to be known is not their object . . . These are the women who bless, dignify and truly adorn society.'[8] Such extreme modesty was not everyone's ambition, or all the time, but it could frame a lifestyle of gentility in simplicity, and in some degree democratized honour by removing the requirement to be pedigreed, rich or famous. Even with very limited financial resources, the genteel person could furnish a life with goods that demonstrated genteel standards; poverty could be evident but it need not degrade status, at least in the eyes of other truly genteel people. In this way, inconspicuous consumption sustained genteel poverty, as among the ladies of Cranford.

Some other conditions touched the genteel value of certain goods, notably patina and fashion. Ancient material could be invested with romantic associations, or it could speak to conservative respectability. The smooth finish of age on the kind of possessions that demonstrated family lineage could suggest ancestry of the aristocratic kind.[9] Fine jewellery is the archetype of such ancestral goods; material prestige contained few such occasions as acknowledging the slightly old-fashioned style of diamonds that had descended from one's grandmother. Such events occurred more in the fantasies of silver fork novels than in middle-class lives but the desirability of patina created the beginnings of the market for antiques, especially furniture.[10] More important than patina was the quality of fashion, the index of up-to-dateness. The role of fashion in the expansion of the world of goods was to promote a flow of variations that demarcated not taste, but contemporaneity, opening up new categories of semiotic indicator. Using fashionable markers to good effect was a function of finely tuned alertness to social currents, but required advanced economic resources to implement if one were to follow the fashion prints available every quarter or year. Serious dedication to fashion was for the few; most women fulfilled its precepts with smaller, cheaper articles of personal adornment such as ribbons, head-dresses for evening wear, buckles and so forth. Such small goods sustained significant production and distribution agencies, pointing to the economic importance of the growing role for middle-class women as consumers.

Even in the eighteenth century, men generally controlled the family purse strings; the usual expenditure was framed by raw supplies, wages and occasional manufactured goods. By the early nineteenth century, the need to acquire and put into use the vast new apparatus of personal and domestic goods required for the genteel life blossomed as a female responsibility, relating as it did to the presentation of the self and the home. Knowing which item or set to select became the test of taste, providing the material evidence of a family's rightful status. This skill fell into the new range of duties of middle-class women to represent family honour as consumers.

The rise of consumerism

Consumerism has been explained by diverse disciplines over a very long period in the history of social science, though until the end of the twentieth century, the attention paid to the production end of the process far outweighed investigation of the use of products.[11] Traditional economics attributes the desire for goods to utilitarian purposes of instrumentality; more and more clearly (not least via personal experience), this explanation can be seen as a modern western cultural category rather than an absolute truth. Philosophers looking beyond economics theorized the possession of goods as central to the construction of individual identity and social relationship. Bourdieu quotes the young Marx: '. . . ownership permits [man] both to preserve his personality and to distinguish himself from other men, as well as to relate to them.'[12] Anthropologists demonstrate applications of this truth among exotic Others, such as the relationship of African Nuer men to their spears; and sociologists trace it, for example, in the evolution of European courtly society distinguished by its use of polite cutlery.[13] But materialist explanations of social construction fell out of favour in the early twentieth century, and revived only towards its end. A dramatic argument is put by Daniel Miller, by way of Hegel and Bourdieu, that the consumption of goods is a major instrument of modern self-formation and a site of reconciling personal autonomy with the social group – a powerful idea in the context of the late eighteenth/early nineteenth-century rise of mass production.[14]

The rise of mass production coincided with a surge in the consumption of goods by middling and lower order people in the late eighteenth century, causing culture and consumerism to grow increasingly interdependent. 'Coincidence' is a deliberately ambiguous term to use in this context, for the causality of production and desire in the history of consumption has been little investigated. Chicken-and-egg questions tend to be dominated by studies of the production end of the process, generating a conventional history of a technologically driven industrial revolution. The other side of the coin is demand; the currency itself is consumerism. A parallel history can be constructed in the following, alternative form.[15] A new capacity to manufacture developed in Britain in the mid-eighteenth century; factories producing consumer goods multiplied thereafter, and multiplied their production again and again throughout the nineteenth century, now also in the United States. Not only did factories produce cheaper versions of luxuries which had formerly been available only to the wealthy, they introduced new types and ranges of goods required for the specialized functions of genteel culture, such as cutlery for different foods and courses, and furniture for private cleanliness in the bedroom. These goods serviced a concomitant consumer revolution, a revolution in demand expressed by an unprecedented number of people, comprising an ever-growing penetration among populations increasingly articulated as classes.[16]

Why did people shift from investing money to spending it on goods, and how could they afford them? The debate about standards of living in the 'industrial revolution' period (essentially the fifty years either side of the turn of the nineteenth century), swings between gloomy and optimistic interpretations, but it is certain that the purchasing power of all classes improved, though more slowly among the working class than the upper classes, and unevenly in time and location.[17] Simultaneously, goods became less expensive, being made of cheaper materials (such as light cottons instead of heavy wools, and veneers instead of solid timbers) as well as mass-produced for economies of scale. The question as to which cause predominated – increasing income or the availability of goods – is answered, both in the eighteenth century and the present, as a function of wealth: the value of consumer goods acquired increases with income, though the proportion of income devoted to goods falls off in the upper registers of wealth.[18] This seems like common sense, and in a striking argument, Neil McKendrick shows its viability even in the realm of the labouring poor, among whom he suggests that the wages of working women and children pushed the family incomes of working-class people above the level of mere subsistence and into the realm of discretionary spending. Even more suggestive, he notes that such income was spent on family maintenance and comforts, such as tablewares and clothing, that were particularly determined by the woman wage-earner.[19] Such consumption recruited working-class people into the enlarging middle class, powered by social ambition and desire for comfort. The rise in new middle-class jobs generated a steady and sometimes spectacular increase in prosperity.[20] A rare explicit insight into the categories of domestic expenditure can be drawn from the English advice book, the 1831 *New System of Practical Domestic Economy*. It prescribes a budget distribution for incomes between £1,000 and £5,000, which was a very comfortable range. In this span, *Practical Domestic Economy* recommends distributing 36 per cent of income to provisions and household expenses; 22 per cent for servants, horses and carriages; 12 per cent for clothing and haberdashery; 8 per cent for education, pocket money and private expenses; 12 per cent to rates, taxes and repairs; and 10 per cent reserved for contingencies.[21]

The causality of rising consumerism can be viewed as less connected with mass production than with the semiotic and empowering possibilities of the vast new universe of goods as agents of gentility. The theorization of the popular desire for goods claims one ancient explanation, and several more recent. The former is Veblen's germinal study of the 'leisure class', which cites emulation as the motive of consumer spending. Veblen traces a sociology of conspicuous consumption by the powerful which was imitated by the aspiring middle ranks, and imitated in turn by the lower orders.[22] The question remains as to why emulative spending should have been so uniquely powerful in propelling industrial/consumer growth in the late eighteenth/early nineteenth-century period. Drawing on Miller's interpretation of the history of consumption presents the archaeologist's insight that objects are specially powerful as the fixers of meanings in unstable cultures with ambiguous hierarchies, an apt description of the multi-stratified middle class at the time.[23] Paul Shackel's interpretation of eighteenth/nineteenth-century archaeological material from Annapolis turns on the same idea that goods play a major role in the struggle for social position and the creation of identity. Referring to Veblen, Shackel theorizes that emulation threatened the existing social hierarchy, and that the elite sought to reassert their dominance by re-establishing differences with new goods.[24]

This attractive explanation is weakened by its potential for circularity, strengthening the claim of historical theorists who identify an entirely new mentality to explain the wave of consumption at this time. Chandra Mukerji proposes such a new mentality through comparison between the asceticism of seventeenth-century entrepreneurs and the 'hedonism' of eighteenth-century consumers, both groups using their relationship to goods as the cultural rationale for increased participation in economic activity.[25] Colin Campbell's investigation into the sources of consumerism identifies this hedonism as a strand of the 'romantic spirit' which he sees as twin to an enduring strand of the

Protestant work ethic; he locates consumption of the new goods as the major expressive focus of romanticism.[26] But to posit the rising middle class – the new consumers – as smug pleasure-seekers ignores their driven and self-controlled struggle to improve themselves, to become genteel and to sustain personal and family honour by consuming correctly. Genteel consumption in this view was middle-class women's labour to generate symbolic capital for the household, as much as respectable employment or business was men's labour generating money.

Mass availability of domestic goods such as ceramic tablewares, printed cottons for furnishings and clothing, and small metal goods such as cutlery and jewellery, enabled the growing or aspiring middle class to affiliate with and discriminate among other people, who revealed by their own consumption how they constructed their vision of genteel living. The unprecedented range of goods available made it possible for people with diverse incomes to afford, say, a dinner service: even if the tablewares were a truncated version of an aristocrat's, each plate, server and tureen was in the same family of goods and presented the same template of genteel characteristics embedded in the minds of their users. The new china amounted to a social statement about the values of its consumers.

The most eloquent explanation of how goods achieve these effects in society comes from Mary Douglas and Baron Isherwood, who present objects as 'a line information system', individually arranged and legible to others as statements of the values to which both individual and group subscribe.[27] The consumption of goods, which at face value may seem a private or idiosyncratic choice, is seen on the scale of society as a force for social cohesion, a group-controlled pressure to conform to certain values and behaviours: it is in this light that Douglas and Isherwood speak of goods as the visible markers of categories of culture.[28] But they view objects as more than a semiotic system. The active arena of object use and exchange is so central to human intercourse, they claim, that it can be called the site 'in which culture is fought over and licked into shape.'[29] In this environment, consumption is about power: the power to reinforce group associations, to include and exclude relationships, to assert dominance and inculcate subordination. This view posits goods as having symbolic meanings far beyond their formal existence as lumps of matter, or as merely functional tools or comforts. Ownership, in short, is not the passive acceptance of objects, but the reflexive agency of acting with and upon them.

Objects are not objective to the theorists of material culture: their meanings are invested in their relationship to other objects and people by the various contexts in which they occur. Further, they have the interesting capacity to operate in both the material and the cognitive worlds, as vehicles of systemic culture through the mechanism of the ordered arrangement of meaningful differences. The variability of objects in general, and manufactured goods in particular, functions as a system of differences, offering eloquent opportunities for the expression of social distinctions. The differences thus selected by individuals reveal group affinities or tastes, the bases of self and social classification. Bourdieu's demonstration of how tastes are conventional according to class fraction, how each variation reveals the individual's degree of mastery of the logic of the economy of goods, enables historical analysis of the competence, nature and manner of consumption. Whole lifestyles or habituses can thus be read in the taste for goods. The consumption of clothing and furnishings is a specially fertile field for such analysis on account of their fashion-bearing but semi-durable nature, and it has been taken up enthusiastically in eighteenth-century studies, though much less thereafter.[30] The following analyses aim to show the values of gentility in early nineteenth-century possessions.

Correct taste in the person

'Clothes maketh the man' expresses the vernacular wisdom that appearances matter, and always have. Whatever the nature of the person within the clothes, the visible coverings transmit deliberate, complex messages about social being. Most theorists now agree that clothing ensembles are not as logically communicative as spoken or written language, but if not actually a text, clothes certainly constitute a code which is intelligible with a fair degree of accuracy within synchronic cultural groupings.[31] Many clothing meanings are constructed by long tradition to define the basic human conditions of gender, age and occupation, though more complex meanings such as status, and specialized purposes such as subversion, tend to be specific to time and context. Meanings are, however, variably understood by social fractions; what is acknowledged as acceptable in one segment may be mocked or dismissed by another. The capacity for such finely differentiated meanings constituted clothing as a finely calibrated evaluative tool in the struggle for middle classness. Yet the semiotics of clothing are not the same as mere differences in fashion. Fashion can be variously defined, but is here understood as a system of novelty driving a rapidly turning-over market, and as such was condemned in 1839 by A Gentleman as 'a system of refined vulgarity'.[32] The ambiguities of the symbolic aspects of clothing are compounded by the metaphorical implications of dressing, in that the act of putting on and taking off clothes represents the spectre of personal and social dissimulation. The misleading possibilities of increasingly available fine feathers were as plausible as put-on manners, and therefore as fraught for aspirants to correct middle-class taste. Clothing was (and is) a crucial system of personal display, but its practice and interpretation were inexplicit and arbitrary.

The special characters of correct genteel clothing at the turn of the nineteenth century are propriety according to circumstance and the absence of ostentation. Advisers recommended 'harmony between your dress and your circumstances' and 'a simple and unaffected manner of wearing your clothes.'[33] This advice follows Lord Chesterfield, whose broad suggestion was to be well dressed 'according to . . . rank and way of life,' and though not neglecting dress, not to take it too seriously.[34] Knowing the right degree of plain or fancy dress for self and others on all occasions was an inexplicit standard, amounting to the most subtle form of cultural capital within the genteel habitus. Induction from birth endowed the most confidence about clothes; otherwise, experience by imitation was the most effective teacher. The safest strategy, therefore, was to be inconspicuous: 'Do not affect singularity of dress by wearing anything that is so conspicuous as to demand attention . . .'[35] Advice books were generally obscure on the problem of correct taste in dress, though it is among the most frequent chapters, advising largely 'propriety, neatness, and elegance, rather than affectation or extravagance', without explaining what these standards actually meant.[36] The inarticulate nature of knowledge about correct taste indicates how extremely circumstantial it was. Yet within each stratum of standards, taste was a highly precise science, grounded in assessment of whole assemblages, nuance by sensitive nuance. Even one item of a costume out of keeping with a viewer's evaluation of the whole could condemn the wearer for displaying incorrect taste, thus exposing ungenteel or suspicious character.

The anti-ostentatious taste in clothing is most essentially demonstrated in the revolution in men's clothing that began with the Puritan and Quaker eschewing of gay clothes in the mid-seventeenth century.[37] But though sombre, these dissenting cultures were not actively penitential; they did not require sackcloth and ashes. They asserted a new distinction between the worldliness of splendid show in dress and the quality of expensive materials, with important consequences for more widespread clothing taste. The plain but affluent style informed the fundamental three-piece suit of knee breeches, waistcoat and coat in dark colours with minimal decoration either on the garments or under them, where the traditional show of frills or lace at the neck and wrists of the shirt muted into simple, white, turned-over collars and cuffs. Both emerging urban capitalists and university-educated professionals adopted the dark suit, appropriating the clerical tradition of black robes to add the honour of vocation and learning to embryonic middle-class lifestyles.[38] Such taste took on secular character as a form of investment in delayed gratification, the essence of the spirit of capitalism. Plain the ensemble might have been, but beyond the purposes of the religiously motivated, it could be made subtly stylish through choice of fabric, variations on elements such as sleeve width and restrained ornaments such as knee and shoe buckles. It never took a place in fashionable society, but the plain dark suit was established as respectable working dress for business and especially professional men by the early eighteenth century in Britain and the United States.

In the thirty years leading to the turn of the nineteenth century, the shape of the suit altered in two fundamentals and it was adopted both by aristocrats and the steadily growing middle class. In the 1770s the full-skirted coat reduced to a shorter, tighter tail coat in practical wool, deriving from hunting costume.[39] The connection with leisured country pursuits gave the simple garment the prestige to climb from occupational dress to fashion. Around the turn of the nineteenth century, country style was, however, urbanized by new English tailoring techniques of cutting, lining and pressing the coat into a short-waisted, body-hugging garment whose visible quality lay in the skill and material of its manufacture; these became the marks of distinction in the new simple fashion. The dark plain fabric and tight cut of the tail coat redirected attention from magnificent clothes to the individual body, which could be happily flattered by tailoring, as in the satirical reference to fashionable tailor Mr Primefit of Regent Street, famous for 'The art sublime, ineffable/Of making middling men look well.'[40] By the 1830s, custom tailors began to systematize their skill with the 'proportional system' of measuring in order to produce readymade but more or less fitted clothes for the wider market.[41] To the horror of the already genteel, readymades launched a new stratum of 'gents', the class of white-collar workers who purchased loud checked trousers and tasteless blue stocks from cheap tailors' warehouses.[42]

The second transformation towards the modern suit was the shift from knee-breeches to long-legged pantaloons in the 1790s, quickly overtaken by looser-cut trousers in the first two decades of the 1800s.[43]

A specimen of the 'trickle-up' movement of working clothes into polite use, the taste for long pants has often been connected to French revolutionary egalitarianism: the *sans culottes* character on the barricades was not naked from the waist down, but instead of *culottes*, breeches, he wore *pantalons*, workmen's trousers. The subversion of conventional high style represented by the elevation of practical working dress is a classic challenge to dominant values, but such subversions have rarely been as overwhelmingly successful as pantaloons. Another source of long pants was the eighteenth-century Hungarian hussar (cavalry) officers' tight trousers, glamorized by stylish coats and mantles with characteristic decorative frogging, and reinvented into the wardrobe of the middle class.[44] Since military forms and details have often migrated into civilian fashions, the hussar origin seems a more likely source than the ideologically loaded *pantalons*, but the role of fashion in the spread of pantaloons is not well understood. In this context Anne Hollander makes a deft argument that the body-hugging shape of pantaloons and tailored coats derives from the aesthetic inspiration of turn-of-the-nineteenth-century neoclassicism, driven by the ideal of the ancient Greek nude body.[45] She suggests that the seventeenth-century vocabulary of the three-piece suit was reshaped to cling to the body, thanks to the new techniques of tailoring and the revived use of wool and knitted fabrics. In this view, the tails of the coat were a redundant appendix, but the careful seams and puffed shoulders stressed statuesque musculature and the stiff neckcloth shaped a heroic neck. The sleek proportions of the neoclassical pantaloon suit demanded both the shapeliness and sexuality of youth to carry off with style, so were transformed by the 1810s for less perfect body shapes and less overt tastes into looser trousers and frock coat, reducing the focus on the crotch and thus becoming respectable for middle-class wear first at leisure and then on business.[46]

Thus in Britain by the year 1800 the English tail coat combined with European pantaloons, mediated by the enduring but shortened waistcoat. Dark colours predominated for coats in the already century-old professional taste for sober shades and high quality fabrics; pantaloons and trousers, however, retained the light and neutral tones of informal wear until a dark shift in the 1840s shaped a new standard of the suit that persists to this day. It possessed both the imprimatur of high style and the image of genteel modesty. The quality of the cloth determined most of its cost, since even impeccable tailoring was relatively cheap, and thus the suit managed to become both elite and available. The embourgeoisement of conventional male clothing produced a flow-on

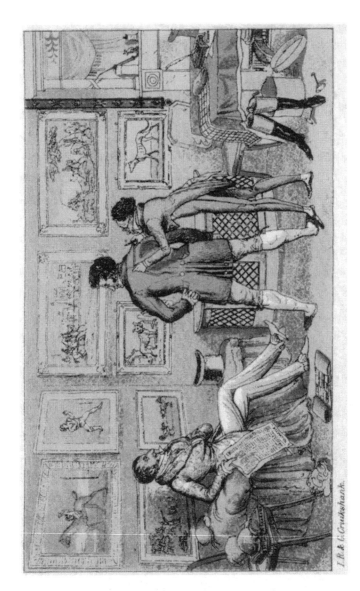

Transformed: Country cousin Gerry, in breeches, is about to be transformed by the tailor, whose fashionable pantaloons are much tighter than the genteel trousers of Tom, the man-about-town.

Robert and George Cruikshank, 'Gerry in training for a swell': Pierce Egan, *Life in London* (London: 1821), opp. p. 117.

effect on the common trousers worn by working-class men, which gained a normative value in becoming standard masculine dress. This democratizing trend was explicit in the French revolutionary adoption of trousers, which travelled to republican America, where Jeffersonian democrats wore long-legged garments while loyalists continued to dress in breeches. In Britain, trousers contained no necessary agenda for democracy, having been rapidly taken up by royalty in the form of the Prince Regent, though perhaps more than any lower-class associations, his salacious reputation influenced older and conservative men to resist the taste. But by the 1840s, knee breeches survived only in fossilized form as ritual dress for very formal occasions.[47] Writing in the 1930s, the psychologist J. C. Flugel named this reorganization of men's attire 'the great masculine renunciation', theorizing it as a middle-class rejection of aristocratic magnificence as the measure of status by asserting plain, democratic values.[48] It is a tempting thesis, and probably true in its largest view, but can a revolution blessed by high fashion and elite aesthetics be called a renunciation? Explicit magnificence had already endured the challenge of ideological simplicity. After the short period of fashionable exposure of legs and genitals in tight pantaloons – suitably recognized with the euphemism 'inexpressibles' for men's nether garments – the enduring revolution in male clothing was trousers. The semiotics of plain style were apparent to all as an expression of anti-magnificence, but within its communities of practice, by no means all democratic, the subtle clues of quality continued to enable hierarchical discrimination. The dark three-piece suit's combination of meaning and capacity to distinguish among its adherents thus placed it as a prime item in the production of middle-class status through consumption.

Women's clothing in the fifty years around the turn of the nineteenth century is broadly analysed by costume historians in two large stylistic movements, the neoclassical (1790s–1810s) and the romantic (1820s–40s). Diverse as these trends were, their significance for the expression of genteel standards lies less in particular forms than in how women responded to them. The middle-class standard of unostentation mandated avoidance of the extremes of fashion with warnings such as 'Take care . . . not to be the first out of fashion, nor the last in it.'[49] At the same time, the imperative of affiliation with society required participation in fashion's dynamic of change:

> When the sleeves called *gigot* first made their appearance, everyone exclaimed against the bizarrerie of the fashion . . . Still, this singular style of sleeve became very general, and no longer appeared

ridiculous: from custom, its elegance was admitted even by those who first ridiculed it. We yield to the authority of the greater number, and it would have been ridiculous not to follow a fashion almost universal.[50]

This example of the careful ambivalence of bourgeois culture towards a fashion acknowledged to be grotesque reveals the anxieties of knowing how to be correct. The extensive advice literature appears to give explicit instructions in how to materialize the self via clothes, with instructions that dress should be suitable to age, complexion and body shape: gay colours and simple floral ornaments for the unmarried while young; sombre tones and richer ornaments for the married or old; colours that enhance skin and hair tone; styles that shift visual focus away from defects such as a short neck or thick waist. Such advice is so generic that it continues to be published today (with the exception of references to the now-unspeakable condition of age). The rare precise instructions focus on the specialization of clothes for particular events or times of day, pronouncing a sequence of simple to elaborate dress from morning wear at home, to promenade or carriage dress (the former suited to walking, the latter less exposed to environmental risk), to dinner dress, to ball dress. Jewellery beyond simple gold chains and opaque stones represents the turning point of good taste in finery, being specially circumscribed to public events. Ultimately, correct taste was a circular phenomenon of cultural capital: 'the best test of delicacy of mind ... exists in the degree of neatness and good taste which [a lady] displays in the choice and arrangement of her dress.'[51] The act of choosing constituted the assertion of genteel taste, and its assessment by others proved its correctness – or not.

An avalanche of rhetoric insisted that 'Elegant dressing is not found in expense; money without judgement may load, but never can adorn.'[52] Nonetheless, money rather than fashion motivated the difficulty of most choices in middle-class dress, even though apart from the injunction that costume should be appropriate to means, the stresses of financial resources were unaddressed in advice books. The conspicuous display of luxuries such as lace and jewellery that had formerly belonged only to the aristocracy was vastly enlarged in the early nineteenth century thanks to new technologies and mass production. Machine-made lace and pseudo-lace in the form of embroidered net and white-work embroidery were by no means cheap, and thus managed to retain an air of ancient richness, but many more people could afford to add them to their vocabulary of elegant details of dress.[53] Lace had always been a mobile item of adornment, and new fashion forms such as the pelerine (a very broad collar) and the chemisette (a false front to tuck into the bodice) enabled a small quantity to be used in a number of combinations with different dresses. From the 1790s embroidered net (fully machine-made or hand-worked on machine toile) fitted the economical bill precisely, used for day wear as bonnet drapes and for evening wear as stoles. By the 1840s, patterned machine lace permitted the magnificence of large lace panels or flounces worn as overskirts for ball and wedding gowns by the wealthy end of the middle-class spectrum.[54] Such lace items attract no moralistic criticism in the costume chapters of advice books, evidently being interpreted as modest and appropriate ornament, perhaps because they were usually white (or if not, black) and except for blonde (silk lace), not conspicuously shiny. Lace came to assert a new respectable image as a genteel ornament while conserving its tradition of exclusivity – the perfect middle-class good.

By contrast, jewellery was a challenging item for middle-class taste. Precious metals and gems had long constituted jewellery as the very definition of splendour, being rich and beautiful for the purpose of sheer display. In every age's expression of conspicuous consumption, wives (and mistresses) have been the vehicles of flaunting the evidence of men's wealth via jewellery. The struggle to reconcile such extravagant meanings with new genteel values was tense: on the one hand, the need for signs of wealth was augmented by the new availability of mass-produced jewellery; on the other, the criterion of good taste demanded propriety and simplicity. The bottom line of the extent and fineness of jewellery was always the wealth of a husband or father, and thus the types of nineteenth-century middle-class jewellery are as various as the range of people united by genteel ideology. Their jewellery ranges from spectacular grandeur to cheap modesty.

Jewellery for women other than the very rich was an innovation of the late eighteenth century. The princely ideal of glittering cut stones was translated into the first middling jewels in the form of paste, a flint glass that could be facetted like a stone and enriched by coloured foil backing, developed in the 1730s. Semi-precious stones such as turquoise, garnet, rock crystal and seed pearl (fresh water mussel pearls) enlarged the repertoire of 'gem' quality jewellery of modest scale and relatively modest price available to the growing market of the early nineteenth century.[55] Another such medium was miniature 'stones' of faceted steel and marcasite (iron pyrites) set into brooches and combs in tolerable, but frank, imitation of glittering stones.[56] Less overtly precious than cut stones, ivory and coral have long traditions of use in popular jewellery, compounded by magical qualities; in the first decades of the nineteenth century they were delicately carved for mounting as brooches and bracelets for the middle class. Tiny scenes of animals in frames of leaves or trees were a speciality of German ivory-workers; English work tended to sprays of flowers. Coral-work centred in Marseilles and Naples was the home of shell cameo, which was worked in a huge range of qualities to produce 'antique'-style gems for the middle-class market, mounted in every form of jewellery. Essentially an imitation of classical engraved gems, the cameo technique was also worked in agate, onyx and other stones.[57] After the neoclassical period, naturalistic forms such as flowers and birds dominated English taste in jewellery, with figurative brooches and pendants worked in gold, employing its different native colours with chemically textured effects to create contrasts, enlivened with enamel and feature stones. A multitude of 'yellow metal' alloys enabled the same forms to be made at vastly cheaper prices, though at the further expense of quality in design and workmanship.

The most characteristic form of early nineteenth-century middle-class jewellery was the genre of sentimental tokens of love and affection, characteristically expressed in lockets, brooches and rings. The emotional content of such pieces removed them from the crass world of expensive display, going some way to resolving the disjunction between riches and goodness by making them precious in the figurative as well as literal sense. Symbolic motifs prescribed by the 'language of flowers' were very popular in the 1830s–40s, e.g. forget-me-not for true love, lily of the valley for the return of happiness, rosebud for youthful beauty.[58] A modest show of cut stones could spell out REGARD in a ruby, emerald, garnet, amethyst, ruby and diamond; or LOVE in a lapis lazuli, opal, vermeil (garnet) and emerald. Many sentimental jewels contained a glass or crystal-covered compartment for a lock of hair from a beloved person, presenting a corporeal presence to nullify separation, whether by distance or death. The art of composing miniature pictures in hair flourished from the later eighteenth century but a tiny wisp or plait was always the predominant form of hair jewellery.[59] Another fundamental form of middle-class jewellery was the cross pendant, available in plain gold, decoratively cast or engraved, set with a variety of jewels, or made of semi-precious stone; the cross was equally effective in conveying piety and modesty, and could be pretty to boot.

In practice, little jewellery other than rings was worn during the day throughout the first half of the nineteenth century. For middle-class women of Jane Austen's degree, an open-necked dress invited a small pendant or locket, and a collar or lace fichu called for a small brooch to pin the edges together. Such small rectangular brooches of cut stone, enamel or painted miniature were typically framed with pastes or small pearls, a format also popular for rings. Perhaps the most common item of jewellery owned by middle-class women in the early nineteenth century was a waist-length gold chain; though hardly surviving at all in museum collections, long chains are seen frequently in portraits.[60] The chain could claim to be functional in attaching to spectacles, watch or seal which would usually reside in a watch pocket inside the waistband of a skirt, but its graceful drape was clearly also an aesthetic advantage. A little further along the spectrum of pseudo-utilitarian jewellery was the chatelaine, a neo-medieval hooked ornament to hang on the belt or waistband, from which were suspended eight or ten miniature domestic tools and trinkets on individual chains, a mixture of the modern Swiss Army knife and the charm bracelet. The chatelaine was the quintessential jewel of domesticity.

It is difficult to move beyond the prescriptions of advice literature to test how middle-class women (or men) translated its exhortations into real wardrobes of clothing. References in diaries and letters provide insights into the use and personal value of clothes, though rarely sufficient to reconstruct an individual's entire range.[61] Nor is there much evidence in historic examples still available for physical study. First, what survives in museum collections is overwhelmingly unprovenanced, and hence it is impossible to assess with certainty the economic and cultural conditions of the original wearer. Second, surviving items tend to be specimens of best or sentimentally important dress. Third, the corpus of museum historic clothing is almost invariably single items, detached from the ensemble of trimmings and outerwear (not to mention underwear) that constituted them so richly as indices of taste.[62] Fourth, systematic documentary evidence of an individual's whole wardrobe, even in a synchronic slice, is extremely scarce. A unique item that approaches such a record is the lifetime clippings of fabric samples, pinned into an old account book, with brief descriptions and a note of the cost of each new dress, made by Barbara Johnson, an English clergyman's daughter, between 1746 and 1823. She was single all her life, and had a steady annual income of about £60, which she described in 1814 as 'slender'; by comparison, Jane Austen had about £20.[63] Johnson's album shows that in 67 years, she acquired 122 garments, averaging in the last twenty years slightly more than one dress per year, plus the occasional mantle or pelisse. How she combined collars, cuffs, shawls and jewellery with each dress is undescribed; so are her under-

THE CHATELAINE. A REALLY USEFUL PRESENT.

Laura. "OH ! LOOK, MA' DEAR; SEE WHAT A *LOVE* OF A CHATELAINE EDWARD
HAS GIVEN ME."

Jewelled? The tools of the kitchen are presented as a jewel of domesticity, but
Punch doubts the reality.

J. Leech, 'The chatelaine: a really useful present', *Punch*, vol. 16 (London: 1849),
p. 16.

wear, outerwear, shoes and bonnets. Johnson's album provides unique detail of fabrics, which assists the interpretation of occasional surviving household accounts and some genres of legal inventories, but both these types of record list clothing so generically that they throw little light on the nature of middle-class taste. Between the ideal prescriptions of advice books and fashion plates, and the rare details such as Barbara Johnson's fabric choices, the reality of early nineteenth-century clothing is remarkably unknown.

Correct taste in the house

Correct taste in the equipment, furnishings and decoration of the middle-class dwelling was a much more clearly articulated standard than for clothing, but it contained many more traps. While the criteria of propriety and unostentation persisted, the enormous complexity of domestic goods for highly differentiated purposes unveiled a universe of choices which even more acutely defined the degree of an individual's – and a family's – genteel standing. The consumption of house fittings and furniture was a large expense by comparison with clothing; they tended to be life-cycle acquisitions rather than regular purchases, first upon marriage, when money or goods were often gifts to the new household, and thereafter mainly in response to advances in household income or other opportunities.[64] The availability of money affected the expression of fully realized domestic gentility, but the knowledge to spend it with correct taste determined its effectiveness in the stakes of status.

Houses had long been a site for the expressive functions of wealth, manifested at their eighteenth-century zenith in the great country and city mansions of the aristocracy in the United Kingdom. Inevitably, they were reproduced in the United States, to the republican horror of the architectural pundit, Andrew Jackson Downing, who fulminated (to no effect): 'they are wholly in contradiction to the spirit of our time and people.'[65] Now the middle-class house and its furnishings acquired new social meaning: the choice of furnishings demonstrated to the inhabitants and to their visitors a vision of correct taste, a demonstration of morality and thus a proof of gentility. Appropriate furnishings came to be perceived not merely as decorative but as evidence of personal and family refinement.

The critic John Ruskin articulated this drive as a new ethic: 'Taste is not only a part and an index of morality; it is the ONLY morality ... Tell me what you like, and I'll tell you who you are.'[66] A house furnished in accordance with genteel principles of gendered behaviour and polite values constituted one of the primary sets in which the genteel performance of women took place; the profile of the public rooms in furnishing advice literature indicates this importance. At the same time, the back rooms of the home demanded new attention as the site of the private rituals of gentility, the proof that the genteel individual truly lived the ideal. Furnishings had never carried so much ideological meaning relevant to daily life. As the desire and capacity to emulate aristocratic tastes expanded with the growth of the middle class, the rhetoric of furniture, household equipment and decorations grew more complex and nuanced. Beside their display meanings, furnishings arranged to represent the spirit of *home* came to be seen as actively shaping the moral character of inhabitants.[67] The moralization of aesthetics had cast the beautiful as contingently good; now the combination of beauty and goodness was set to construct the righteousness of people who beheld and used beautiful things. Again in Ruskin's words: 'Is the liking for ornaments – for pictures, or statues, or furniture, or architecture – a moral quality? . . . Taste for *any* pictures or statues is not a moral quality, but taste for good ones is.'[68]

The concept of the home as the spiritual centre of daily life introduced a practice of sanctity that had previously been confined to church; it was expressed in Gothic forms, altar-like arrangements of tables and parlour organs and church furniture modified for home use, such as the priedieu chair.[69] The separation of the home away from worldly interaction and into women's sphere of private life promoted a new view of privacy between inhabitants and visitors and within the family itself. From the visitor's point of view, this began with the formalization of the hall as an ante-room to the private drawing room and the distancing of the drawing room from a family sitting room.[70] Within the family, unmarried adults came to expect to have individual bedrooms. The softening, beautifying aspect of the genteel project was expressed in a new commitment to physical comfort, realized both in plumper styles of upholstery and in novel articles of furniture.[71] Genteel values endowed the house with the aura of homeliness, reflecting its removal from communal, productive status to the modern conception of a family retreat.

At the same time, the acquisition of goods such as ornaments and furniture inculcated genteel habits of consumption, joining the domestic world to the economy of mass production. Furniture manufacture increased hugely throughout the nineteenth century, driven less by mechanization than by middle-class demand.[72] Here the commodity nature of furnishings demanded a crossover of the individual's financial and cultural capital to achieve the correct result. Cheaper materials with imitation finishes such as staining and graining enabled the middle and lower ends of the furniture trade to flourish as they met the expanding market for genteel forms. Unaffected by the War of Independence, the British trade exported huge quantities of less expensive furniture to America and to the colonies. English trade manuals and pattern books crossed the oceans and were reprinted for decades.[73] Despite a republican sentiment that named American tastes 'French', the neoclassical and revivalist styles of furniture in the first half of the nineteenth century were barely distinguishable from British designs. The critical issue for people who desired respectability was not nationalism but the risks contained in acquiring items which might be judged too decorative (condemned as garish) or too expensive (extravagant). At the other end of the financial spectrum, a touch of gentility was increasingly available to people without large means by purchasing a small but matching dinner service, or an inexpensive set of dining chairs. The beautifying, specializing and gendering of daily life enabled by such goods represented determined steps on the ladder of genteel practice.

Advice on the style of architecture, room arrangement and furniture demonstrates how a consistent cultural standard of gentility could be met at a variety of financial levels. Advice and pattern books such as Englishman John Claudius Loudon's *Encyclopedia of Cottage, Villa and Farm Architecture* (1833) and American Andrew Jackson Downing's *The Architecture of Country Houses* (1850) offered house plans ranging from very modest size to palatial grandeur. All but the very smallest cottages contain a living room or parlour, separate from the kitchen, but only the villas – the larger houses designed for persons 'of competence or wealth' – possess a dining room, the threshold of middle-class distinction.[74] Wealth is fundamental in consumption choices, but different degrees of genteel cultural capital can be discerned in internal arrangements such as the function and furnishing of rooms. The orientation of rooms clearly demarcates the private (bedroom, kitchen) and the public (hall, dining room, drawing room), with private rooms at the back and upstairs and public rooms at the front and downstairs. In this, Loudon's and Jackson's recommendation follows the conventions of the Georgian remodelling of medieval domestic room arrangements, a trend that became increasingly marked in the Regency/Federal and Victorian/Ante-Bellum periods.[75] The suite of public rooms demonstrates specific, differentiated functions: the hall for receiving, the dining room for eating, the drawing room for entertaining. The dedication of space and resources to public rooms without direct domestic functions such as food preparation or sleeping accommodation constitutes claims to both the aspirational style of aristocratic largesse and the rhetoric of genteel correctness and specificity.

The hall or lobby is the decisive domestic architectural expression of the private family, the normative expectation, even for cottages, of both Loudon and Downing. A hall interposes private space between the living room and the front door to the outside world, in which the visitor's further penetration could be negotiated. It is therefore a formal space, mediating the external and internal relations of the family with the public world. Thomas Sheraton, early nineteenth-century upholsterer to the nobility and style-setter to many more, recommended that the hall 'ought always to be expressive of the dignity of its possessor,' and Downing commended a lobby in even the most modest cottage, to protect 'the privacy and dignity of the inmates.'[76] To fulfil this role, specific new furniture forms developed in the early nineteenth century. The determining form was the hall chair, characteristically small and hard but decorated with aristocratic scrolls and flourishes, offering a cautious hospitality to the waiting visitor. Loudon, dedicated to genteelizing through cheap, rational solutions, proposed that cottage lobbies should be furnished with iron furniture grained to imitate oak, a reform that never really took off indoors.[77] A dedicated hall table or hallstand enabled the crucial new function of presenting a card tray or specially-designed card receiver for visiting cards, and of respectfully accommodating visitors' hats or umbrellas. For these functions, Kenneth Ames interprets the hallstand as a mechanism of 'image management', a piece of furniture mediating the departure of family members into the public world and the entry of visitors into the private domain.[78] The test for immaculate gentility in the use of the hall is the combination of these pieces of furniture and equipment; a family's degree of cultural and financial capital became evident in its consumption of the range of possibilities. In studies of middle-class household inventories in Scotland, Delaware and New South Wales in the 1830s and 1840s, the fully fledged expression of hall furnishings occurs in about a third of households; partial combinations indicate the willingness but not yet competence in one or the other capital resources.[79]

The drawing room was crucial to the practice of gentility; Karen Halttunen identifies it as 'the arena within which the aspiring middle class worked to establish their claims to social status.'[80] A drawing room was the defining element of genteel house space: described by Sheraton, it was 'the chief apartment of a noble, or genteel house, to which it is usual for company to draw after dinner, and in which formal visits are paid.'[81] Its function was leisure in the form of entertainment, implying the luxury of idle time which had once been available only to the very wealthy or to courtly society, but at the turn of the nineteenth century was increasingly appropriated into the realm of middle-class women. This group had to learn the arts of gentility, including the sense of being refined without stilted effort; in this environment of aspiration, a correctly furnished drawing room was visible proof of the family's refinement, a demonstration that they understood how to be polite. 'The drawing room should always exhibit more beauty and elegance than any other apartment in the house . . . The furniture should be richer and more delicate in design . . . ,' urged Downing.[82]

At the beginning of the century, Sheraton advised that the drawing room should be furnished with sofas, chairs to match, a commode (table), pier tables, elegant fire screens, elaborate light fittings (such as figures with lights in their hands) and large glasses (mirrors) fixed so as to maximize 'the reflection or perspective representation of the room.'[83] By the 1830s, Loudon proposed a larger and more complex scheme for the drawing room: reposing chairs, lighter cane-seated chairs, sofas with a sofa table, a large round table in the middle, two card tables, other tables of various sizes (with 'something upon them, to make them appear of use'), a bookcase, fire screens, a pier looking-glass, pictures, busts, curios, vases of flowers, draperies with inner curtains of figured muslin and an Axminster carpet and rug.[84] The variety of drawing room tables recommended by Loudon is vivid evidence of the new bourgeois tendency to specialize the functions of furnishings. It can be seen very clearly in Sydney auction records of the 1840s, where the median number of tables per drawing room is four and a half; the largest number is ten (and they were not in the wealthiest households). The Sydney catalogues list 15 kinds of table (some names overlap meanings); the major types are card, sofa, work, small and round tables.[85] One of the larger of these tables anchored the room as the defining piece of drawing room furniture. The central table was the cynosure of drawing room gentility, draped with a decorative cover, the site of an oil lamp and thus the source of radiant light, the focus of refined equipment such as books and portable writing desks, and the nexus of family gathering for shared pastimes from games to prayers. 'The centre-table is to us the emblem of the family circle,' asserted Downing.[86] Yet measured in practice, the outstanding index of the genteel character of a drawing room is the cohort of small fancy tables that flanked the central table: small round, Pembrokes, Chinese, sofa, card, work and so forth. This point is

Fancy: A host of small tables studded the drawing room, encircling the centre table: (from top right) work table, small table, flower stand, chess table, sofa table.

Loudon, *Encyclopedia of Cottage, Villa and Farm Architecture* (London: 1833), pp. 312–13, 1067, 1068–9, 1071; Webster, *Encyclopedia of Domestic Economy* (London: 1844) p. 231.

not made explicitly in the advisory literature, whose limitations are also evident in the actual scarcity of highly advocated items. An example is pier or console tables, shown in inventory analyses to be much less common than the advice books suggest they ought to have been: 'Pier and console tables are great ornaments in drawing rooms, and ought never to be omitted where splendour is an object to be desired, and money is not wanting', wrote Loudon; Sheraton too emphasized their importance, though Thomas Webster's more down-to-earth *Encyclopedia of Domestic Economy* suggested an alternative in the form of the chiffonier.[87]

More famous in the history of middle-class culture than fancy tables is the piano. Every drawing room novel contains a piano for its heroine, with the usual corrective insight of Jane Austen, who depicts Mrs Collins, a county clergyman's wife, without one and Miss de Bourgh, an aristocrat's daughter, with one but unable to play it.[88] On the frontier and in the colonies, accounts are legion of heroic efforts to transport pianos to unpromising destinations, indicating the tremendous significance of musical accomplishment.[89] This fame represents a strongly gender-marked need, for pianos signified specially the genteel skill of women (though men played the instrument too), evidence both of personal refinement and of the ability to entertain others.[90] Practising music was a deliciously unproductive means of passing time at home, displaying a lady as rich enough to afford idle time; as a performer at domestic entertainments, she was constructed as the refined servant and cultural guide of her family and guests. Loudon was more forthright in his assessment of the meaning of pianos, describing them bluntly as 'articles of luxury, . . . made . . . ornamental for this reason, [of] the most beautiful forms [and] rare and curious woods.'[91] Yet the real extent of piano ownership among early nineteenth-century middle-class people throughout the Anglo world was almost certainly less than implied by the ideal and its ideologues, as in Downing's assertion, 'Even in simple cottages, where such a thing would excite astonishment in Europe, the piano will be found.'[92] Pianos were expensive, starting at around £10 and leaping upwards. According to *A New System of Practical Domestic Economy*, £125 p.a. was the threshold 'which will afford to a man with a wife and three children, an ample sufficiency of all the necessities of life, but without any superfluity,' and between £150 and £250 enabled them a servant, or two for £300.[93] As a proportion of income, then, pianos must be seen as luxuries of either considerable wealth or very determined gentility, and the Scottish, Delaware and New South Wales studies of middle-class furnishings show that less than a quarter of middle-class households actually owned them.

The spread of refined leisure activities such as reading novels and writing letters marks another development of the late eighteenth/early nineteenth-century rise of individualistic culture. Both pastimes required new furniture forms or, rather, adaptations for domestic use from old official or professional forms, notably bookcases and writing desks. Massive forms of bookcases and desks survived for masculine use in offices or libraries, but entirely new, light, consciously decorative forms were designed from the mid-eighteenth century onwards for the use of ladies in their bedrooms and drawing rooms.[94] Downing prescribed that anyone with the means and taste to live in a villa would devote 'a library or cabinet sacred to books' and Loudon, the determined gentrifier, advised even cottagers that 'no cottage parlour ought to be without one.'[95] Possession of such goods in middle-class households follows the pattern of pianos in being less than might have been assumed. Half to two-thirds listed bookcases, distributed predominantly in drawing rooms, but also in dining rooms and libraries. A fifth to a third listed a desk or writing table or a portable desk (fitted writing box). These studies further suggest that a secretaire-bookcase, despite the apparent convenient combination of functions, was an advanced piece of furniture appreciated only by those already in the habit of owning the furniture of literacy.

The decision to allocate resources to dining and entertaining in separate rooms is among the most characteristic in the history of the specialization and embourgeoisement of domestic space. Requiring less wealth than the aristocracy but more than the lowest sort, by the mid-eighteenth century the middling kind pioneered smaller, more private apartments fitted out for different functions. Simpler tastes remained satisfied with common-purpose rooms, but people who were financially capable could choose to cultivate this mark of refinement, and by the turn of the nineteenth century a suite of specialized rooms had become a baseline for a genteel standard of living. Separation of eating from the kitchen was a fundamental of aristocratic hierarchy, desirable even at the cost of cold meals. To eat in the kitchen was to acknowledge the production of food, a suitable state for servants and the poor, but not for their betters; hence the significance of the separate dining room. Where cultural capital exceeded financial resources, it was a compromise in the face of necessity to eat in the parlour, as did the ladies of Cranford, and as suggested by Scottish furnishing inventories naming a dining table in the living room. The inability to dedicate a room to formal dining would have had considerable implications for a family's honour as ritualists and hosts. Formal meals in a specific dining room could take on various orientations: family events, hospitable occasions and assertions of distinction between servants and masters. The family dinner contains ancient meanings of patriarchal authority in which the head of the household demonstrates his ability to provide his family with food. The cause of middle-class refinement could interpose a servant between the hands of the provider and the service of the food but his repute was buttressed by the head position at the table, seated on grander furniture than any other diner's. The role of provider was also an element of the ritual of feeding guests, when it was enlarged by the dimension of conspicuous generosity and enriched with the material battery of table display. The formal rules of the table functioned not only to control the acts of the diners but of their servants too, making every meal a performance of class distinction.

A specialized room required specialized furniture. Downing advised that 'the furniture should be substantial, without being clumsy, but much simpler in decoration than in the drawing room.'[96] Loudon prescribed a pair of carved mahogany sideboards, a pair of side tables, and a 'handsome wide dining table' with 'very handsome' chairs.[97] He further recommended equipment such as cellarets for wine storage, ottomans for easy feet, lamps for the sideboards, a mantel mirror, richly framed pictures and a stand for the table's additional leaves when not in use. Sideboards, like self-consciously elegant (as opposed to purely utilitarian) dining tables, were items of furniture that became available to the middling sphere of society in the eighteenth century, elements of the 'consumer revolution' drawing on industrializing wealth. The sideboard was particularly a piece of display furniture, both for conspicuously housing valuable table plate when not in use and for presenting tableware and food during meals. The hospitable character of dining required a large number of chairs, two of which were conventionally arm chairs for the master and mistress of the household and the others, armless side chairs for children and guests, indicating the subaltern status of both in relation to the host and hostess. The range of documented dining room ensembles indicates that sets of eight, ten and twelve chairs were standard numbers. Like other recommended furniture groups, the evidence of inventories indicates that prescriptions were met to varying degrees within the vocabulary of genteel consumption. The Scottish study suggests that the neoclassical style of a set of push-together tables persisted into the era of the modern Victorian taste for a massive single-piece table – perhaps a rare instance of the ability to distinguish older furniture in the bare bones of written lists, and a caveat for the interpretation of all such lists.

Dining was the site of one of the earliest expressions of genteel self-control in the form of cutlery and table napkins; Norbert Elias traces its development from the fourteenth century.[98] In feudal times, use of a fork had distinguished the gentleperson's self-discipline; in the eighteenth century, fork-use trickled down the ranks of society, a major indicator of the spread of civilized manners; and by the early nineteenth century, matching sets of forks, spoons and, less frequently, knives occupied the genteel diner's hands.[99] (Knives always retained the potential to be non-matching implements, because they required blades of steel set into handles of many possible materials, not necessarily en suite with other implements.) Sets of cutlery assert the flatteringly inclusive expectation that all individuals at table subscribe to the same high standards of manipulating food, and the generous expectation that a host can satisfy these standards for all the diners. Within the set of cutlery was an intricate structure of specialized purposes, though the essential pair of knife and fork is marked in lists with a limited variety of purposes: table and dessert, or large and small. Spoons are the most highly differentiated articles, specific shapes being named for table, soup, dessert, tea, egg and marrow, plus a variety of particular serving spoons for sugar, salt, mustard and gravy.

Rich materials quickly became the standard for aristocratic eating implements and by the turn of the nineteenth century, industrial mass production rose to meet the expanding demand with elegant imitations of rich cutlery. Thus inventories and catalogues list goods made not only of solid silver but also of Sheffield plate, Britannia metal and German silver, along with the word 'plate', which carries the useful ambiguity of its traditional meaning, 'silver', together with its modern, nineteenth-century meaning of electroplate.[100] Domestic adviser to the would-be genteel, Miss Leslie, reassures her readers of the credibility of such compromises: 'Forks of this composition [German silver] are much in use . . . It is by no means costly, and when properly taken care of, it looks very well.'[101] Solid silver table forks were the heaviest and hence most expensive items of cutlery, thus incarnating genteel significance as the tool of rich, refined eating; Agogos asserts confidently, 'At every respectable table you will find silver forks.'[102] In practice, sterling silver was still so expensive in the 1830s–40s that many documented households owned only a token few items of silver table equipment such as fish slices, sugar tongs and wine coasters – just enough to create an air of luxury to infuse the atmosphere of the imitation goods.

The ceramic and glass equipage of the table for formal dining constituted yet further sites for the simultaneous display of conspicuous wealth and of the subtle range of behaviours that marked genteel practice. Dinner services, dessert services, breakfast services and tea and/or coffee services listed in records show the range of ceramics that could frame a genteel performance at table, matched by glassware for table service and for particular drinks. A standard dinner service comprised 80 to 140 or more pieces, mainly sets of different-sized plates, plus a variety of serving dishes, bowls, lidded dishes and sauceboats. The dessert service was conventionally highly decorated, comprising a dozen plates and a few serving dishes or stands. A breakfast service might contain large cups and saucers in addition to a range of plates, and

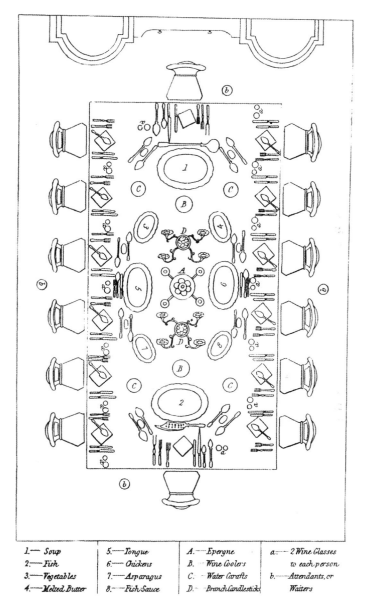

1.— Soup	5.——Tongue	A.——Epergne	a.—— 2 Wine Glasses
2.——Fish	6.—— Chickens	B. Wine Coolers	to each person
3.——Vegetables	7.——Asparagus	C. Water Carafts	b.——Attendants, or
4.——Melted Butter	8.——Fish Sauce	D. Branch Candlesticks	Waiters

Lavish: A genteel dinner required large quantities of knives and forks for eating, and equal numbers for serving, plus specialized glasses, carafes, decanters (here, wine coolers), serving dishes and ornaments.

'Dinner party for fourteen': James Williams, *The Footman's Guide* (London: *c.* 1845), frontispiece.

was sometimes coterminous with the tea service, whose difference amounted to the size of the cups – also the indicator of a coffee service. Table glass includes finger bowls, custard and blancmange cups, trifle and jelly glasses and glasses for preserves, pickles and ginger. Drinking glasses are identified for specific liquids: wine (sherry, claret, hock, champagne), whiskey, cider, water and soda water, though Miss Leslie noted the challenge that, 'the fashionable glass for each wine varying so frequently, it is difficult in this respect to give any rules.'[103] The decorative layout of the serving dishes, plates and glasses on the table, sketched in many an instruction manual, was ritualized by the elegant repetition of each 'remove' or course, eloquently displaying the host's knowledge as well as means. Among the professional and commercial gentlemen of Sydney in the 1840s, a large quarter of households owned all four types of service and another quarter more owned three types, and nearly half practised the refinement of drinking different wines from specific glasses, suggesting that a good half of these colonial middle-class households invested seriously in the genteel style of using specialized dining equipment. But quantities of differentiated plates composed only one aspect of a genteel mentality in the use of table china, for the mass output of the potteries of Staffordshire and the Ohio valley encompassed sets available in so many registers of price that the semiotic quality of multiple specific items was effectively available to anyone possessing the motivation and knowledge to use it.

Pure white ceramics, for instance, echoed the seventeenth-century European passion for Chinese porcelain, which few could then afford. Hence, throughout the eighteenth century, a raft of techniques developed to manufacture white ceramic bodies of more or less convincing quality: creamware, pearlware, ironstone, bone china and other patent recipes made imitation porcelain out of earthenware available at steadily decreasing prices. Transfer-printed designs westernized intricate oriental motifs and domesticated traditional Chinese cobalt blue and intensely-coloured enamel decoration.[104] At the same time, authentic Chinese wares made for export to Europe were traded on an enormous scale, and until the 1790s were more available in England than locally manufactured imitation porcelain.[105] After the War of Independence decapitated the East India Company's monopoly on the China trade, United States merchants initiated direct contact with China, and by the early nineteenth century America was the largest market for customized export porcelain wares.[106] Such an avalanche of tableware available in so many levels of quality and price revolutionized genteel capacities at table. While it is impossible to know how much porcelain, and of exactly what standard, was acquired by aspirant and accomplished middle-class people, archaeological investigations throughout the Anglo world demonstrate its frequency.[107]

Private gentility

Genteel standards shaped private practice; indeed, maintaining a refined private life was the acid test of the sincerity of aspirant gentility. The separation of public from private rooms in the house meant that family private life had to cross over into one or the other sphere. For all but the very wealthy this required the compromise of expediency, in the use of the publicly oriented drawing room for family living as well as public entertaining. When resources permitted, the genteel ambition was to dedicate an additional, private sitting room, morning room or parlour out of the total space available in the building, and/or to construct a library.[108] The parlour and library were strongly gender-defined, respectively feminine and masculine, evidence of the penetration of the concept of separate spheres into the home. The proportion of middle-class aspirants or practitioners able to afford additional private rooms in their houses was essentially a function of wealth; but the ideal to maintain a private as well as a public room for family activity indicates the importance of the genteel specificity of space for domestic communal activity.[109]

The bedroom was a private space, but some of the genteel values expressed in drawing room furnishings were also manifested in the master's and mistress's personal domain. Among Scottish, Delaware and New South Wales inventories little decorative furniture is listed in the bedrooms, evidence that they served essentially functional purposes; in this category, Miss Leslie advised a rocking chair, a stuffed easy chair, some low chairs for sewing or footbaths, one or two footstools and a sofa for naps or a settee if ill.[110] Though removed from the public sphere of the medieval single-room house, where the large, curtained bed constituted the visible honour of the progenitors of a family, the privatized major bed retained the prestige of massive proportions and rich furnishings. The need for warmth and privacy was logically reduced by the move into a separate bedroom, but the traditional wooden four poster, fully furnished with fine textiles, remained the standard for middle-class refinement: 'no bedstead looks so well as the square, high post with curtains.'[111] It was also among the most valuable items of household furniture. Cheap, light iron beds became steadily more available from the 1820s, growing from utilitarian portability to some degree of style, and thanks to a further reputation for healthy airiness, began to be considered appropriate for children's as well as servants' beds. Loudon was a great advocate of iron beds, claiming that they were already 'to be found in the houses of people of wealth and fashion in London, sometimes even for best beds.'[112] Nonetheless, even in New South Wales, where ease of transport was often a desideratum and metal beds were numerous in inventories, they never supplant the full mahogany item in middle-class main bedrooms. The value of a bed was composed not merely of the bedstead, but of its bedding and dressings, the fabrics that made it cosy, beautiful or even majestic. Bed textiles have long been traced as a significant component of household wealth, traditionally the one that belonged specifically to women.[113] They amounted to a considerable investment, for a fully furnished bed required fifty-plus metres of fabric. Bedding conventionally comprised a straw or seagrass palliasse; one or two mattresses of horsehair, wool or flock; a feather bed, sheets, blankets and counterpane; a bolster and two pillows. Scottish insolvency inventories show that the blanket and napery wealth of many households was large, e.g., three characteristic middle-wealth inventories contain blankets, sheets, pillow and bolster slips, bed covers, towels and tablecloths worth £8/5/6, £10/5/- and £16/6/-, often equivalent to the value of the furnished main bed.[114] The same major investment in household textiles is evident in the Delaware records, typified by Jesse Mendenhall, a gentleman of Wilmington, whose main bedchambers contained $130 worth of furniture and $50 worth, a third as much again, of bed linen alone.[115]

Another large item of furniture inhabited main bedrooms by the 1830s–40s: a wardrobe, usually accompanied by a chest of drawers. The wardrobe was a new form, appearing in the late eighteenth century; the chest of drawers was a specializing development of the medieval chest or coffer, dating from a little earlier.[116] Webster's *Encyclopedia* urges readers that 'Wardrobes are far more convenient for keeping apparel than the chests of drawers formerly in use,' but he was campaigning for the modern taste more than describing a real truth.[117] The need for free-standing, fitted furniture for clothes storage was in some part a response to the enlarging quantities of clothing available to people, thanks to the consumer revolution, as well as a testimony to the value placed on that clothing. But the massive character of wardrobes may be more significant than their practical function, introducing to the private domain expensive cabinetwork such as had hitherto been present only in the public rooms of the house. Conspicuous consumption is usually assumed to have a public face, but use of a wardrobe in private contains

Imposing: A polished (or faux) mahogany wardrobe comprised a monument to substantial resources, even in the privacy of the bedroom.

Webster, *Encyclopedia of Domestic Economy* (London: 1844), p. 279; Loudon, *Encyclopedia of Cottage, Villa and Farm Architecture* (London: 1833), p. 304.

an echo of the inner necessities of genteel practice, of the need to conduct the self in the same refined manner in private as in public. In such ways, bedrooms were as crucial as drawing rooms in living the genteel habitus. The specific roles fulfilled by the furniture of personal cleanliness, the high post bed decked with rich textiles and the careful expense of storing clothing were as necessary to genteel self-consciousness as the knowledge of etiquette and the habits of self-control.

Like manners, genteel goods mediated the lived experience of middle-class and would-be middle-class people, testing and proving to themselves as much as to others whether they achieved *comme il faut*. So essential were precise forms that they travelled wherever the middle class went. Consumer goods were now efficiently distributed through the networks of global capitalism, exemplified in Loudon's observation of the market for Elizabethan furniture: 'as London has a direct and cheap communication with every part of the world by sea, the American citizen or the Australian merchant, who wishes to indulge in this taste, may do it.'[118] The reassurance of familiar objects with which to frame daily life induced women emigrants and pioneers to make heroic efforts to keep up standards: a story, 'The Settlers of Van Diemen's Land' in the London *Court Magazine and Belle Assemblée*, depicts a paragon of a wife emerging from a bogged bullock cart on a stormy night in the bush, not only bright and cheerful, but equipped with a box of dry clothes for her husband and a white tablecloth, 'a luxury hitherto unknown in the hut'.[119] The symbolism of the genteel woman bearing the snowy tablecloth to the ends of the earth is potent. Crisp cleanliness demarcated culture from nature; pure whiteness marked the power of humans over the environment; the fabric layer that separated the meal from the rude table demonstrated the power of gentility over barbarism. The absence of a fresh tablecloth on the frontier table would indicate despairing failure in the project to re-create the genteel habitus. Wherever the tablecloth was victorious, the success of genteel culture was proved across the globe.

Conclusion

Victorian gentility – which is to say the middle class – flourished and grew throughout Greater Britain's long nineteenth century, becoming the ideal and then the norm as the standard of desirable lifestyle. Outwardly, a rigid structure of explicit and implicit rules seemed to govern genteel culture, but in practice, it was an extraordinarily flexible system. The axes of financial and cultural capital which defined the genteel habitus enabled a tremendous range of expressions, capable of including almost anyone motivated to aspire. Precise degrees of mastery of the necessary money and knowledge resources set up endless subcategories with which to vary internal advancement, amounting to a self-regulating mechanism to manage peer acknowledgement. The central value of self-control imbued male lives with the righteousness of work and female lives with ideals of domesticity. Nonetheless, in each sphere, genteel people managed the presence of contradictions such as the psychic drive to self-indulgence and the strategic necessity of manipulating others. Suppressed for the sake of respectability, such ungenteel behaviour was hypocritical, but human. Overall, the rules and the accommodations evidently satisfied their practitioners, because they continued to use them, and if the young and the restless complained about personal constriction, it was ever so in the conditioning of humans to society.

Yet by the last decades of the nineteenth century a discourse of resistance asserted itself with a masculinist flavour of bohemian free spirit. In fact, the romantic, rebellious character of bohemianism constitutes the opposite side of the coin of bourgeois culture: 'not a realm outside bourgeois life but the expression of a conflict that arose at its very heart.'[1] Fledged in Paris in the 1830s–40s, the tastes of the artist, the student, the wanderer, came to express freedom from convention, often distilled into opposition to marriage and the domestic values and behaviour it now represented. The pure morality of domesticity cast men outside its sphere as immoral.[2] Paris itself took on an aura of licentiousness in Anglo mythology, and all things French came to stand for passion, freedom, decadence. *La bohème* was romanticized as the female partner in the comparatively more available lifestyle of *le bohème*, for the free-spirited man needed a mate of the same persuasion; but, for all that she enjoyed the permission of unconvention, she bore the consequences of her sex harder than men did (even in bohemian art, she dies). The liminal status of the student enabled bourgeois young men, if so inclined, to spend some bohemian years beyond the bounds of middle-class containment, and some were inspired to persist with lives as artists, but many drifted back into the fold. The conflict between personal liberation and social conformity emerged as a choice that shaped middle-class youth culture throughout the twentieth century. By its end, argues Elizabeth Wilson, bohemian ideals had converted mass culture.[3] It is beyond the scope of this book to explore bohemianism as a reaction to gentility but the contrast points up features of gentility that merit further examination, in particular its feminist character and its pervasive influence.

It may seem absurd to suggest that gentility contained advantages for women which could be called 'feminist', in the sense of meaning improvements in women's social circumstances that empowered them with personal agency or positively validated them in public esteem. The claim skates close to the thin ice of suggestions that women are best off under the 'shelter' of prescriptive social systems such as most religions offer. But in the long wake of second-wave feminism of the 1970s, we have grappled with the politics of biology as well as the politics of oppression, and come to much more complex views of women's power and powerlessness. The history of female status is an uphill road of slow advances, but unarguably of advance. No rhetorical progressivism underlies the claim, for it can be seen at least partly as another aspect of Elias's civilizing process, by which modern social construction is shaped by self-constraint.[4] Gentility challenged the ancient Christian presentation of women as sexual temptresses and elevated instead the warm, loving ideal of the domestic mother. In the politics of daily life, this was a much stronger position than the essentially medieval concept of women's worth as creatures who could work and breed, and (sometimes) exert sexual power over men. Such a simple exchange fails to represent the compromises of religion, society and individuals which made variations and exceptions to such a bleak female situation, but it remains true in essentials – though it was not without cost.

Gentility offered women the new status of moral beings, even if the spirit was released only in certain directions, defined by the family. The daily work of the loving wife, the dedicated mother, the responsible housekeeper, opened no new routes beyond the traditional domain of women, but the moral power it now claimed *did*. The spirituality of the calling to domesticity validated unexpectedly extra-domestic projects, exemplified by the strategies of family positioning and the vocations of philanthropy. The first is an argument of the end justifying the means: if women's holy destiny was to nourish and protect their families, their excursions into the world in the family interest were undertaken in the line of blessed duty. With this kind of example in mind, domestic management took on an analogy with national government, grandifying the one and feminising the other, fortuitously illuminated by the aura of Queen Victoria. The second is a more essentialist logic: since female purity underwrote women's interventions in charity, then the spiritual nature of true womanhood both led and protected them in maternalist encounters with vice. In practice, action in both these spheres demonstrated to selves and others the effectiveness of women in semi-public life and paved the way for female politicking in the later nineteenth century in the fields of child health, public hygiene and women's suffrage.[5] The feminist advance of these developments shouldn't be exaggerated, but it was real.

The power of the genteel ideal in women's lives is strikingly demonstrated in its (at least partial) adoption by working-class women. Gentility not only suffused the middle class but shaped working-class standards of female respectability with the concept of the domestic wife. The sacrifices made to embrace genteel domesticity could mean women giving up external, wage-earning work in order to devote nice attention to the family, or to the hard row of attempting both. But it was evidently worth the cost, and probably for similar reasons as domesticity was advantageous to middle-class women: it gave new meaning and value to unwaged work by improving women's status.[6] Working-class men who declined the respectable mantle might continue with rough ways whatever their women chose, but in asserting the genteel identity, working-class women cloaked themselves with a spectrum of standards, from the nice lifestyle of tablecloths and doilies to an expectation of being treated with love. By the end of the nineteenth century the 'angel in the house' beatification of women was accepted as natural by both middle-class and working-class women.[7]

The costs of gentility to women were more apparent in the later nineteenth century than in the formative turn-of-the-century period.

Domesticity, consumerism and etiquette opened up new horizons for women's agency by making them responsible for whole segments of life inside and outside the family, but the genteel habitus stripped them of a somatic character of sensuality and sexuality and thus of the licence they give to pleasure. The burden of 'true womanhood' was the risk of perfectionism, whereby the individual is formed by the expectations of others to standards so demanding that she is in danger of falling off the pedestal for any breach. The extreme self-control necessary to be (or seem) perfect is difficult to learn and a hard state in which to live, specially when masked with the required air of naturalness. Despite the escape permitted in the form of intense emotional relationships among women, the armour that many developed to contain feeling and project the correct manner was oppressive. First-generation aspirants or those motivated by further social advance were sustained in their efforts by the goal ahead, but generations already comfortably ensconced in the genteel habitus acquired the detachment to criticize it. Perception of the self-control of genteel femininity shifted from being a new ideal to a normal standard, and came to be regarded as an artificial shell of repression. Of course, it was all those things, according to the degree of self-discipline the agent was prepared to invest in living genteely. The ratio of costs to benefits transmuted in various circumstances and over time, but the challenge of bohemianism offered an articulate statement of an alternative.

The character of bohemianism as freedom from social control and self-discipline facilitated a rambunctious culture of expressive energy dedicated to exploration of the self and its world. Warren I. Susman identifies this shift as between the Victorian cultivation of 'character' and the modern cult of 'personality', where the purpose of the one was to develop self-control, and of the other self-fulfilment.[8] Bohemianism stood for the inverse of gentility, and damned genteel stricture, with the effect of condemning middle-class women's power in the genteel lifestyle. The goal to *épater les bourgeois* indicates the scope and techniques of the contest, often expressed in sexist mockery. Thus middle-class women found themselves trapped between the discourses of feminine respectability and free spirit, repressed by one but exploited by the other. Yet even as non-domestic opportunities opened up to middle-class women in the early twentieth century, they hung onto genteel personal and social standards (or reverted to them after a youthful fling). As long as there was achievement in being middle class, its values and behaviours maintained purpose. At the same time, the liberating nature of bohemian non-conformism and its ethic of anti-authoritarianism glittered with the romance of the forbidden. The decisive break with gentility came only with the beat-beatnik-hippie culture of the 1960s–70s, as mourned by modern Jeremiahs: 'it all began to go bad around 1965.'[9] Thereafter, liberation culture began to characterize even the adult middle class, and genteel behaviour devolved to the sphere of the elite, for whom self-control was still a means to profitable ends. The codes and practices of essentially Victorian gentility now distinguish the elite from the undisciplined masses who feel 'free' in not observing such rules. Magnates and their minions again discover the power of genteel cultural capital, and take classes in table manners; their wives are schooled in folding serviettes. How this happened is a further question beyond the present work. Answers must connect to the durability of the middle class itself, as suggested by sociologists Melanie Archer and Judith Blau in reviewing its historical trajectory, concluding: 'Norms about respectability and conventionality are put severely to the test in a society of cultural diversity and under conditions of decline.'[10]

In this context it is revealing to examine the two mechanisms identified in this book for working the Victorian genteel habitus: etiquette and consumption. At the turn of the twenty-first century, the former is a dodo and the latter a dragon. Codified genteel etiquette had come to represent the iniquity of an oppressive social order long before the crisis of the 1960s; nonetheless, etiquette manuals continued to be produced throughout the twentieth century, flexibly describing new manners for new circumstances.[11] Today, Victorian-style etiquette is fossilized for use in rituals, still more or less knowledgeably employed in ceremonies such as formal dinners and balls, though it is also subverted on such occasions by playful disobedience.[12] In consequence, the turn of the twenty-first century has seen an episode of lamentation for declining standards of manners, now discussed in terms of civility, strangely echoing the style of lament of a hundred years before.[13] Consumption, on the other hand, has become more and more a central site for self-expression, serviced by an infinitely expanded universe of goods and informed by an unparalleled cosmology of personalities or identities. The genteel consciousness of appropriate consumption as sufficient to show without being showy has been subsumed by the availability of goods and transformed into a diversity of 'looks'. Multiple personalities are not (usually) a psychotic sign in the modern individual, but positively self-expressive. Where the multitude of nineteenth-century middle-class strata was depicted as an onion, the many subcultures of today's mass middle class are distinct and fragmented, like the seeds of a pomegranate. The variety of consumer-defined self-presentations available these days is largely unhierarchical and thus inspires less motivation for social movement. And since the concept of income-earning work as a defining morality disappeared in the economic crises of the later twentieth century, it is doubtful whether a cultural identification of the middle class via its consumption is viable today.

Success has ever been measured in wealth; today is no exception. Yet does cultural capital continue to have any necessary relation to high status? The answer is both yes and no. The body of classical or liberal knowledge inculcated at university among genteel men from the early to mid nineteenth century, and later among women, steadily lost prestige in popular opinion after the Second World War, when practical technology began to seem more useful and popular culture more fun. The late twentieth century witnessed another bout of lament for the decline of such knowledge and the incursion of cultural relativism which presented the truths of western civilization merely as one tradition among many for understanding the world.[14] In general, higher learning as a distinctive asset of cultural capital is regarded as having no strategic purpose other than job training – and yet a liberal arts education can still possess some relic of symbolic capital. In certain circumstances, the cultural assets of a genteel-style upbringing and education remain valuable, and for the same reasons as in the nineteenth century: they distinguish their owners. A cultivated mind and nice manners suggest the more substantial qualities of character, as opposed to the facile veneer of personality. In particular, the Victorian project persists of the self-made rich man seeking the status-honour of old wealth by acquiring its trappings and (at least some of) its manners. A special route to this end today is via the appreciation of art: to collect artworks and antiquities uniquely combines the flaunting of expensive goods with the lustre of educated taste, and to collect almost anything glows with the same aura. This is such a powerful process that it can project (very rich) louts and criminals into the company of old world wealthy culture, and (less rich) nobodies into the reflected light of same – or so they hope.

Humans will always need distinctions to make us unique and yet desirable among our fellows, and to define why we don't want to affiliate with all of them. The culture of gentility constructed the framework of such a body of distinctions in the long nineteenth century and hung on into the twentieth, but it has only residual relevance in the twenty-first. Democratic society must, however, tolerate all, within the bounds of legal standards. It may be the irony of our age that the right to self-realization is bought at the cost of self-control.

Notes

Introduction

1. Linda Young, 'Life in the English Country House – in Australia: the case of Martindale Hall', *Heritage Australia*, vol. 9, no. 3 (1990); 'Constructing Ancestral Grandeur: the performance of two assemblages of furnishings', *Public History Review*, no. 1 (1992).
2. See Judith Martin, *Miss Manners' Guide to Excrutiatingly Correct Behaviour* (London: Hamish Hamilton, 1983) pp. 7–8.

Chapter 1   Cultural Baggage: the Genteel World

1. Charlotte Bosanquet, *The drawing room of Admiral Bosanquet at Clay Hill, Enfield*, 1843, watercolour: Ashmolean Museum; Anon (possibly Edward Hawkins), *Interior, New South Wales*, c.1830, pencil sketch, Mitchell Library, Sydney; Auguste Edouart, *A New York family*, 1842, silhouette, Winterthur Museum, Delaware.
2. Peter Laslett, *The World We Have Lost* (London: Methuen, 1965) p. 22. See also Geoffrey Crossick, 'From Gentlemen to the Residuum: Languages of Social Description in Victorian Britain', in Penelope J. Corfield, *Language, History and Class* (Oxford: Basil Blackwell, 1991).
3. An old but perceptive account of this period of transition is offered by Maurice J. Quinlan, *Victorian Prelude: A History of English Manners, 1700–1830* (Hamden, CT: Archon Books, 1965 [1941]). In adopting the shorthand of 'Victorian' I do not mean to limit my period to 1837–1901, but to connect the period of the Queen's reign with the somewhat longer history of genteel culture.
4. Jane Austen, *Pride and Prejudice* (1813) vol. 1, ch. 8; vol. 3, ch. 1.
5. See discussion in K. C. Phillipps, *Language and Class in Victorian England* (Oxford: Basil Blackwell, 1984) p. 15.
6. Agogos, *Hints on Etiquette and the Usages of Society with a Glance at Bad Habits* (London: Printed for the Booksellers, 1834) pp. 29–30.
7. Norbert Elias, *The Civilizing Process*, vol. 2, *State Formation and Civilization* (Oxford: Basil Blackwell, 1994 [1939]).
8. For example, Asa Briggs, *The Age of Improvement* (London: Longmans, 1959); Joan Evans, *The Victorians* (London: Cambridge University Press, 1966).
9. See Walter L. Arnstein, 'The Myth of the Triumphant Middle Class', *The Historian* 38 (February 1975); also his 'The Survival of the Victorian Aristocracy', in Frederic Cople Jaher (ed.), *The Rich, the Well Born, and the Powerful: Elites and Upper Classes in History* (Urbana: University of Illinois Press, 1973).
10. Leonore Davidoff and Catherine Hall, *Family Fortunes: Men and Women of*

the English Middle Class, 1750–1850 (London: Hutchinson, 1987) part 1, ch. 1.

11. E. P. Thompson, 'The Peculiarities of the English', in *The Poverty of Theory* (London: Merlin, 1978) p. 85.
12. Pierre Bourdieu, *Distinction: A Social Critique of the Judgement of Taste* (London: Routledge & Kegan Paul, 1984 [1979]), pp. 1–2, 170.
13. Pierre Bourdieu, *The Logic of Practice* (Cambridge: Polity Press, 1990 [1980]), pp. 53, 58–9.
14. Pierre Bourdieu, *Language and Symbolic Power* (Cambridge: Polity Press, 1991 [1982]) p. 14.
15. Bourdieu, *Distinction*, p. 56.
16. Bourdieu, *Distinction*, p. 2. Mary Douglas and Baron Isherwood employ this understanding of the consumption of goods: *The World of Goods: Towards an Anthropology of Consumption* (Harmondsworth: Penguin, 1980) p. 10.
17. Elias, *The Civilizing Process*, pp. 85–8.
18. Richard L. Bushman, *The Refinement of America: Persons, Houses, Cities* (New York: Knopf, 1992).
19. Michael Curtin, *Propriety and Position: A Study of Victorian Manners* (New York: Garland, 1987).
20. 'The Nature of Deference and Demeanour', in *Interaction Ritual: Essays on Face-to-Face Behaviour* (London: Allen Lane, 1967) pp. 57, 71.
21. Davidoff and Hall, *Family Fortunes*, pp. 108, 114–15; Mary Ryan, *Cradle of the Middle Class: The Family in Oneida County, New York, 1790–1865* (Cambridge: Cambridge University Press, 1981) pp. 11–12.
22. E. Anthony Rotundo, 'Learning about Manhood: Gender Ideals and the Middle Class Family in Nineteenth Century America', in J. A. Mangan and James Walvin (eds), *Manliness and Morality: Middle Class Masculinity in Britain and America, 1800–1940* (Manchester: Manchester University Press, 1987) pp. 38–9; Peter Gay, *The Cultivation of Hatred*, vol. 3: *The Bourgeois Experience* (New York: Norton, 1993) p. 112.
23. F. K. Prochaska, *Women and Philanthropy in Nineteenth Century England* (Oxford: Clarendon, 1980) pp. 11–12.
24. Ann Douglas, *The Feminization of American Culture* (New York: Knopf, 1977) ch. 1.
25. Dorothy Thompson, *Queen Victoria: Gender and Power* (London: Virago, 1990) pp. 143–5.
26. For example, Esther Aresty, *The Best Behaviour: The Course of Good Manners from Antiquity to the Present as Seen through Courtesy and Etiquette Books* (New York: Simon & Schuster, 1970).
27. For example, David Castronovo, *The English Gentleman: Images and Ideals in Literature and Society* (New York: Ungar, 1987).
28. John F. Kasson, *Rudeness and Civility: Manners in Nineteenth-Century America* (New York: Hill & Wang, 1990); Bushman, *Refinement of America*.
29. Kasson, *Rudeness and Civility*, p. 4.
30. Bushman, *Refinement of America*, p. xiii.
31. Bushman, *Refinement of America*, pp. xv–xix.
32. As observed by de Tocqueville: *Democracy in America* (New York: Harper & Row, 1966 [1835]), p. 424. See also Stuart M. Blumin, *The Emergence of the*

Middle Class: Social Experience in the American City, 1760–1900 (Cambridge: Cambridge University Press, 1989) ch. 1, ch. 5.

33. Ian Tyrrell, *The Absent Marx: Class Analysis and Liberal History in Twentieth Century America* (New York: Greenwood Press, 1986) pp. 15–16.

34. See Martin J. Burke, *The Conundrum of Class: Public Discourse on the Social Order in America* (Chicago: University of Chicago Press, 1995). The history of class history in US historiography is traced by Stuart M. Blumin in 'The Hypothesis of Middle-Class Formation in Nineteenth Century America: A Critique and Some Proposals', *American Historical Review*, vol. 90, no. 2 (April 1985).

35. Richard L. Bushman, 'American High Style and Vernacular Cultures', in Jack P. Greene and J. R. Pole (eds), *Colonial British America: Essays in the History of the Early Modern Era* (Baltimore, MD: Johns Hopkins University Press, 1984) p. 360.

36. Penny Russell, 'A Wish of Distinction: Genteel Femininity in Melbourne Society, 1860–1880', PhD thesis, University of Melbourne (1989); Emma Curtin, 'In Awe of Mrs Grundy: British Gentility and Emigrant Gentlewomen in Australia, 1830–1880', PhD thesis, LaTrobe University (1995); Linda Young, 'The Struggle for Class: The Transmission of Genteel Culture to Early Colonial Australia', PhD thesis, Flinders University of South Australia (1997).

37. H. L. Malchow, *Gentlemen Capitalists: The Social and Political World of the Victorian Businessman* (London: Macmillan – now Palgrave Macmillan, 1991) p. 6.

38. Martin J. Wiener, *English Culture and the Decline of the Industrial Spirit* (Cambridge: Cambridge University Press, 1981).

39. Ryan, *Cradle of the Middle Class*.

40. R. J. Morris, *Class, Sect and Party: The Making of the British Middle Class, Leeds, 1820–1850* (Manchester: Manchester University Press, 1990) p. 12.

41. Blumin, *Emergence of the Middle Class*.

42. Benjamin DeMott, *The Imperial Middle: Why Americans Can't Think Straight about Class* (New York: William Morrow, 1990).

43. Louis Hartz, *The Liberal Tradition in America: An Interpretation of Political Thought since the Revolution* (New York: Harcourt, Brace & Co., 1955), ch. 1.

44. Daniel Walker Howe, 'Victorian Culture in America', in Daniel Walker Howe (ed.), *Victorian America* (Philadelphia: University of Pennsylvania Press, 1976).

45. For example, W. K. Hancock, *Australia* (London: Ernest Benn, 1930), ch. 2, ch. 3; George Nadel, *Australia's Colonial Culture: Ideas, Men and Institutions in Mid-Nineteenth Century Eastern Australia* (Melbourne: Melbourne University Press, 1957).

46. A. Barcan, 'Development of the Australian Middle Class', *Past and Present*, no. 8 (1955), pp. 67–8; David Denholm, *The Colonial Australians* (Harmondsworth: Penguin, 1979), p. 12; Peter Beilharz, 'Theorising the Middle Class', Arena, no. 72 (1985).

47. John Hirst, 'Egalitarianism', in S. L. Goldberg and F. B. Smith (eds), *Australian Cultural History* (Cambridge: Cambridge University Press, 1988); Penny Russell, *A Wish of Distinction: Colonial Gentility and Femininity* (Melbourne: Melbourne University Press, 1994).

48. Louis Hartz, *The Founding of New Societies: Studies in the History of the United States, Latin America, South Africa, Canada and Australia* (New York: Harcourt Brace & World, 1964) ch. 1.

49. Hartz, *Founding of New Societies*, pp. 3, 24, 26–41.

50. Jack P. Greene, *Pursuits of Happiness: The Social Development of Early Modern British Colonies and the Formation of American Culture* (Chapel Hill: University of North Carolina Press, 1988) ch. 7.

51. Charles Dilke, *Greater Britain: A Record of Travel in the English-Speaking Countries during 1866 and 1867*, 2 vols (London: Macmillan, 1869).

52. David Armitage, 'Greater Britain: A Useful Category of Historical Analysis?', *American Historical Review*, no. 104 (April 1999).

53. J. G. A. Pocock, 'British History: A Plea for a New Subject', *New Zealand Journal of History*, vol. 8, no. 1 (1973).

54. For example of such absence, see John H. Mackenzie, 'Empire and Metropolitan Cultures', in Andrew Porter (ed.), *The Nineteenth Century*, vol. 3, *The Oxford History of the British Empire* (Oxford: Oxford University Press, 1999).

55. Described in an earlier period by Bushman, 'American High Style and Vernacular Cultures', p. 348.

56. See James Horn, 'British Diaspora: Emigration from Britain, 1680–1815', in P. J. Marshall (ed.), *The Eighteenth Century*, vol. 2, *Oxford History of the British Empire* (Oxford: Oxford University Press, 1998).

57. Melville Herskovits, *The Myth of the Negro Past* (New York: Harper, 1941); Peter Kolchin, *American Slavery, 1619–1877* (New York: Hill & Wang, 1993), pp. 40–9.

58. David Hackett Fischer, *Albion's Seed: Four British Folkways in America* (New York: Oxford University Press, 1989).

59. Gina Buijs (ed.), *Migrant Women: Crossing Boundaries and Changing Identities* (Oxford: Berg, 1993) p. 2.

60. Robin Cohen, *Global Diasporas: An Introduction* (London: UCL Press, 1997) esp. ch. 3.

61. Briggs, *Age of Improvement*; Harold Perkin, *The Origins of Modern English Society, 1780–1880* (London: Routledge & Kegan Paul, 1969); William Roger Lewis (ed.), *Oxford History of the British Empire*, 5 vols (Oxford: Oxford University Press, 1998).

62. For example, John Field, 'Wealth, Styles of Life and Social Tone amongst Portsmouth's Middle Class, 1800–1875', in R. J. Morris (ed.), *Class, Power and Social Structure in British Nineteenth-Century Towns* (Leicester: Leicester University Press, 1986).

63. Arjun Appadurai, 'Disjuncture and Difference in the Global Cultural Economy', *Public Culture*, vol. 2, no. 2 (1992) pp. 6–10.

64. Malcolm Waters, *Globalization* (London: Routledge, 1995) chs 2–3.

65. Agogos, *Hints on Etiquette and the Usages of Society, With a Glance at Bad Habits*, 9th edn (London: reprinted by William Elliston Gore, Hobarton, 1838).

66. Frances Trollope, *Domestic Manners of the Americans* (London: Folio Society, 1974 [1832]) p. 222; Louisa Meredith, *Notes and Sketches of New South Wales* (London: John Murray, 1844) p. 50.

67. For example, Cary Carson, Ronald Hoffman and Peter J. Albert (eds), *Of Consuming Interest: The Style of Life in the Eighteenth Century* (Charlottesville: University of Virginia Press, 1994).

Chapter 2   In Between: the Problem of the Middle Class

1. G. Kitson Clark, *The Making of Victorian England* (London: Methuen, 1962) p. 119; Peter N. Stearns, 'The Middle Class: Towards a Precise Definition', *Comparative Studies in Society and History*, vol. 21 (1979) p. 380.
2. H. L. Malchow, *Gentleman Capitalists: The Social and Political World of the Victorian Businessman* (London: Macmillan, – now Palgrave Macmillan, 1991) p. 5.
3. Asa Briggs, 'The Language of "Class" in Early Nineteenth Century England', in Asa Briggs and John Saville (eds), *Essays in Labour History* (London: Macmillan, 1960) footnote 3, p. 52; Raymond Williams, *Keywords: A Vocabulary of Culture and Society* (London: Fontana, 1976) pp. 60–9. Steven Wallech adds a convincing context to Briggs's account of the change: '"Class versus Rank": The Transformation of Eighteenth Century English Social Terms and Theories of Production', *Journal of the History of Ideas*, vol 47, no. 3 (1986) pp. 409–10.
4. Marx's recognition of the petty bourgeoisie explains how the term 'bourgeois' comes to be commonly used to mean the middle class. Though technically incorrect, I join common use in this meaning.
5. Joyce Appleby, 'The Social Consequences of American Revolutionary Ideals in the Early Republic', in Burton J. Bledstein and Robert D. Johnston, *The Middling Sorts: Explorations in the History of the American Middle Class* (New York: Routledge, 2001) p. 34.
6. G. M. Young, *Victorian England: Portrait of an Age*, 2nd edn (Oxford: Oxford University Press, 1953 [1936]); Elie Halévy, *A History of the English People in 1815* (London: Penguin, 1937) and *The Age of Peel and Cobden: A History of the English People 1841–1852* (London: Ernest Benn, 1947).
7. For example, Roy Lewis and Angus Maude, *The English Middle Classes* (London: Phoenix House, 1950) ch. 2; Walter E. Houghton, *The Victorian Frame of Mind, 1830–1870* (New Haven, CT: Yale University Press, 1957) p. 4.
8. For example, Harold Perkin, *The Origins of Modern English Society 1780–1880* (London: Routledge & Kegan Paul, 1969) chs 6–9.
9. Asa Briggs, *The Age of Improvement* (London: Longman, 1959).
10. Lawrence Stone and Jeanne C. Fawtier Stone, *An Open Elite? England 1540–1880* (Oxford: Clarendon Press, 1984) p. 20. Adam Smith, *An Inquiry into the Nature and Causes of the Wealth of Nations*, eds R. H. Campbell and A. S. Skinner (Oxford: Clarendon Press, 1976 [1776]) Book 4, ch. 9.
11. W. D. Rubinstein, 'Wealth, Elites and the Class Structure of Modern Britain', *Past and Present*, no. 76 (August 1977); see also his *Elites and the Wealthy in Modern British History: Essays in Social and Economic History* (Brighton: Harvester Press, 1987).
12. Martin J. Wiener, *English Culture and the Decline of the Industrial Spirit* (Cambridge: Cambridge University Press, 1981); Neil McKendrick, '"Gentlemen and Players" Revisited: The Gentlemanly Ideal, the Business Ideal, and the Professional Ideal in English Literary Culture', in Neil McKendrick and R. B. Outhwaite (eds), *Business Life and Public Policy* (Cambridge: Cambridge University Press, 1986) p. 119. The arguments are reviewed in F. M. L. Thompson, *Gentrification and the Enterprise Culture: Britain 1780–1980* (Oxford: Oxford University Press, 2001) ch. 1.

13. Benjamin De Mott, *The Imperial Middle: Why Americans Can't Think Straight About Class* (New York: William Morrow, 1990) p. 9.

14. Alexis de Tocqueville, *Democracy in America* (New York: Harper & Row, 1966 [1835]) pp. 48–9.

15. Edward Pessen, 'The Egalitarian Myth and the American Social Reality: Wealth, Mobility and Equality in the "Era of the Common Man"', in *The Many-Faceted Jacksonian Era: New Interpretations* (Westport, CT: Greenwood, 1977); C. Wright Mills, *White Collar: The American Middle Classes* (New York: Oxford University Press, 1951); W. Lloyd Warner, *American Life: Dream and Reality* (Chicago: University of Chicago Press, 1953) esp. ch. 3; E. Digby Baltzell, *Philadelphia Gentlemen: The Making of a National Upper Class* (Glencoe, IL: Free Press, 1958).

16. Louis Hartz, *The Liberal Tradition in America: An Interpretation of American Political Thought since the Revolution* (New York: Harcourt, Brace, 1955), ch. 1; Herbert J. Gans, *Middle American Individualism: The Future of Liberal Democracy* (New York: Free Press, 1988) ch. 1.

17. Robert D. Johnston, 'Historians and the Middle Class', in Bledstein and Johnston, *Middling Sorts*, p. 297.

18. Stuart M. Blumin, 'The Hypothesis of Middle Class Formation in Nineteenth Century America', *American Historical Review*, vol. 90, no. 2 (April 1985); *The Emergence of the Middle Class: Social Experience in the American City, 1760–1900* (Cambridge: Cambridge University Press, 1989).

19. Russel Ward, *The Australian Legend* (Melbourne: Oxford University Press, 1977 [1958]) p. 39.

20. John Hirst, 'Egalitarianism', in S. L. Goldberg and F. B. Smith (eds), *Australian Cultural History* (Cambridge: Cambridge University Press, 1988).

21. Penny Russell, *A Wish of Distinction: Colonial Gentility and Femininity* (Melbourne: Melbourne University Press, 1994).

22. For example, Robert Ross, *Status and Respectability in the Cape Colony, 1750–1870* (Cambridge: Cambridge University Press, 1999).

23. For example, Paul E. Johnston, *A Shopkeeper's Millennium: Society and Revivals in Rochester, New York, 1815–1837* (New York: Hill & Wang, 1978); Kathleen D. McCarthy, *Noblesse Oblige: Charity and Cultural Philanthropy in Chicago 1848–1929* (Chicago: University of Chicago Press, 1982); R. J. Morris, *Class, Sect and Party: The Making of the British Middle Class, Leeds, 1820–1850* (Manchester: Manchester University Press, 1990) ch. 13; Theodore Koditschek, *Class Formation and Urban-Industrial Society: Bradford, 1750–1850* (Cambridge: Cambridge University Press, 1990) ch. 6.

24. See David Cannadine, 'The Present and the Past in the Industrial Revolution', *Past and Present*, vol. 103 (1984).

25. Mary Ryan, *Cradle of the Middle Class: The Family in Oneida County, New York 1790–1865* (Cambridge: Cambridge University Press, 1981) ch. 4.

26. Leonore Davidoff and Catherine Hall, *Family Fortunes: Men and Women of the English Middle Class, 1780–1850* (London: Hutchinson, 1987) part 1, 'Religion and Ideology' and part 2, 'Economic Structure and Opportunity'.

27. For example, Clyde Griffen and Sally Griffen, 'Small Business and Occupational Mobility in mid 19th century Poughkeepsie', in Stuart W. Bruchey, *Small Business in American Life* (New York: Columbia University Press, 1980);

John Field, 'Wealth, Styles of Life and Social Tone amongst Portsmouth's Middle Class, 1800–1875', in R. J. Morris (ed.), *Class, Power and Social Structure in British Nineteenth-Century Towns* (Leicester: Leicester University Press, 1986); Howard M. Wach, 'Culture and the Middle Classes: Popular Knowledge in Industrial Manchester', *Journal of British Studies*, vol. 27, no. 1 (January 1988); H. B. Rock (ed.), *The New York City Artisan, 1789–1825* (Albany: State University of New York Press, 1989); Timothy R. Mahoney, *Provincial Lives: Middle-Class Experience in the Ante-Bellum Middle West* (Cambridge: Cambridge University Press, 1999).

28. Melanie Archer and Judith R. Blau, 'Class Formation in Nineteenth Century America: The Case of the Middle Class', *Annual Review of Sociology*, vol. 19 (1993).

29. Joan Scott, 'Gender: A Useful Category of Analysis', *American Historical Review*, vol. 91, no. 5 (December 1986).

30. Joan Kelly, 'The Doubled Vision of Feminist Theory', in Judith L. Newton, Mary P. Ryan and Judith R. Walkowitz (eds), *Sex and Class in Women's History* (London: Routledge & Kegan Paul, 1983) pp. 259–60.

31. For example, Martha Vicinus (ed.), *Suffer and Be Still: Women in the Victorian Age* (Bloomington: Indiana University Press, 1972); Patricia Branca, *Silent Sisterhood: Middle Class Women in the Victorian Home* (London: Croom Helm, 1975); Nancy Cott, *The Bonds of Womanhood; 'Women's Sphere' in New England, 1780–1835* (New Haven, CT: Yale University Press, 1977). For the historiographical context of these works, see Catherine Hall, 'Feminism and Feminist History', in *White, Male and Middle Class* (Cambridge: Polity Press, 1992).

32. Mary Poovey, *Uneven Developments: The Ideological Work of Gender in Mid-Victorian England* (Chicago: University of Chicago Press, 1988) p. 10.

33. John E. Toews, 'Intellectual History after the Linguistic Turn: The Autonomy of Meaning and the Irreducibility of Experience', *American Historical Review*, vol. 92, no. 4 (October 1987) p. 882.

34. Patrick Joyce, 'A People and a Class: Industrial Workers and the Social Order in Nineteenth-Century England', in M. L. Bush (ed.), *Social Orders and Social Classes in Europe since 1500: Studies in Social Stratification* (London: Longman, 1992) p. 200.

35. John Seed, 'From "Middling Sort" to Middle Class in Late Eighteenth- and Early Nineteenth-Century England', in Bush, *Social Orders and Social Classes*, p. 125.

36. Geoffrey Crossick, 'From Gentlemen to the Residuum: Languages of Social Description in Victorian Britain', in Penelope J. Corfield (ed.), *Language, History and Class* (Oxford: Blackwell, 1991) p. 161.

37. Dror Wahrman, *Imagining the Middle Class: The Political Representation of Class in Britain, c.1780–1840* (Cambridge: Cambridge University Press, 1995) pp. 10–11; Joyce, 'A People and a Class', pp. 205–6; Johnston, 'Historians', in Bledstein and Johnston, *Middling Sorts*, pp. 303–4.

38. J. V. Beckett, *The Aristocracy in England 1660–1914* (Oxford: Blackwell, 1986) p. 30.

39. F. M. L. Thompson, *English Landed Society in the Nineteenth Century* (London: Routledge & Kegan Paul, 1963) p. 14.

40. W. L. Guttsman, *The British Political Elite* (London: Macgibbon & Kee,

1963) pp. 41–2; Peter J. Jupp, 'The Landed Elite and Political Authority in Britain, *c*.1760–1850', *Journal of British Studies*, vol. 29, no. 1 (January 1990).

41. R. H. Tawney, 'The Rise of the Gentry', *Economic History Review*, vol. 11 (1941) p. 6.

42. Beckett, *Aristocracy in England*, pp. 40–1; Leonore Davidoff, *The Best Circles: Society Etiquette and the Season* (London: Croom Helm, 1973) p. 16.

43. Thompson, *English Landed Society*, pp. 27, 31, 112.

44. Thompson, *English Landed Society*, p. 113.

45. G. E. Mingay, *The Gentry: The Rise and Fall of a Ruling Class* (London: Longman, 1976) p. 14.

46. E. Digby Baltzell, *Philadelphia Gentlemen: The Making of a National Upper Class* (Glencoe, IL: Free Press, 1958) pp. 12–18; Stow Persons, *The Decline of American Gentility* (New York: Columbia University Press, 1973) pp. 134–6.

47. Pessen, 'Egalitarian Myth', pp. 20–1.

48. Lillian B. Miller, *Patrons and Patriotism: The Encouragement of the Fine Arts in the United States, 1790–1860* (Chicago: University of Chicago Press, 1966) pp. 4–6.

49. The first *Social Register* was published in New York in 1887: Baltzell, *Philadelphia Gentlemen*, p. 19.

50. R. S. Neale, 'The Colonies and Social Mobility: Governors and Executive Councillors in Australia, 1788–1856', in *Class and Ideology in the Nineteenth Century* (London, Routledge & Kegan Paul, 1972) pp. 118–20.

51. J. F. C. Harrison, *The Early Victorians 1832–1851* (London: Weidenfeld & Nicolson, 1971) p. 104.

52. *A New System of Practical Domestic Economy*, new edn (London: H. Colburn, 1824) pp. 390–463.

53. Thomas Webster, *Encyclopedia of Domestic Economy*, new edn (London: 1847 [1844]) pp. 330–1.

54. Harold Perkin, *The Rise of Professional Society: England since 1880* (London: Routledge, 1989) pp. 28–30.

55. Pessen, 'Egalitarian Myth', pp. 11–16.

56. Pamela Horn, *The Rise and Fall of the Victorian Servant* (London: Gill & Macmillan, 1975) pp. 17–18.

57. J. A. Banks, *Prosperity and Parenthood: A Study of Family Planning among the Victorian Middle Classes* (London: Routledge, 1954) p. 75.

58. A Gentleman, *The Laws of Etiquette: or, Short Rules and Reflections for Conduct in Society* (Philadelphia: Cary, Lea & Blanchard, 1836) p. 89.

59. Daniel E. Sutherland, *Americans and Their Servants: Domestic Service in the United States from 1800–1920* (Baton Rouge: Louisiana State University Press, 1981) pp. 3–5; Barbara G. Carson, Ellen Kirven Donald and Kym S. Rice, 'Household Encounters: Servants, Slaves and Mistresses in Early Washington', in Eleanor McD. Thompson (ed.), *The American Home: Material Culture, Domestic Space, and Family Life* (Winterthur, DE: Winterthur Museum, 1998) pp. 86–8; Joyce Appleby, 'The Social Consequences of American Revolutionary Ideals in the Early Republic', in Bledstein and Johnston, *Middling Sorts*, p. 39.

60. C. Dallett Hemphill, *Bowing to Necessities: A History of Manners in the United States, 1620–1860* (New York: Oxford University Press, 1999) p. 130.

61. Beverley Kingston, *My Wife, My Daughter and Poor Mary Ann: Women and Work in Australia* (Melbourne: Nelson, 1975) pp. 30–1.

62. R. S. Neale, *Class and Ideology* (London: Routledge & Kegan Paul, 1972) pp. 30–1. Perkin recognizes two middle classes, composed of capitalists and professionals; these are better regarded as status groups rather than classes: Perkin, *Origins of Modern English Society*, p. 252.

63. Arno J. Mayer, 'The Lower Middle Class as a Historical Problem', *Journal of Modern History*, vol. 47, no. 3 (September 1975) pp. 411, 433.

64. Geoffrey Crossick and Hans-Gerhard Haupt, *The Petite Bourgeoisie in Europe, 1780–1914: Enterprise, Family and Independence* (London: Routledge, 1995) pp. 195–6.

65. E. J. Hobsbawm, 'The Labour Aristocracy in Nineteenth Century Britain', in E. J. Hobsbawm, *Labouring Men: Studies in the History of Labour* (London: Weidenfeld & Nicolson, 1968) p. 273; Robert Q. Gray, *The Labour Aristocracy in Victorian Edinburgh* (Oxford: Clarendon Press, 1976) p. 91.

66. Paul Faler, 'Working Class Culture and Politics in the Industrial Revolution: Sources of Loyalism and Revolution', *Journal of Social History*, vol. 9 (1976) pp. 466–80.

67. Sally Alexander, 'Women, Class and Sexual Difference', *History Workshop*, vol. 17 (1984).

68. E. P. Thompson, *The Making of the English Working Class* (Harmondsworth: Penguin, 1980 [1963]) p. 900.

69. Wally Seccombe, 'Patriarchy Stabilised: The Construction of the Male Breadwinner Wage Norm in Nineteenth Century Britain', *Social History*, vol. 11, no. 1 (January 1986) p. 54.

70. Sonya Rose, *Limited Livelihoods: Gender and Class in Nineteenth-Century England* (Berkeley: University of California Press, 1992) p. 187.

71. See Janet McCalman, 'Respectability and Working Class Politics in Late-Victorian London', *Historical Studies*, vol. 19, no. 74 (April 1980) p. 108.

72. Trygve Tholfsen, *Working Class Radicalism in Mid-Victorian England* (London: Croom Helm, 1976) pp. 218–19.

73. Patrick Joyce, *Visions of the People: Industrial England and the Question of Class, 1848–1914* (Cambridge: Cambridge University Press, 1991) p. 79.

74. Peter Bailey, *Popular Culture and Performance in the Victorian City* (Cambridge: Cambridge University Press, 1998) p. 36.

75. Gray, *The Labour Aristocracy*, p. 136; Susan E. Hirsch, *Roots of the American Working Class: The Industrialization of Crafts in Newark, 1800–1860* (Philadelphia: Temple University Press, 1978) p. 54.

76. Ivy Pinchbeck, *Women Workers and the Industrial Revolution, 1750–1850* (London: George Routledge & Sons, 1930) p. 97.

77. Pinchbeck, *Women Workers*, p. 311; Neil McKendrick, 'Home Demand and Economic Growth: A New View of the Role of Women and Children in the Industrial Revolution', in Neil McKendrick (ed.), *Historical Perspectives: Studies in English Thought and Society* (London: Europa, 1974) pp. 172, 208. See also Carole Shammas, *The Pre-Industrial Consumer in England and America* (Oxford: Clarendon Press, 1990) p. 298.

78. Sidney Kronos, *The Black Middle Class* (Columbus, OH: Charles E. Merrill, 1971) pp. 2–4.

79. *De Tocqueville's L'Ancien Regime*, trans. M. W. Patterson (Oxford: Basil Black-well, 1947 [1856]) p. 95.
80. Davidoff, *The Best Circles*, p. 15.
81. Young, *Victorian England*, p. 4; David Spring, 'Aristocracy, Social Structure and Religion in the Early Victorian Period', *Victorian Studies*, vol. 6, no. 3 (March 1963) p. 267.
82. Michael Curtin, *Propriety and Position: A Study of Victorian Manners* (New York: Garland, 1987) p. 101.
83. Cited in Norman Gash, *Aristocracy and the People: Britain 1815–1865* (London: Edward Arnold, 1979) p. 24.
84. Max Weber, 'Class, Status, Party', in H. H. Gerth and C. Wright Mills, *From Max Weber: Essays in Sociology* (New York: Oxford University Press, 1946) p. 188.
85. Davidoff and Hall, *Family Fortunes*, p. 36.
86. Magali Sarfatti Larson, *The Rise of Professionalism: A Sociological Analysis* (Berkeley: University of California Press, 1977) p. 5.
87. Burton J. Bledstein, *The Culture of Professionalism: The Middle Class and the Development of Higher Education in America* (New York: Norton, 1976) p. 33.
88. McKendrick, '"Gentlemen and Players" Revisited', pp. 119–22.
89. However, competition was based on education, now even more the domain of the genteel; see Wiener, *English Culture*, p. 22.
90. Penelope J. Corfield, *Power and the Professions in Britain 1700–1850* (London: Routledge, 1995) p. 245.
91. Marjorie Morgan, *Manners, Morals and Class in England, 1774–1858* (New York: St. Martin's Press – now Palgrave Macmillan, 1994) ch. 5.
92. Albert Smith, *The Natural History of the Gent* (London: David Bogue, 1847) p. 2.
93. Samuel Smiles, *Self-Help* (London: J. Murray, 1958 [1859]).
94. Smiles, *Self-Help*, p. 373.
95. For example, Blumin's and Pessen's studies in Edward Pessen (ed.), *Three Centuries of Social Mobility in America* (Lexington, MA: Heath, 1974) pp. 59–92, 110–21.
96. Kitson Clark, *Making of Victorian England*, p. 6.
97. Eric Hobsbawm, 'The Example of the English', in Jurgen Kocka and Allan Mitchell (eds), *Bourgeois Society in Nineteenth Century Europe* (Oxford: Berg, 1993) p. 134.
98. Joyce Appleby, Lynn Hunt and Margaret Jacob, *Telling the Truth about History* (New York: Norton, 1994) p. 225.

Chapter 3   The Civilizing Process: the Morphology of Gentility

1. For an analysis of meanings of 'gentleman' and 'lady' in Victorian litera-ture, see K. C. Phillipps, *Language and Class in Victorian England* (Oxford: Basil Blackwell, 1984) pp. 5–14.
2. Thorstein Veblen, *The Theory of the Leisure Class: An Economic Study of Institutions* (London: Allen & Unwin, 1924) p. 53.

3. R. H. Tawney, 'The Rise of the Gentry 1558–1640', *Economic History Review*, vol. 11 (1941) p. 2.
4. Quoted in David Castronovo, *The English Gentleman: Images and Ideals in Literature and Society* (New York: Ungar, 1987) p. 31.
5. Giovanni della Casa, *Galateo or the Book of Manners*, trans. R. S. Pine-Coffin (Harmondsworth: Penguin, 1958). The history of English translations is traced pp. 14–17.
6. Mark Girouard, *The Return to Camelot: Chivalry and the English Gentleman* (New Haven, CT: Yale University Press, 1981) ch. 2.
7. On the social and economic construction of 'gentlemanly capitalism' from the late seventeenth century to the late nineteenth, see P. C. Cain and A. G. Hopkins, 'Gentlemanly Capitalism and British Expansion Overseas', parts 1 and 2, *Economic History Review*, vol. 39, no. 4 (1986) and vol. 40, no. 1 (1987).
8. Ian Bradley, *The Call to Seriousness: The Evangelical Impact on the Victorians* (London: Jonathon Cape, 1967) pp. 153–4.
9. Henry Brougham, 1831, cited in the *Oxford English Dictionary*, defining 'middle class' vol. 6, p. 421; Walt Whitman, 1858, cited in Stuart M. Blumin, *Emergence of the Middle Class: Social Experience in the American City, 1760–1900* (Cambridge: Cambridge University Press, 1989) p. 1.
10. Karen Halttunen, *Confidence Men and Painted Ladies: A Study of Middle Class Culture in America, 1830–1870* (New Haven, CT: Yale University Press, 1982) pp. 102–6; Penny Russell, *A Wish of Distinction: Colonial Gentility and Femininity* (Melbourne: Melbourne University Press, 1994) ch. 1.
11. Janet Wolff, *Feminine Sentences: Essays on Women and Culture* (Cambridge: Polity Press, 1990) p. 12; Jane Rendall, *Women in an Industrializing Society: England 1750–1880* (Oxford: Basil Blackwell, 1990) p. 45.
12. Patricia Branca, *Silent Sisterhood: Middle Class Women in the Victorian Home* (London: Croom Helm, 1975) ch. 2; Theresa M. McBride, *The Domestic Revolution: The Modernization of Household Service in England and France, 1820–1920* (New York: Holmes & Meier, 1976) pp. 27–8.
13. Elizabeth Langland, *Nobody's Angels: Middle Class Women and Domestic Ideology in Victorian Culture* (Ithaca, NY: Cornell University Press, 1995) pp. 8–10.
14. The first group is represented by Mrs Ellis, *The Women of England, The Daughters of England*, and *The Wives of England* (London: Fisher, 1839–43); the second by Miss Leslie, *The House Book: or A Manual of Domestic Economy* (Philadelphia: Carey & Hart, 1841), one of a small handful before Mrs Beeton's *Book of Household Management* of 1859.
15. Nancy Armstrong, 'The Rise of the Domestic Woman', in Nancy Armstrong and Leonard Tennenhouse (eds), *The Ideology of Conduct: Essays on Literature and the History of Sexuality* (New York: Methuen, 1987) p. 114.
16. Barbara Welter, 'The Cult of True Womanhood, 1820–1860', *American Quarterly*, vol. 18, no. 2 (1966) p. 152.
17. Peter Gay, *The Tender Passion*, vol. 1, *The Bourgeois Experience* (New York: Oxford University Press, 1986) p. 299; Janet Wolff, 'The Culture of Separate Spheres', in Janet Wolff and John Seed (eds), *The Culture of Capital: Art, Power and the Nineteenth Century Middle Class* (Manchester: Manchester University Press, 1988) pp. 135–7.

18. Caroline Chisholm, *Emigration and Transportation Relatively Considered* (London: John Olliver, 1847) p. 21.
19. Leonore Davidoff and Catherine Hall, *Family Fortunes: Men and Women of the English Middle Class, 1750–1850* (London: Hutchison, 1987) pp. 114–15.
20. F. K. Prochaska, *Women and Philanthropy in Nineteenth Century England* (Oxford: Clarendon, 1980) pp. 223–6.
21. The arguments are surveyed by Mary Poovey, *Uneven Developments: The Ideological Work of Gender in Mid-Victorian England* (Chicago: University of Chicago Press, 1988) pp. 21–2.
22. Michelle Perrot, 'The Family Triumphant', in Philippe Ariès and Georges Duby (eds), *A History of Private Life*, vol. 4, *From the Fires of the Revolution to the Great War* (ed. Michelle Perrot) (Cambridge, MA: Belknap Press, 1990) pp. 100–2.
23. 'The Angel in the House' is an epic tale of domestic love, inspired not by heroes, but by: '. . . your gentle self, my Wife / . . . the most heart-touching theme / That ever turned a poet's voice': Coventry Patmore, *The Angel in the House* (London: George Routledge & Sons, n.d.) p. 29.
24. Nancy F. Cott, *The Bonds of Womanhood: 'Women's Sphere' in New England, 1780–1835* (New Haven, CT: Yale University Press, 1977) pp. 64–70.
25. Catherine Hall, 'The Early Formation of Victorian Domestic Ideology', in Sandra Burman (ed.), *Fit Work for Women* (London: Croom Helm, 1979) pp. 28–31; Mary P. Ryan, *Cradle of the Middle Class: The Family in Oneida County, New York, 1790–1865* (Cambridge: Cambridge University Press, 1981) ch. 5.
26. Carroll Smith Rosenberg, 'The Hysterical Woman: Sex Roles and Role Conflict in Nineteenth-Century America', *Social Research*, vol. 39, no. 4 (1972); Barbara Leslie Epstein, *The Politics of Domesticity: Women, Evangelism and Temperance in Nineteenth-Century America* (Middletown, CT: Wesleyan University Press, 1981) p. 47.
27. Ann Douglas, *The Feminization of American Culture* (New York: Knopf, 1977) ch. 1.
28. Yvonne Knibiehler, 'Bodies and Hearts', in Geneviève Fraisse and Michelle Perrot (eds), *A History of Women in the West*, vol. 4: *Emerging Feminism from Revolution to World War* (Cambridge, MA: Belknap, 1993) p. 364.
29. Betty Friedan, *The Feminine Mystique* (New York: Norton, 1963).
30. Ryan, *Cradle of the Middle Class*, p. 15.
31. William Acton, *The Functions and Disorders of the Reproductive Organs in Youth, in Adult Age, and in Advanced Life*, 6th edn (London: J. and A. Churchill, 1903 [1857]) p. 74.
32. R. H. Wilkinson, 'The Gentleman Ideal and the Maintenance of a Political Elite', in P. W. Musgrave (ed.), *Sociology, History and Education: A Reader* (London: Methuen, 1970) p. 131.
33. Peter N. Stearns, *Battleground of Desire: The Struggle for Self-Control in Modern America* (New York: New York University Press, 1994) pp. 58–9.
34. Budgets for a range of incomes between £1000 and £5000 are presented in *A New System of Practical Domestic Economy*, new edn (London: H. Colburn, 1824).
35. J. A. Banks, *Prosperity and Parenthood: A Study of Family Planning among the Victorian Middle Class* (London: Routledge & Kegan Paul, 1954) ch. 12;

William M. Langer, 'The Origins of the Birth Control Movement in the Early Nineteenth Century', *Journal of Interdisciplinary History*, vol. 5, no. 4 (1975) p. 669.

36. Catherine Hall, 'The Sweet Delights of Home', in Michelle Perrot (ed.), *From the Fires of Revolution to the Great War* (Cambridge, MA: Belknap, 1990) pp. 60–1.

37. Davidoff and Hall, *Family Fortunes*, pp. 76–7.

38. Hall, 'Sweet Delights', pp. 51–2; Doreen M. Rosman, *Evangelicals and Culture* (London: Croom Helm, 1984) pp. 10–11.

39. Steven Mintz, *A Prison of Expectations: The Family in Victorian Culture* (New York: New York University Press, 1983) ch. 2; Rosman, *Evangelicals and Culture*, ch. 4.

40. Bradley, *The Call to Seriousness*, pp. 152–3.

41. Norman Vance, *The Sinews of the Spirit: The Ideal of Christian Manliness in Victorian Literature and Religious Thought* (Cambridge: Cambridge University Press, 1985) pp. 1, 27.

42. J. A. Mangan and James Walvin (eds), 'Introduction', *Manliness and Morality: Middle Class Masculinity in Britain and America 1800–1940* (Manchester: Manchester University Press, 1987) p. 4.

43. The classic history of the period by Asa Briggs is titled *The Age of Improvement*, though ironically, Briggs barely touches on private self-improvement.

44. Richard Bushman, *The Refinement of America: Persons, Houses, Cities* (New York: Knopf, 1992) pp. 64–5.

45. Kenneth Ames, *Death in the Dining Room and Other Tales of Victorian Culture* (Philadelphia: Temple University Press, 1992) pp. 206–10.

46. John Kasson, 'Rituals of Dining: Table Manners in Victorian America', in Kathryn Grover (ed.), *Dining in America, 1850–1900* (Amherst: University of Massachusetts Press, 1987) pp. 125–6.

47. John Kasson, *Rudeness and Civility: Manners in Nineteenth Century Urban America* (New York: Hill & Wang, 1990) p. 148.

48. For example, Captain Wickham in Jane Austen, *Pride and Prejudice* (1813).

49. E. P. Thompson, 'Time, Work Discipline and Industrial Capitalism', *Past and Present*, vol. 38 (1967) pp. 56–97; Paul A. Shackel, *Personal Discipline and Material Culture: An Archaeology of Annapolis, Maryland, 1695–1870* (Knoxville: University of Tennessee Press, 1993) pp. 130–5.

50. Baldassare Castiglione, *The Book of the Courtier*, trans. Sir Thomas Hoby, 1561 (London: J. M. Dent & Sons, 1974): Hoby translates *sprezzatura* as 'a certain lovely freenesse', p. 98.

51. Michael Curtin lists 87 nineteenth-century etiquette publications: *Propriety and Position: A Study of Victorian Manners* (New York: Garland, 1987); C. Dallett Hemphill counts more than a hundred conduct works (not necessarily focusing on etiquette alone) published in or imported to the US between 1820 and 1860: *Bowing to Necessities: A History of Manners in America, 1620–1860* (New York: Oxford University Press, 1999) p. 131.

52. Jane Austen, *Pride and Prejudice* (1813), v. 1, ch. 5; v. 2, ch. 6.

53. See the detailed tables of precedence in manuals such as Burke's *Peerage* and etiquette guides such as *Court Etiquette: A Guide to the Intercourse with Royal*

or *Titled Persons, to Drawing Rooms, Levées, Courts and Audiences, the Usages of Social Life* (London: Mitchell [1849]).

54. A Member of the Philadelphia Bar, *The American Chesterfield, or, Way to Wealth, Honour and Distinction; Being Selections from the Letters of Lord Chesterfield . . . with Alterations and Additions Suited to the Youth of the United States* (Philadelphia: J. Grigg, 1827); Samuel R. Wells, *The Laws of Etiquette*, 2nd edn (Philadelphia: 1836) p. 10.

55. Hemphill, *Bowing to Necessities*, p. 130.

56. Hemphill, *Bowing to Necessities*, pp. 135–6.

57. Pierre Bourdieu, *Distinction: A Social Critique of the Judgement of Taste* (London: Routledge & Kegan Paul, 1984 [1979]) p. 56.

58. Bushman, *Refinement of America*, p. 96.

59. Neil McKendrick, John Brewer and J. H. Plumb, *The Birth of a Consumer Society: The Commercialisation of Eighteenth-Century England* (London: Europa, 1982) p. 1.

60. Werner Sombart, *Luxury and Capitalism* (Ann Arbor: University of Michigan Press, 1967 [1913]) ch. 4.

61. Colin Campbell, *The Romantic Ethic and the Spirit of Modern Consumerism* (Oxford: Basil Blackwell, 1987), pp. 89, 136–7, 201–3.

62. On bourgeois consumption as the expression of taste, see Whitney Walton, *France at the Crystal Palace: Bourgeois Taste and Artisan Manufacture in the Nineteenth Century* (Berkeley: University of California Press, 1992) ch. 1.

63. Katherine Grier, *Culture and Comfort: People, Parlours and Upholstery, 1850–1930* (Rochester, NY: Strong Museum, 1988) pp. 5–7.

64. On the historical prejudice against female consumers see Amanda Vickery, 'Women and the World of Goods: A Lancashire Consumer and her Possessions', p. 247 in John Brewer and Roy Porter (eds), *Consumption and the World of Good* (London: Routledge, 1993).

65. Chandra Mukerji, *From Graven Images: Patterns of Modern Materialism* (New York: Columbia University Press, 1983) ch. 5.

66. Penny Corfield, 'The Democratic History of the English Gentleman', *History Today*, vol. 42 (1992).

Chapter 4   Under Control: the Genteel Body

1. Sigmund Freud, *Civilization and Its Discontents* (New York: W.W. Norton, 1962 [1930]) pp. 44, 70.

2. Norbert Elias, *The Civilizing Process*, vol. 2, *State Formation and Civilization* (Oxford: Basil Blackwell, 1994 [1939]) ch. 2.

3. *Advice to a Young Gentleman on Entering Society* (London: A.H. Bailey, 1839) p. 73.

4. Lawrence Wright, *Clean and Decent: The Fascinating History of the Bathroom and Water Closet* (London: Routledge & Kegan Paul, 1960) p. 24.

5. Siegfried Giedion, *Mechanization Takes Command: a Contribution to Anonymous History* (New York: Norton, 1969 [1948]) p. 628. Richard Bushman and Claudia Bushman, 'The Early History of Cleanliness in America', *Journal of American History*, vol. 74, no. 4 (1988) p. 1219.

6. *Chambers Information for the People*, vol. 29 (Edinburgh: 1835) p. 225.

7. Catharine Beecher, *A Treatise on Domestic Economy* (New York: Source Books, 1970 [1841]) p. 103.

8. Mrs Copley, *Female Excellence, or Hints to Daughters* (London: Religious Tract Society, n.d.) p. 49.

9. Copley, *Female Excellence*, p. 49; A Lady of Distinction, *The Mirror of the Graces, or, the English Lady's Costume* (New York: I. Riley, 1815) pp. 34–5; Emily Thornwell, *The Lady's Guide to Perfect Gentility* (New York: Derby & Jackson, 1858) pp. 21–2; A. F. Crell and W. M. Wallace, *The Family Oracle of Good Health, Economy, Medicine and Good Living*, vol. 1 (London: Knight & Lacey, 1824) p. 310.

10. George Hepplewhite, *The Cabinet-Maker and Upholsterer's Guide*, 3rd edn ([1794] facs. New York: Dover, 1969) pl. 83, 84; Thomas Sheraton, *The Cabinet-Maker and Upholsterer's Drawing Book*, part 3 (London: T. Bensley, 1793) pl. 42–3, pp. 393–4; pl. 53, pp. 109–10.

11. See examples in Edward Joy, *Pictorial Dictionary of British Nineteenth Century Design* (Woodbridge, Suffolk: Antique Collectors Club, 1984) pp. 70–5.

12. W. Smee and Sons, *Designs for Furniture*, 1850, in *Pictorial Dictionary*, pp. 73–4.

13. National Archives of Scotland (NAS), Court of Sequestration: CS96; State Library of New South Wales (SLNSW), Mitchell: auction catalogues: 018.2Pa1; Delaware Public Archives (DPA), Probate records, New Castle County.

14. John Gloag, *A Short Dictionary of Furniture* (London, George Allen & Unwin, 1969) pp. 235–6.

15. Florence M. Montgomery, *Textiles in America 1650–1870* (New York: W.W. Norton & Co., n.d.) pp. 361–3.

16. See recipes for toilet and laundry soaps in Thomas Webster, *Encyclopedia of Domestic Economy* (London: Longman, Bowman and Green & Longman, 1844) pp. 1035, 1079–80.

17. Neville Williams, *Powder and Paint: A History of the Englishwoman's Toilet* (London: Longman, Green & Co., 1957) p. 89.

18. Thomas Sheraton, *The Cabinet Dictionary* (London: W. Smith, 1803) p. 43.

19. Gloag, *Short Dictionary of Furniture*, p. 139.

20. NAS, Court of Sequestration: CS96; SLNSW, Mitchell: auction catalogues: 018.2Pa1; DPA, Probate records, New Castle County.

21. Maureen Ogle, 'Domestic Reform in American Household Plumbing', *Winterthur Portfolio*, vol. 28, no. 1 (Spring 1993) pp. 36–8.

22. Horatio Mahomed, *The Bath: A Concise History of Bathing* (London: Smith, Elder & Co., 1843) p. 27.

23. Miss Leslie, *The House Book, or A Manual of Domestic Economy* (Philadelphia: Carey & Hart, 1841) p. 318.

24. See, for example, Giedion, *Mechanization Takes Command*, part VII; Wright, *Clean and Decent*, pp. 158–76.

25. Giedion, *Mechanization Takes Command*, pp. 660–2.

26. Thornwell, *Lady's Guide*, p. 26.

27. Webster, *Encyclopedia*, p. 1220.

28. See historic house re-creations in Christina Hardyment, *Behind the Scenes:*

Domestic Arrangements in Historic Houses (London: National Trust, 1997) p. 203. Mahomed, *The Bath*, p. 47.

29. Young, 'The Struggle for Class', p. 206.
30. Ogle, 'Domestic Reform', p. 33. Loudon describes an ideal complete bathroom fit-out: John Claudius Loudon, *The Suburban Gardener and Villa Companion* (London: Longman, Orme, Brown, Green & Longmans, 1838), pp. 675–9.
31. May Stone, 'The Plumbing Paradox: American Attitudes towards Late Nineteenth Century Domestic Sanitary Arrangements', *Winterthur Portfolio*, vol. 14, no. 3 (Autumn 1979) p. 285; Mark Girouard, *Life in the English Country House* (Harmondsworth: Penguin, 1980) pp. 265–6.
32. NAS, Court of Sequestration: CS96/4288, 1839.
33. Beecher, *Treatise*, p. 293.
34. See Stone, 'Plumbing Paradox', pp. 297–303.
35. Jacqueline Wilkie, 'Submerged Sensuality: Technology and Perceptions of Bathing', *Journal of Social History*, no. 19 (1986) p. 649.
36. Caroline Davidson, *A Woman's Work is Never Done: A History of Housework in the British Isles 1650–1950* (London: Chatto & Windus, 1982) p. 12.
37. Ogle, 'Domestic Reform', p. 36.
38. *A New System of Practical Domestic Economy*, new edn (London: Colburn & Bentley, 1831) p. 79.
39. Thornwell, *Lady's Guide*, p. 43.
40. Crell and Wallace, *Family Oracle*, vol. 1, p. 296.
41. M. G. Jones, *The Story of Brushmaking: a Norfolk Craft* (Norwich: Briton Chadwick, 1974).
42. NAS, Court of Sequestration: CS96/725.
43. Paul Shackel, *Personal Discipline and Material Culture: An Archaeology of Annapolis, Maryland, 1695–1870* (Knoxville: University of Tennessee Press, 1993) pp. 48–9.
44. Williams, *Powder and Paint*, p. 90; Thornwell, *Lady's Guide*, p. 43.
45. *New System of Practical Domestic Economy*, p. 79.
46. NAS, Court of Sequestration: CS96/725.
47. Thornwell, *Lady's Guide*, p. 35.
48. 'Cleanliness is indeed next to godliness.' John Wesley, 1 Sermon xciii. *On Dress*.
49. Beverley Lemire, *Fashion's Favourite: The Cotton Trade and the Consumer in Britain, 1660–1800* (Oxford: Oxford University Press, 1991) pp. 95–6.
50. Christina Walkley and Vanda Foster, *Crinolines and Crimping Irons: Victorian Clothes: How They Were Cleaned and Cared For* (London: Peter Owen, 1978) p. 40.
51. Linda Young, 'Decency and Necessity: Material Life in South Australia, 1859', *Journal of Interdisciplinary History*, vol. XXV, no. 1 (1994).
52. Anne Hollander, *Seeing Through Clothes* (New York: Viking, 1975) pp. 132–3.
53. C. Willet Cunnington and Phillis Cunnington, *The History of Underclothes* (New York: Dover, 1992 [1951]) pp. 111, 130.
54. Captain Jesse, *The Life of George Brummell Esquire* (London: Saunders & Otley, 1844) p. 69.
55. William Cobbett, *Advice to Young Men*, 'Letter III: To a Lover' (London: Henry Froude, 1906 [1829]) p. 112.

56. Lucy Frost, *No Place for a Nervous Lady: Voices from the Australian Bush* (Melbourne: McPhee Gribble, 1984) p. 47.
57. Kathy Peiss, *Hope in a Jar: The Making of America's Beauty Culture* (New York: Metropolitan Books, 1998) pp. 26–31.
58. Gloag, *Short Dictionary of Furniture*, pp. 302–3, 573, 672–3; cf. three designers' formulations: Thomas Chippendale, *The Gentleman and Cabinet-Maker's Director*, 3rd edn ([1762], facs. New York: Dover, 1966) pl. 52; Hepplewhite, *Guide*, pl. 72–3; Sheraton, *Drawing Book, Appendix*, pl. 7, p. 156.
59. NAS, Court of Sequestration: CS96; SLNSW, Mitchell: auction catalogues: 018.2Pa1; DPA, Probate records, New Castle County.
60. Jane B. Donegan, *'Hydropathic Highway to Health': Women and Water-Cure in Antebellum America* (New York: Greenwood Press, 1986) ch. 9.
61. *Encyclopedia Britannica*, 8th edn, vol. XIV (Edinburgh: Adam & Charles Black, 1853) p. 440.
62. Giovanni della Casa, *Galateo, or the Book of Manners* (Harmondsworth: Penguin, 1958) p. 24.
63. Elias, *Civilising Process*, pp. 105–9.
64. Lucinda Lambton, *Temples of Convenience and Chambers of Delight* (New York: St. Martin's Press – now Palgrave Macmillan, 1995) p. 12.
65. Gloag, *Short Dictionary of Furniture*, pp. 233–5.
66. Sheraton, *Drawing Book*, p. 394.
67. John Claudius Loudon, *Encyclopedia of Cottage, Farm and Villa Architecture* (London: 1833) entry 2135, p. 1083.
68. NAS, Court of Sequestration: CS96; SLNSW, Mitchell: auction catalogues: 018.2Pa1; DPA, Probate records, New Castle County.
69. Ibid.
70. Lambton, *Temples of Convenience*, pp. 16–19. For American examples, see Ogle, 'Domestic Reform', pp. 54–8.
71. Loudon, *Encyclopedia*, p. 18; Stone, 'Plumbing Paradox', p. 285.
72. [Eleazar Moody], *The School of Good Manners* (Newburyport: Thomas Whipple, 1818) p. 10; R.W.G. Vail, 'Moody's *School of Good Manners*: A Study in American Colonial Etiquette', in *Studies in Cultural History* (Menasha, WN: ACLS, 1942) p. 266.
73. Anne Buck, *Victorian Costume and Costume Accessories*, 2nd edn (Bedford: Ruth Bean, 1984) p. 172.
74. Buck, *Victorian Costume*, p. 175.
75. Lord Chesterfield, *Letters to his Son, 1737–1768*, letter LXXIV.
76. *Chambers Information*, vol. 38, p. 303.
77. David Yosifon and Peter N. Stearns, 'The Rise and Fall of American Posture', *American Historical Review*, vol. 103, no. 4 (1998) p. 1057.
78. Moody, *School of Good Manners*, p. 10.
79. Mrs Almira Lincoln Phelps, *Hours With My Pupils: The Young Lady's Guide* (New York: Charles Scribner & Co., 1859) p. 110.
80. Bushman, Richard, *The Refinement of America: Persons, Houses, Cities* (New York: Knopf, 1992) p. 295.
81. Elizabeth Ewing, *Dress and Undress: A History of Underclothes* (London: Bibliophile, 1978) p. 57.

82. C. Willet Cunnington and Phillis Cunnington, *The History of Underclothes* (New York: Dover, 1992 [1951]) p. 106.

83. Albert E. Scheflen, *Body Language and Social Order: Communication as Behavioural Control* (Englewood Cliffs, NJ: Prentice-Hall, 1972) p. 9.

84. Kenneth L. Ames, *Death in the Dining Room, and Other Tales of Victorian Culture* (Philadelphia: Temple University Press, 1992) pp. 201–6.

85. Katherine C. Grier, *Culture and Comfort: People, Parlours and Upholstery, 1850–1930* (Rochester, NY: Strong Museum, 1988) pp. 108–9.

86. Gloag, *Short Dictionary*, pp. 561–2.

87. Leslie, *Housebook*, p. 194.

88. Ames, *Death in the Dining Room*, pp. 216–17, 227.

89. Gloag, *Short Dictionary*, p. 597.

90. Giedion, *Mechanization*, p. 410; Grier, *Culture and Comfort*, pp. 118–19.

91. Cf. John E. Crowley, 'The Sensibility of Comfort', *American Historical Review*, vol. 104, no. 3 (1999).

92. A Lady, *The Young Lady's Friend* (Boston: American Stationers' Company, 1837) p. 363.

93. Jane Austen, *Pride and Prejudice* (1813) vol. 2, ch. 11.

94. Thomas Henry Lister, *Granby*, rev. edn, 1 volume (n.d. [1825]) p. 143.

95. Mrs Ellis, *The Mothers of England: Their Influence and Responsibility* (London: Fisher, Son & Co., 1843) p. 164.

96. Carroll Smith-Rosenberg, 'The Female World of Love and Ritual: Relations between Women in Nineteenth-Century America', in *Disorderly Conduct: Visions of Gender in Victorian America* (New York: Knopf, 1985) pp. 60–2.

97. Daniel C. Eddy, *The Young Man's Friend* (Boston: Dayton & Wentworth, 1855) p. 117.

98. Peter N. Stearns, *Battleground of Desire: The Struggle for Self-Control in Modern America* (New York: New York University Press, 1999) pp. 58–9.

99. For example, T. H. Lister, *Granby*, 1825.

100. Richard Waterhouse, *Private Pleasures, Public Leisures: A History of Australian Popular Culture since 1788* (Melbourne: Longman, 1995) pp. 23, 38–9.

101. F. M. L. Thompson, *The Rise of Respectable Society: a Social History of Victorian Britain 1830–1900* (London: Fontana, 1988) p. 334.

102. Barbara Leslie Epstein, *The Politics of Domesticity: Women, Evangelism and Temperance in Nineteenth-Century America* (Middletown, CT: Wesleyan University Press, 1981) pp. 1, 89.

103. Cited in John D'Emilio and Estelle B. Freedman, *Intimate Matters: A History of Sexuality in America* (New York: Harper & Row, 1988) p. 70.

104. D'Emilio and Freedman, *Intimate Matters*, p. 71.

105. D'Emilio and Freedman, *Intimate Matters*, p. 56; Stearns, *Battleground of Desire*, p. 72.

106. Jeffrey Weekes, *Sex, Politics and Society: The Regulation of Sexuality since 1800*, 2nd edn (London: Longman, 1989) p. 49.

107. D'Emilio and Freedman, *Intimate Matters*, pp. 58–9.

108. William L. Langer, 'The Origins of the Birth Control Movement in England in the Early Nineteenth Century', *Journal of Interdisciplinary History*, vol. 5, no. 4 (1975) p. 684.

Chapter 5 Best Behaviour: Public Relationships

1. [T. C. Morgan], 'Etiquette', *New Monthly Magazine and Humorist*, part 3 (1838) p. 21.
2. *Dictionary of National Biography*, vol. 54 (London: Smith, Elder & Co., 1898) pp. 24–37. Chesterfield became a byword for good manners, as in *The American Chesterfield, or, Ways to Wealth, Honour and Distinction*, by A Member of the Philadelphia Bar (Philadelphia: John Grigg, 1828).
3. Lord Chesterfield, *Letters to his Son, 1737–1768*, letter LXXX, 4.11.1741.
4. Chesterfield, *Letters*, Letter LXXIV, 25.7.1741.
5. 'Millbank was the son of one of the wealthiest manufacturers of Lancashire. His father, whose opinions were of a very democratic bent, sent his son to Eton, though he disapproved of the system of education there, to show that he had as much right to do so as any duke in the land. He had, however, brought up his only boy with a due prejudice against every sentiment or institution of an aristocratic character . . .' Benjamin Disraeli, *Coningsby, or, The New Generation* (London: Dent, 1967 [1844]) p. 35.
6. A Gentleman, *The Laws of Etiquette, or, Short Rules and Reflections for Conduct in Society* (Philadelphia: Carey, Lee & Blanchard, 1839) p. 13.
7. Mary Douglas, *Purity and Danger: An Analysis of the Concepts of Pollution and Taboo* (New York: Praeger, 1966) pp. 121–2.
8. See Norbert Elias, *The Court Society* (Oxford: Basil Blackwell, 1983 [1969]) ch. 5.
9. Joan Wildblood, *The Polite World* (London: Oxford University Press, 1965) p. 177.
10. Michael Curtin, *Propriety and Position: A Study of Victorian Manners* (New York: Garland, 1987) pp. 2–3.
11. Elias, *Court Society*, pp. 114–16.
12. Curtin, *Propriety and Position*, p. 35.
13. Marjorie Morgan, *Manners, Morals and Class in England, 1774–1858* (New York: St. Martin's Press – now Palgrave Macmillan, 1994) pp. 23, 119–20. Morgan concludes that this recombination demonstrates the merging of aristocratic and middle-class ideals; the evidence of the development of professional culture is an interesting case but is better explained by the model of cultural appropriation.
14. C. Dallett Hemphill, *Bowing to Necessities: A History of Manners in the United States, 1620–1860* (New York: Oxford University Press, 1999) p. 131.
15. Elias, *Court Society*, p. 95.
16. Disraeli, *Coningsby*, p. 68.
17. A Member of the Royal Household, *The Book of Fashionable Life: Comprising the Etiquette of the Drawing Room, Dining Room and Ball Room* (London: Hugh Cunningham, [c.1844]) p. 42.
18. A Lady, *The Young Lady's Friend* (Boston: American Stationers' Company, 1837) p. 97.
19. For example, 'Table of Precedency', in Member of the Royal Household, *Fashionable Life*, pp. 131–6.
20. William Charles Day, *The American Ladies' and Gentlemen's Manual of Elegance, Fashion and True Politeness* (Auburn and Rochester, NY: Alden & Beardsley, 1856) pp. 5–6.

21. Asteios, *The Philosophy of Manner, or, a Sequel to the Laws of Etiquette* (Glasgow: John Symington, 1838) p. 9.
22. Chesterfield, *Letters*, Letter CXI, 29.9.1746.
23. Reverend Dr John Trusler, *A System of Etiquette, with Maxims of Prudence, and Some Observations of Duelling* (London: 1828) p. 15.
24. Lawrence Stone and Jeanne Fawtier Stone, *An Open Elite? England 1540–1800* (Oxford: Oxford University Press, 1984) p. 423.
25. [Samuel R. Wells] *How to Behave: A Pocket Manual of Republican Etiquette* (New York: Fowler & Wells, 1856) p. 48.
26. A Citizen of Washington, *Etiquette at Washington, together with the Customs Adopted by Polite Society in Other Cities of the United States*, 2nd edn (Baltimore, MD: John Murphy & Co., 1850) p. 114.
27. Elias, *Court Society*, pp. 91–2.
28. Pierre Bourdieu, *Language and Symbolic Power* (Cambridge: Polity Press, 1991) pp. 230, 238.
29. Mrs Ellis, *The Daughters of England: Their Position in Society, Character and Responsibilities* (London: Fisher, Sons & Co., 1845) p. 255.
30. Jane Austen, *Emma* (1816).
31. Baldassare Castiglione, *The Book of the Courtier* (trans. Sir Thomas Hoby, 1561) (London: J. M. Dent & Sons, 1974); Giovanni della Casa, *Galateo, or The Book of Manners* (trans. R. S. Pine-Coffin) (Harmondsworth: Penguin, 1958) pp. 15–17; Curtin, *Propriety and Position*, ch. 2.
32. *Instructions in Etiquette for the Use of All*, 3rd edn (London: Simpkin, Marshall & Co., 1847) p. iv.
33. *Advice to a Young Gentleman on Entering Society* (London: A. H. Bailey, 1839) p. 77.
34. R. W. G. Vail, 'Moody's *School of Good Manners*: A Study in American Colonial Etiquette, *Studies in the History of Culture* (Menasha, WN: ACLS, 1942) p. 266.
35. *A Manual of Manners, or, a Child's Book of Etiquette* (Glasgow: John Reid, 1838).
36. Mrs H. C. Caddick, *The Bride's Book; A Code of Morals and Conduct from the Works of Eminent Writers for the Use of Young Married Women* (London: H. Fisher, R. Fisher & P. Jackson, 1835); Horace Mayhew, *Model Men* (London: D. Bogue, 1848).
37. Curtin, *Propriety and Position*, p. 40.
38. Agogos, *Hints on Etiquette and the Usages of Society with a Glance at Bad Habits*, 26th edn Revised (with Additions) by A Lady of Rank (London: Orme, Brown, Green & Longmans, 1849).
39. Day, *American Ladies' and Gentlemen's Manual*.
40. Agogos, *Hints on Etiquette and the Usages of Society, With a Glance at Bad Habits*, 9th edn (London: reprinted by William Elliston Gore, Hobarton, 1838).
41. Agogos, *Hints on Etiquette*, pp. 25, 35.
42. Matthew Rosa, *The Silver-Fork School: Novels of Fashion preceding Vanity Fair* (New York: Columbia University Press, 1936); Alison Adburgham, *Silver Fork Society: Fashionable Life and Literature from 1814–1840* (London: Constable, 1983).
43. Edward Bulwer, *England and the English* (Shannon: Irish University Press, 1971 [facs. 2nd edn, London: Richard Bentley, 1833]) p. 108.

44. Catherine Gore, *Pin Money: A Novel* (London: Henry Colburn, 1831), Preface.
45. William Hazlitt, *The Examiner*, 18.11.1827, cited by Margaret Drabble (ed.), *The Oxford Companion to English Literature* (Oxford: Oxford University Press, 1995) p. 345.
46. [Abraham Hayward], 'Codes of Manners and Etiquette', *Quarterly Review*, vol. 59, no. 18 (October 1837).
47. 'Codes of Manners', p. 397.
48. 'Codes of Manners', p. 398.
49. 'Codes of Manners', p. 426.
50. *The Spirit of Etiquette, or, Politeness Exemplified* (London: Moore, 1837) p. ii.
51. *Hints*, p. 46.
52. *Encyclopedia Britannica*, 9th edn (1878) vol. 5, p. 607.
53. A Lady of Distinction, *The Mirror of the Graces, or, the English Lady's Guide to Costume* (New York: I. Riley, 1815) p. 169.
54. Jane Austen, *Pride and Prejudice* (1813), ch. 29.
55. Charles Dickens, *David Copperfield* (1850) ch. 16.
56. Jane Austen, *Pride and Prejudice* (1813), ch. 29.
57. *Etiquette for Ladies; with Hints on the Preservation, Improvement and Display of Female Beauty* (Philadelphia: Carey, Lea & Blanchard, 1838) p. 35.
58. *Hints*, p. 49.
59. Mrs Maberly, *The Art of Conversation, with Remarks on Fashion and Address* (New York: Wilson & Co., 1845) pp. 5, 31.
60. Henry Savery, *The Hermit in Van Diemen's Land* (St Lucia, Queensland: University of Queensland Press, 1964 [1829]) p. 140.
61. A Citizen of Washington, *Etiquette at Washington, Together with Customs Adopted by Polite Society in the Other Cities of the United States* (Baltimore, MD: J. Murphy, 1850) pp. 32–3; Jane Austen, *Persuasion* (1818) ch. 26.
62. Wilfred Hudspeth, *Early Van Diemen's Land: Hudspeth Memorial Volume* (Hobart: L. G. Shea, 1954) p. 111.
63. A Lady, *The Young Lady's Friend* (Boston: American Stationers' Company, 1837) p. 389.
64. Leonore Davidoff, *The Best Circles* (London: Croom Helm, 1973) pp. 16, 40.
65. Chesterfield, *Letters*, Letter CCIV, 22.9.1752.
66. Catharine Beecher, *A Treatise on Domestic Economy* (New York: Source Books, 1970 [1841]) p. 124.
67. Asteios, *Philosophy of Manners*, p. 15.
68. Elias, *Court Society*, pp. 87–93.
69. *The Female Instructor; or Young Woman's Companion and Guide to Domestic Happiness* . . . (London: Thos Kelly, 1824) p. 35.
70. *Hints*, p. 22.
71. *Hints*, p. 23.
72. Hemphill, *Bowing to Necessities*, p. 194.
73. *Hints*, p. 5.
74. *Pride and Prejudice*, ch. 25.
75. For example, Jane Austen, *Northanger Abbey* (1818), ch. 8.
76. Reverend Dr John Trusler, *The Honours of the Table, or Rules for Behaviour during Meals* (London: The Author, 1791) p. 5.
77. *Debrett's Peerage and Baronetage* was first published in 1769; new editions continue to be produced today.

78. William Denison, *Varieties of Vice-Regal Life* (London: Longmans Green & Co., 1870) pp. 36–7.

79. John Kasson, *Rudeness and Civility: Manners in Nineteenth Century Urban America* (New York: Hill & Wang, 1990) p. 182; *Hints*, p. 29.

80. Norbert Elias, *The Civilizing Process* (Oxford: Blackwell, 1994 [1939]) part 2, ch. 4.

81. Moody, *School of Good Manners*, p. 7.

82. H. M. Boot, 'Real Incomes of the British Middle Class, 1760–1850: The Experience of Clerks at the East India Company', *Economic History Review*, vol. LII, no. 4 (1999) p. 662.

83. John Dixon, *The Condition and Capability of Van Diemen's Land* (London: Smith, Elder & Co., 1839) p. 51.

84. Penny Russell, *A Wish of Distinction: Colonial Gentility and Femininity* (Melbourne: Melbourne University Press, 1994) p. 14.

85. Karen Halttunen, *Confidence Men and Painted Women: A Study of Middle Class Culture in America, 1830–1870* (New Haven, CT: Yale University Press, 1982) p. 92.

86. Chesterfield, *Letters*, Letter CLXXXIII, 22.5.1749.

87. Timothy R. Mahoney, *Provincial Lives: Middle-Class Experience in the Ante-Bellum Middle West* (Cambridge: Cambridge University Press, 1999) pp. 3–5.

88. Annette Kolodny, *The Land before Her: Fantasy and Experience on the American Frontiers 1630–1860* (Chapel Hill: University of North Carolina Press, 1984) p. xiii.

89. Halttunen, *Confidence Men and Painted Women*, p. xv.

90. Mrs A. Prinsep, *Journal of a Voyage from Calcutta to Van Diemen's Land* (London: Smith Elder, 1833) p. 51.

91. Elizabeth Fenton, *Mrs Fenton's Tasmanian Journal 1829–1830* (Adelaide: Sullivans Cove, 1986) p. 36.

92. Hemphill, *Bowing to Necessities*, p. 131.

93. A Gentleman, *The Laws of Etiquette*, p. 10.

94. *The Laws of Etiquette, or Short Rules and Reflections for Conduct in Society*, 2nd edn (Philadelphia: Carey, Lea & Blanchard, 1836) p. 10.

95. Stow Persons, *The Decline of American Gentility* (New York: Columbia University Press, 1973) pp. 2–3.

96. De Tocqueville, *Democracy in America* (New York: Harper & Row, 1966 [1835]), p. 219.

97. Arthur M. Schlesinger, *Learning How to Behave: A Historical Study of American Etiquette Books* (New York: Macmillan, 1946) p. 17.

98. Richard Bushman, *The Refinement of America: Persons, Houses, Cities* (New York: Knopf, 1992) pp. 412–13, 425–31.

99. Hemphill, *Bowing to Necessities*, p. 130.

Chapter 6   Correct Taste: the Material Conditions of Gentility

1. Leonore Davidoff and Catherine Hall, *Family Fortunes: Men and Women of the English Middle Class, 1750–1850* (London: Hutchison, 1987) p. 398.

2. Elizabeth Gaskell, *Cranford* (London: OUP, 1934 [1853]) p. 4.

3. Catherine Gore, *Pin Money: A Novel* (London: Henry Colburn, 1831) p. 7.

4. A. J. Downing, *The Architecture of Country Houses* (New York: Dover Publications, 1969 [1850]) p. 407.

5. Charles White, *Almack's Revisited* (London: Henry Colburn, 1828) p. 151.

6. Thorstein Veblen, *The Theory of the Leisure Class* (New York: Modern Library, 1934 [1899]) ch. 4.

7. Frederick B. Tolles, *Quakers and the Atlantic Culture* (New York: Macmillan, 1960) p. 88.

8. Asteios, *The Young Wife's Book: A Manual of Domestic Duties* (Glasgow: John Symington, 1838) pp. 43–4.

9. Grant McCracken, *Culture and Consumption: New Approaches to the Symbolic Character of Consumer Goods and Activities* (Bloomington: Indiana University Press, 1988) pp. 32–7.

10. Clive Wainwright, *The Romantic Interior: The British Collector at Home 1750–1850* (New Haven, CT: Yale University Press, 1989) chs 2, 3.

11. The older tradition of consumption history is exemplified by E. J. Hobsbawm, *The Age of Revolution, Europe 1789–1848* (London: Weidenfeld & Nicolson, 1962) ch. 2. Production-driven history is reviewed by Cary Carson, 'The Consumer Revolution in Colonial British America: Why Demand?', in Cary Carson, Ronald Hoffman and Peter J. Albert (eds), *Of Consuming Interest: The Style of Life in the Eighteenth Century* (Charlottesville: University Press of Virginia, 1994) pp. 483–6.

12. Karl Marx, 'Excerpts from James Mill's Elements of Political Economy', cited by Pierre Bourdieu, *Distinction: A Social Critique of the Judgement of Taste* (London: Routledge & Kegan Paul, 1984 [1979]) p. 267.

13. E. E. Evans-Pritchard, *The Nuer: A Description of the Modes of Livelihood and Political Institutions of a Native People* (New York: Oxford University Press, 1956) p. 233; Norbert Elias, *The Civilizing Process* (Oxford: Basil Blackwell, 1994 [1939]) pp. 104–5.

14. Daniel Miller, *Material Culture and Mass Consumption* (Oxford: Basil Blackwell, 1987) pp. 205, 216.

15. Consumerism as a framework for historical analysis is traced by Ann Smart Martin, 'Makers, Buyers, and Users: Consumerism as a Material Culture Framework', *Winterthur Portfolio*, vol. 28, no. 2–3 (1993).

16. Carole Shammas, *The Pre-Industrial Consumer in England and America* (Oxford: Clarendon Press, 1990) p. 185. Consumer revolutions have been identified by historians since at least the sixteenth century, by Joan Thirsk, *Economic Policy and Projects: The Development of a Consumer Society in Early Modern England* (Oxford: Clarendon Press, 1978); the seventeenth century by Chandra Mukerji, *From Graven Images: Patterns of Modern Materialism* (New York: Columbia University Press, 1983) and Margaret Spufford, *The Great Reclothing of Rural England: Petty Chapmen and their Wares in the Seventeenth Century* (London: Hambledon Press, 1984); the nineteenth century by Rosalind Williams, *Dream Worlds: Mass Consumption in Late Nineteenth Century France* (Berkeley: University of California Press, 1982) and T. J. Jackson Lears, 'From Salvation to Self-Realization: Advertising and the Therapeutic Roots of the Consumer Culture, 1880–1930', in Richard Wightman Fox and T. J. Jackson Lears (eds), *The Culture of Consumption:*

Critical Essays in American History, 1880–1980 (New York: Pantheon, 1983); and the twentieth century by Susan Strasser, *Satisfaction Guaranteed: The Making of the American Mass Market* (New York: Pantheon, 1989) and Daniel Miller, *Material Culture and Mass Consumption* (Oxford: Basil Blackwell, 1987).

17. Arthur J. Taylor (ed.), *The Standard of Living in the Industrial Revolution* (London: Methuen, 1975) p. *l*. The same trend appears in the United States, best documented for a slightly earlier period: see Lorena S. Walsh, Gloria L. Main, Lois Green Carr, Jackson Turner Main and John J. McCusker, 'Forum' on the standard of living in the colonial era, *William and Mary Quarterly*, vol. XLV, no. 1 (January 1988).

18. Shammas, *Pre-Industrial Consumer*, pp. 102–4.

19. Neil McKendrick, 'Home Demand and Economic Growth: A New View of the Role of Women and Children in the Industrial Revolution', in Neil McKendrick (ed.), *Historical Perspectives: Studies in English Thought and Society* (London: Europa, 1974) pp. 172, 208. See also Ivy Pinchbeck, *Women Workers and the Industrial Revolution 1750–1850* (London: G. Routledge, 1930) pp. 215–21; Shammas, *Pre-Industrial Consumer*, p. 298.

20. H. M. Boot, 'Real Incomes of the British Middle Class, 1760–1850: The Experience of Clerks at the East India Company', *Economic History Review*, vol. LII, no. 4 (1999).

21. *A New System of Practical Domestic Economy*, new edn (London: H. Colburn, 1824) p. 436.

22. Veblen, *Leisure Class*, ch. 2.

23. Miller, *Material Culture*, p. 136.

24. Paul A. Shackel, *Personal Discipline and Material Culture: An Archaeology of Annapolis, Maryland, 1695–1870* (Knoxville: University of Tennessee Press, 1993) pp. 3, 7.

25. Mukerji, *From Graven Images*, p. 2.

26. Colin Campbell, *The Romantic Ethic and the Spirit of Modern Consumerism* (Oxford: Basil Blackwell, 1987) p. 201.

27. Mary Douglas and Baron Isherwood, *The World of Goods: Towards an Anthropology of Consumption* (Harmondsworth: Penguin, 1980) pp. 5–10.

28. Douglas and Isherwood, *World of Goods*, pp. 5, 59.

29. Douglas and Isherwood, *World of Goods*, p. 57; Arjun Appadurai's analysis of goods as commodities shares this view: 'Introduction: Commodities and the Politics of Value', in Arjun Appadurai (ed.), *The Social Life of Things: Commodities in Cultural Perspective* (Cambridge: Cambridge University Press, 1986) p. 3.

30. For example, Ann Bermingham and John Brewer (eds), *The Consumption of Culture 1600–1800: Image, Object, Text* (London: Routledge, 1995).

31. McCracken, *Culture and Consumption*, pp. 62–4; Fred Davis, *Fashion, Culture and Identity* (Chicago: University of Chicago Press, 1992) pp. 4–8.

32. A Gentleman, *The Laws of Etiquette, or, Short Rules and Reflections for Conduct in Society*, new edn (Philadelphia: Carey, Lea & Blanchard, 1839) p. 38.

33. [Samuel R. Wells], *How to Behave: A Pocket Manual of Republican Etiquette* (New York: Fowler & Wells, 1856) pp. 34, 38.

34. Lord Chesterfield, *Letters to his son, 1737–1768*, letter CIV, 29.11.1745.
35. An American Gentleman, *True Politeness: A Handbook of Etiquette for Gentlemen* (Philadelphia: George S. Appleton, 1848) p. 18.
36. *The Female Instructor; or Young Woman's Companion and Guide to Domestic Happiness* (London: Thos Kelly, 1824) p. 9.
37. Joan Kendall, 'The Development of a Distinctive Form of Quaker Dress', *Costume*, no. 19 (1985). However, plain dress was not universal among either Puritans or Quakers: C. Willet Cunnington and Phillis Cunnington, *Handbook of English Costume in the Seventeenth Century* (London: Faber, 1966) p. 11.
38. James Laver, *Modesty in Dress: An Inquiry into the Fundamentals of Fashion* (Boston: Houghton Mifflin, 1969) pp. 55–6.
39. Aileen Ribeiro, *The Art of Dress: Fashion in England and France 1750–1820* (New Haven, CT: Yale University Press, 1995) pp. 46–7.
40. Pierce Egan, *Life in London* (London: Sherwood, Neely & Jones, 1821) p. 109.
41. Claudia B. Kidwell and Margaret C. Christman, *Suiting Everyone: The Democratization of Clothing in America* (Washington: Smithsonian Institution Press, 1974) pp. 39–41; Jane Ashelford, *The Art of Dress: Clothes and Society 1500–1914* (London: National Trust/Laura Ashley, 1996) pp. 196–200.
42. Albert Smith, *The Natural History of the Gent* (London: David Bogue, 1847) pp. 7–8.
43. C. Willet Cunnington and Phillis Cunnington, *Handbook of English Costume in the Nineteenth Century* (London: Faber, 1959) pp. 45–50; Ribeiro, *Art of Dress*, p. 95.
44. Laver, *Modesty in Dress*, p. 69; Ribeiro, *Art of Dress*, pp. 104–5.
45. Anne Hollander, *Sex and Suits* (New York: Knopf, 1994) pp. 87–91.
46. Naomi Tarrant, *The Development of Costume* (London: Routledge, 1994) p. 98.
47. Laver, *Modesty in Dress*, pp. 44, 61.
48. J. C. Flugel, *The Psychology of Clothes* (London: Hogarth Press, 1930) pp. 111–12; followed by David Kuchta, 'The Making of the Self-Made Man: Class, Clothing and English Masculinity, 1688–1832', in Victoria de Grazia (ed.), *The Sex of Things: Gender and Consumption in Historical Perspective* (Berkeley: University of California Press, 1996) ch. 2.
49. Rev. Dr John Trusler, *A System of Etiquette, with Maxims of Prudence, and Some Observations of Duelling* (London: 1828) p. 59.
50. Mrs Alexander Walker, *Female Beauty As Preserved and Improved by Regimen, Cleanliness and Dress (revised and amended by an American editor)* (New York: Scofield & Voorhies, 1840) pp. 25–6. The *gigot* or leg o'mutton sleeve arrived in the late 1820s and persisted into the late 1830s: Naomi E. Tarrant, *The Rise and Fall of the Sleeve, 1825–1840* (Edinburgh: Royal Scottish Museum, 1983).
51. *The Art of Dress; or Guide to the Toilette: With directions for adapting the various parts of the female costume to the complexion and figure* (London: Charles Tilt, 1839) p. 1.
52. A Lady of Distinction, *The Mirror of the Graces, or, the English Lady's Guide to Costume* (New York: I. Riley, 1815) p. 56.

53. Patricia Wardle, *Victorian Lace* (London: Herbert Jenkins, 1968) pp. 221–7; Pat Earnshaw, *Lace Machines and Machine Laces* (London: BT Batsford, 1986) chs 1–5.
54. Santina Levey, *Lace: a History* (London: Victoria & Albert Museum/W.S. Maney & Sons, 1983) pp. 77–88.
55. Hugh Tait (ed.), *The Art of the Jeweller: A Catalogue of the Hull Grundy Gift to the British Museum: Jewellery, Engraved Gems and Goldsmiths' Work*, vol. 2 (Plates) (London: British Museum, 1984) pp. 22–31.
56. Tait, *Art of the Jeweller*, vol. 2, pp. 34–7.
57. Tait, *Art of the Jeweller*, vol. 2, pp. 52–61, 219–27.
58. Hugh Tait (ed.), *The Art of the Jeweller: A Catalogue of the Hull Grundy Gift to the British Museum: Jewellery, Engraved Gems and Goldsmiths' Work*, vol. 1 (Text) (London: British Museum, 1984) p. 105.
59. Shirley Bury, *An Introduction to Sentimental Jewellery* (London: HMSO, 1985) pp. 33–45.
60. For example, just one such chain appears in the British Museum's Hull Grundy Gift, which focuses on popular Victorian jewellery: Tait, *Art of the Jeweller*, vol. 2, p. 41 (an unusual iron and gold chain). It is likely that long gold chains were broken up and re-used after they went out of style.
61. For example, 1794–1835 diary of Sarah Snell Bryant of Cummington, MA, analysed by Jane C. Nylander, 'Everyday Life on a Berkshire County Hill Farm', in Eleanor McD. Thompson (ed.), *The American Home: Material Culture, Domestic Space, and Family Life* (Winterthur, DE: Winterthur Museum, 1998) pp. 108–15.
62. Trims, outer garments and underwear survive, but also in isolation from each other. Dresses composed of a skirt and a bodice are considered a single unit.
63. Natalie Rothstein (ed.), *Barbara Johnson's Album of Fashions and Fabrics* (London: Thames & Hudson, 1987) p. 14.
64. Stana Nenadic notes that neighbours often purchased bargain furnishings at insolvents' compulsory house sales: 'Middle-rank Consumers and Domestic Culture in Edinburgh and Glasgow, 1720–1840', *Past and Present*, vol. 145 (1994) pp. 131–2.
65. Downing, *Country Houses*, p. 267.
66. John Ruskin, *The Crown of Wild Olive: Three Lectures on Work, Traffic, and War* (London: Smith, Elder & Co., 1866) p. 83.
67. Katherine C. Grier, *Culture and Comfort: People, Parlours and Upholstery, 1850–1930* (Rochester, NY: Strong Museum, 1988).
68. Ruskin, *Crown of Wild Olive*, p. 86.
69. Loudon and Downing both assert the sacral value of Gothic style in the home. See also Colleen McDannell, *The Christian Home in Victorian America, 1840–1900* (Bloomington: Indiana University Press, 1986) ch. 2.
70. Clifford E. Clark, 'Domestic Architecture as an Index to Social History: The Romantic Revival and the Cult of Domesticity in America, 1840–1870', *Journal of Interdisciplinary History*, vol. 7, no. 1 (1976) pp. 49–52.
71. Grier, *Culture and Comfort*, ch. 4.; Witold Rybcyzinski, *Home: The Short History of an Idea* (New York: Viking, 1986) ch. 5.
72. Edward T. Joy, *English Furniture 1800–1851* (London: Sotheby Parke Bernet

Publications, 1977) p. 217.

73. Joy, *English Furniture*, p. 256.
74. John Claudius Loudon, *Encyclopedia of Cottage, Farm and Villa Architecture* (London: Longman, Rees, Orme, Brown & Green, 1833); Downing, *Country Houses*, p. 257. Loudon's villas are very grand by comparison with Downing's, but his designs establish the distinction of the dining room, which is not to be found in any of his cottage plans.
75. John Cornforth, *English Interiors 1790–1848: The Quest for Comfort* (London: Barrie & Jenkins, 1978) p. 15; Siegfried Giedion, *Mechanization Takes Command: A Contribution to Anonymous History* (New York: Norton, 1969 [1948]) p. 292; Henry Glassie, *Folk Housing in Middle Virginia* (Knoxville, TN: University of Tennessee Press, 1975) p. 89.
76. Thomas Sheraton, *The Cabinet Dictionary* (London: W. Smith, 1803) p. 217; Downing, *Country Houses*, p. 44.
77. Loudon, *Encyclopedia*, p. 318.
78. Kenneth L. Ames, *Death in the Dining Room, and Other Tales of Victorian Culture* (Philadelphia: Temple University Press, 1992) pp. 17–32.
79. National Archives of Scotland, Court of Sequestration: CS96; State Library of New South Wales, Mitchell Library, Auction Catalogues: 018.2Pa1; Delaware Public Archives: Probate Records, New Castle County.
80. Karen Halttunen, *Confidence Men and Painted Women: A Study of Middle-Class Culture in America, 1830–1870* (New Haven, CT: Yale University Press, 1982) pp. 59–60.
81. Sheraton, *Cabinet Dictionary*, p. 201.
82. Downing, *Country Houses*, p. 403.
83. Sheraton, *Cabinet Dictionary*, p. 218.
84. Loudon, *Encyclopedia*, p. 797.
85. State Library of New South Wales, Mitchell Library, Auction Catalogues: 018.2Pa1.
86. Downing, *Country Houses*, p. 429.
87. Loudon, *Encyclopedia*, p. 1065; Sheraton, *Cabinet Dictionary*, p. 201; Thomas Webster, *Encyclopedia of Domestic Economy*, new edn (London: 1847 [1844]) p. 240.
88. Jane Austen, *Pride and Prejudice* (1813) vol. 2, ch. 6.
89. Terence Lane and Jessie Serle, *Australians at Home: A Documentary History of Australian Domestic Interiors from 1788 to 1914* (Melbourne: Oxford University Press, 1990) pp. 374–6; Kevin Fahy, 'Furniture and Furniture-Makers', in James Broadbent and Joy Hughes (eds), *The Age of Macquarie* (Melbourne: Melbourne University Press, 1992) pp. 122–4.
90. Arthur Loesser, *Men, Women and Pianos: A Social History* (London: Victor Gollancz, 1955) pp. 267–79.
91. Loudon, *Encyclopedia*, p. 1071.
92. Downing, *Country Houses*, p. 429.
93. Randell, *Practical Domestic Economy*, pp. 418–20, 424–7.
94. John Gloag, *A Short Dictionary of Furniture*, rev. edn (London: George Allen & Unwin, 1969) pp. 147, 731–2.
95. Downing, *Country Houses*, p. 259; Loudon, *Encyclopedia*, p. 302.
96. Downing, *Country Houses*, p. 404.
97. Loudon, *Encyclopedia*, p. 800.

98. Elias, *Civilizing Process*, pp. 85–8; John F. Kasson, 'Rituals of Dining: Table Manners in Victorian America', in Kathryn Grover (ed.), *Dining in America, 1850–1900* (Amherst: University of Massachusetts Press, 1987) pp. 130–41.

99. Paul A. Shackel, *Personal Discipline and Material Culture: An Archaeology of Annapolis, Maryland, 1695–1870* (Knoxville: University of Tennessee Press, 1993) pp. 106–7, 144–50.

100. Sheffield plate (silver-plated copper, invented 1742); Britannia metal (tin, antimony and copper alloy, invented 1790); German silver (nickel 'silver' alloy, invented 1824); electroplating (invented 1840).

101. Miss Leslie, *The House Book, or A Manual of Domestic Economy* (Philadelphia: Carey & Hart, 1841) p. 206.

102. Agogos, *Hints on Etiquette and the Usages of Society with a Glance at Bad Habits* (London: 1834) p. 16.

103. Leslie, *House Book*, p. 258.

104. A. W. Coysh and R. K. Henrywood, *The Dictionary of Blue and White Printed Pottery, 1780–1880* (Woodbridge, Suffolk: Antique Collectors Club, 1982) pp. 8–9.

105. Geoffrey Godden, 'Chinese Export Porcelain', in David Battie (ed.), *Sotheby's Concise Encyclopedia of Porcelain* (Boston: Little, Brown, 1990) p. 67.

106. Jean McClure Mudge, *Chinese Export Porcelain for the American Trade, 1785–1835* (Newark: University of Delaware Press, 1962) ch. 4.

107. The salvage of wrecked cargoes of the early nineteenth century indicates that millions of pieces of fairly ordinary quality ceramics were loaded for the markets of the West; see Hugh Edwards, *Treasures of the Deep: The Extraordinary Life and Times of Captain Mike Hatcher* (Sydney: HarperCollins, 2000) chs 9 and 10.

108. The nomenclature of parlour, drawing, sitting and morning rooms shifts frequently over place, time and class segment; the use here is to indicate different aims framed by public or private use.

109. Cf. Mark Girouard, *Life in the English Country House* (Harmondsworth: Penguin, 1980) pp. 293–4.

110. Leslie, *House Book*, pp. 296–7.

111. Leslie, *House Book*, p. 303; Carole Shammas, 'The Domestic Environment in Early Modern England and America', *Journal of Social History*, vol. 14, no. 1 (1980) p. 9; Jack Larkin, *The Reshaping of Everyday Life, 1790–1840* (New York: Harper & Row, 1988) p. 138.

112. Loudon, *Encyclopedia*, p. 654. Downing, *Country Houses*, p. 419. See also Georg Himmelheber, *Cast-iron Furniture and All Other Forms of Iron Furniture* (London: Philip Wilson, 1996) pp. 41–4.

113. Shammas, *Pre-Industrial Consumer*, p. 169.

114. National Archives of Scotland, Court of Sequestration: CS96/2074; CS96/4744; CS96/4697.

115. Delaware Public Archives, Mendenhall probate record, 14.12.1852.

116. Gloag, *Short Dictionary*, pp. 706, 213.

117. Webster, *Encyclopedia*, p. 278.

118. Loudon, *Encyclopedia*, p. 1102.

119. 'The Settlers of Van Diemen's Land', *Court Magazine and Belle Assemblée* (November 1832) p. 228.

Conclusion

1. Jerrold Seigel, *Bohemian Paris: Culture, Politics and the Boundaries of the Bourgeois Life, 1830–1930* (New York: Viking, 1986) p. 10.
2. Richard Sennett, *The Fall of Public Man* (Cambridge: Cambridge University Press, 1974) p. 23.
3. Elizabeth Wilson, 'The Bohemianisation of Mass Culture', *International Journal of Cultural Studies*, vol. 2, no. 1 (April 1999).
4. Norbert Elias, *The Civilizing Process* (Oxford: Basil Blackwell, 1982 [1939]) vol. 2, *State Formation and Civilization*, part 2.1.1.
5. Glenna Matthews, *'Just a Housewife': The Rise and Fall of Domesticity in America* (New York: Oxford University Press, 1987) p. 89.
6. Joanna Bourke, 'Housewifery in Working Class England, 1860–1914', *Past and Present*, no. 143 (May 1994) p. 172.
7. Catherine Hall, 'The Sweet Delights of Home', in Philippe Ariès and Georges Duby (eds), *A History of Private Life*, vol. 4, *From the Fires of the Revolution to the Great War* (Cambridge, MA: Belknap Press, 1990) p. 77.
8. Warren I. Susman, '"Personality" and the Making of Twentieth-Century Culture', in John Highman and Paul K. Conkin (eds), *New Directions in American Intellectual History* (Baltimore, MD: Johns Hopkins University Press, 1979) p. 220.
9. Stephen Carter, *Civility: Manners, Morals, and the Etiquette of Democracy* (New York: Basic Books, 1998) p. 38.
10. Melanie Archer and Judith R. Blau, 'Class Formation in Nineteenth Century America: The Case of the Middle Class', *Annual Review of Sociology*, vol. 19 (1993) p. 35.
11. Arthur M. Schlesinger, *Learning How to Behave: A Historical Study of American Etiquette Books* (New York: Macmillan, 1946) ch. 5, 'Relax!'
12. See Judith Martin, *Miss Manners' Guide to Excrutiatingly Correct Behaviour* (London: Hamish Hamilton, 1983), 'Dinner Parties', 'Debuts and Dances.'
13. Carter, *Civility*; John Kasson, *Rudeness and Civility: Manners in Nineteenth-Century Urban America* (New York: Hill & Wang, 1990) p. 258.
14. Allan Bloom, *The Closing of the American Mind: How Higher Education has Failed Democracy and Impoverished the Souls of Today's Students* (New York: Simon & Schuster, 1987).

Bibliography

Primary sources

A New System of Practical Domestic Economy, new edn (London: H. Colburn, 1824).

Acton, William, *The Functions and Disorders of the Reproductive Organs in Youth, in Adult Age, and in Advanced Life*, 6th edn (London: J. and A. Churchill, 1903 [1857]).

Advice to a Young Gentleman on Entering Society (London: A. H. Bailey, 1839).

Agogos [William Charles Day], *Hints on Etiquette and the Usages of Society with a Glance at Bad Habits* (London: Printed for the Booksellers, 1834).

Agogos, *Hints on Etiquette and the Usages of Society, With a Glance at Bad Habits*, 9th edn (London: reprinted by William Elliston Gore, Hobarton, 1838).

Agogos, *Hints on Etiquette and the Usages of Society with a Glance at Bad Habits*, 26th edn Revised (with Additions) by A Lady of Rank (London: Orme, Brown, Green & Longmans, 1849).

American Gentleman, An, *True Politeness: A Handbook of Etiquette for Gentlemen* (Philadelphia: George S. Appleton, 1848).

Art of Dress; or Guide to the Toilette: With directions for adapting the various parts of the female costume to the complexion and figure (London: Charles Tilt, 1839).

Asteios, *The Philosophy of Manner, or, a Sequel to the Laws of Etiquette* (Glasgow: John Symington, 1838).

Asteios, *The Young Wife's Book: A Manual of Domestic Duties* (Glasgow: John Symington, 1838).

Austen, Jane, *Emma* (1816) (any edition).

Austen, Jane, *Northanger Abbey* (1818) (any edition).

Austen, Jane, *Persuasion* (1818) (any edition).

Austen, Jane, *Pride and Prejudice* (1813) (any edition).

Beecher, Catharine, *A Treatise on Domestic Economy* (New York: Source Books, 1970 [1841]).

Bulwer [Lytton], Edward, *England and the English*, 2nd edn (Shannon: Irish University Press, 1971 [1833]).

Caddick, Mrs H. C., *The Bride's Book; A Code of Morals and Conduct from the Works of Eminent Writers for the Use of Young Married Women* (London: H. Fisher, R. Fisher & P. Jackson, 1835).

Casa, Giovanni della, *Galateo, or The Book of Manners* (trans. R. S. Pine-Coffin) (Harmondsworth: Penguin, 1958).

Castiglione, Baldassare, *The Book of the Courtier* (trans. Sir Thomas Hoby, 1561) (London: J. M. Dent & Sons, 1974).

Chesterfield, Lord [Philip Dormer Stanhope], *Letters to His Son, 1737–1768* (1774).

Chippendale, Thomas, *The Gentleman and Cabinet-Maker's Director*, 3rd edn (New York: Dover, 1966 [1762]).

Chisholm, Caroline, *Emigration and Transportation Relatively Considered* (London: John Olliver, 1847).

Citizen of Washington, A, *Etiquette at Washington, together with the Customs Adopted by Polite Society in Other Cities of the United States*, 2nd edn (Baltimore, MD: John Murphy & Co., 1850).

Cobbett, Anne, *The English Housekeeper, or, Manual of Domestic Management*, 2nd edn (London: A. Cobbett, *c.*1838).

Cobbett, William, *Advice to Young Men* (London: Henry Froude, 1906 [1829]).

Court Etiquette: A Guide to the Intercourse with Royal or Titled Persons, to Drawing Rooms, Levees, Courts and Audiences, the Usages of Social Life (London: Mitchell, n.d. [1849]).

Crell, A. F. and W. M. Wallace, *The Family Oracle of Good Health, Economy, Medicine and Good Living*, vol. 1 (London: Knight & Lacey, 1824).

Day, William Charles, *The American Ladies' and Gentlemen's Manual of Elegance, Fashion and True Politeness* (Auburn and Rochester, NY: Alden & Beardsley, 1856).

Denison, William, *Varieties of Vice-Regal Life* (London: Longmans Green & Co., 1870).

Dickens, Charles, *David Copperfield* (1850) (any edition).

Dictionary of National Biography (London: Smith, Elder & Co., 1898).

Dilke, Charles, *Greater Britain: A Record of Travel in the English-Speaking Countries during 1866 and 1867*, 2 vols (London: Macmillan, 1869).

Disraeli, Benjamin, *Coningsby, or, The New Generation* (London: Dent, 1967 [1844]).

Dixon, John, *The Condition and Capability of Van Diemen's Land* (London: Smith, Elder & Co., 1839).

Downing, A. J., *The Architecture of Country Houses* (New York: Dover, 1969 [1850]).

Eddy, Daniel C., *The Young Man's Friend* (Boston: Dayton & Wentworth, 1855).

Egan, Pierce, *Life in London* (London: Sherwood, Neely & Jones, 1821).

Ellis, Mrs [Sarah Stickney], *The Mothers of England: Their Influence and Responsibility* (London: Fisher, Son & Co., 1843).

Ellis, Mrs [Sarah Stickney], *The Daughters of England: Their Position in Society, Character and Responsibilities* (London: Fisher, Sons & Co., 1845).

Encyclopedia Britannica, 8th edn (Edinburgh: Adam & Charles Black, 1853).

Encyclopedia Britannica, 9th edn (Edinburgh: Adam & Charles Black, 1878).

Etiquette for Ladies; with Hints on the Preservation, Improvement and Display of Female Beauty (Philadelphia: Carey, Lea & Blanchard, 1838).

Female Instructor; or Young Woman's Companion and Guide to Domestic Happiness . . . (London: Thos Kelly, 1824).

Fenton, Elizabeth, *Mrs Fenton's Tasmanian Journal 1829–1830* (Adelaide: Sullivans Cove, 1986).

Footman's Directory, and Butler's Remembrancer, 4th edn (London: T. Consett, 1825).

Gaskell, Elizabeth, *Cranford* (London: OUP, 1934 [1853]).

Gentleman, A, *The Laws of Etiquette, or, Short Rules and Reflections for Conduct in Society* (Philadelphia: Carey, Lee & Blanchard, 1839).

Gore, Catherine, *Pin Money: A Novel* (London: Henry Colburn, 1831).

[Hayward, Abraham], 'Codes of Manners and Etiquette', *Quarterly Review*, vol. 59, no. 18 (October 1837).

Hepplewhite, George, *The Cabinet-Maker and Upholsterer's Guide*, 3rd edn (New York: Dover, 1969 [1794]).

Instructions in Etiquette for the Use of All, 3rd edn (London: Simpkin, Marshall & Co., 1847).

Jesse, Captain, *The Life of George Brummell Esquire* (London: Saunders & Otley, 1844).

Lady, A, *Instructions in Household Matters, or the Young Girl's Guide to Domestic Service*, 5th edn (London: John W. Parker & Son, 1852).

Lady, A [Eliza Ware Farrar], *The Young Lady's Friend* (Boston: American Stationers' Company, 1837).

Lady, A [Maria Rundell], *A New System of Practical Domestic Cookery*, new edn (London: John Murray, 1822).

Lady of Distinction, A, *The Mirror of the Graces, or, the English Lady's Costume* (New York: I. Riley, 1815).

Laws of Etiquette, or Short Rules and Reflections for Conduct in Society, 2nd edn (Philadelphia: Carey, Lea & Blanchard, 1836).

Leslie, Miss [Eliza], *The House Book, or A Manual of Domestic Economy* (Philadelphia: Carey & Hart, 1841).

Lister, Thomas Henry, *Granby*. rev. edn (n.d. [1825]).

Loudon, John Claudius, *Encyclopedia of Cottage, Farm and Villa Architecture* (London: Longman, Orme, Brown, Green & Longmans, 1833).

Loudon, John Claudius, *The Suburban Gardener and Villa Companion* (London: Longman, Orme, Brown, Green & Longmans, 1838).

Maberly, Mrs, *The Art of Conversation, with Remarks on Fashion and Address* (New York: Wilson & Co., 1845).

Mahomed, Horatio, *The Bath: A Concise History of Bathing* (London: Smith, Elder & Co., 1843).

Mayhew, Horace, *Model Men*, (London: D. Bogue, 1848).

Member of the Philadelphia Bar, A, *The American Chesterfield, or, Ways to Wealth, Honour and Distinction* (Philadelphia: John Grigg, 1828).

Member of the Royal Household, A, *The Book of Fashionable Life: Comprising the Etiquette of the Drawing Room, Dining Room and Ball Room* (London: Hugh Cunningham [c.1844]).

Meredith, Louisa, *Notes and Sketches of New South Wales* (London: John Murray, 1844).

[Moody, Eleazar], *The School of Good Manners* (Newburyport: Thomas Whipple, 1818).

[Moody, Eleazar] *Manual of Manners, or, a Child's Book of Etiquette* (Glasgow: John Reid, 1838).

[Morgan, T. C.], 'Etiquette', *New Monthly Magazine and Humorist*, part 3 (1838).

Parkes, Frances Byerley, *Domestic Duties: or, Instructions to Young Married Ladies on the Management of their Households* (New York: J. & J. Harper, 1828).

Phelps, Mrs Almira Lincoln, *Hours With My Pupils: The Young Lady's Guide* (New York: Charles Scribner & Co., 1859).

Prinsep, Mrs A., *Journal of a Voyage from Calcutta to Van Diemen's Land* (London: Smith Elder, 1833).

Ruskin, John, *The Crown of Wild Olive: Three Lectures on Work, Traffic, and War* (London: Smith, Elder & Co., 1866).

Savery, Henry, *The Hermit in Van Diemen's Land* (St Lucia, Qld: University of Queensland Press, 1964 [1829]).

Servants' Guide and Family Manual (London: John Limbird, 1832).
'The Settlers of Van Diemen's Land', *Court Magazine and Belle Assemblée*, (London: E. Bull, November 1832).
Sheraton, Thomas, *The Cabinet-Maker and Upholsterer's Drawing Book* (London: T. Bensley, 1793).
Sheraton, Thomas, *The Cabinet Dictionary* (London: W. Smith, 1803).
Smiles, Samuel, *Self-Help* (London: J. Murray, 1958 [1859]).
Smith, Adam, *An Inquiry into the Nature and Causes of the Wealth of Nations*, eds R. H. Campbell and A. S. Skinner (Oxford: Clarendon Press, 1976 [1776]).
Smith, Albert, *The Natural History of the Gent* (London: David Bogue, 1847).
Spirit of Etiquette, or, Politeness Exemplified (London: Moore, 1837).
Thornwell, Emily, *The Lady's Guide to Perfect Gentility* (New York: Derby & Jackson, 1858).
Tocqueville, Alexis de, *Democracy in America*, tran. George Lawrence, eds J. P. Mayer and Max Lerner (New York: Harper & Row, 1966 [1835]).
Tocqueville's L'Ancien Régime, trans. M. W. Patterson (Oxford: Basil Blackwell, 1947 [1856]).
Trollope, Frances, *Domestic Manners of the Americans* (London: Folio Society, 1974 [1832]).
Trusler, Rev. Dr John, *The Honours of the Table, or Rules for Behaviour during Meals* (London: The Author, 1791).
Trusler, Rev. Dr John, *A System of Etiquette, with Maxims of Prudence, and Some Observations of Duelling* (London: 1828).
Walker, Mrs Alexander, *Female Beauty As Preserved and Improved by Regimen, Cleanliness and Dress (revised and amended by an American editor)* (New York: Scofield & Voorhies, 1840).
Webster, Thomas, *Encyclopedia of Domestic Economy* (London: Longman, Bowman & Green & Longman, 1844).
Wells, Samuel R., *The Laws of Etiquette*, 2nd edn (Philadelphia: 1836).
[Wells, Samuel R.], *How to Behave: A Pocket Manual of Republican Etiquette* (New York: Fowler & Wells, 1856).
White, Charles, *Almack's Revisited* (London: Henry Colburn, 1828).
The Work Woman's Guide (London: Simpkins, Marshall & Co., 1838).

Secondary sources

Adburgham, Alison, *Silver Fork Society: Fashionable Life and Literature from 1814–1840* (London: Constable, 1983).
Alexander, Sally, 'Women, Class and Sexual Difference', *History Workshop*, vol. 17 (1984).
Ames, Kenneth L., *Death in the Dining Room, and Other Tales of Victorian Culture* (Philadelphia: Temple University Press, 1992).
Appadurai, Arjun (ed.), *The Social Life of Things: Commodities in Cultural Perspective* (Cambridge: Cambridge University Press, 1986).
Appadurai, Arjun, 'Disjuncture and Difference in the Global Cultural Economy', *Public Culture*, vol. 2, no. 2 (1992).
Appleby, Joyce, 'The Social Consequences of American Revolutionary Ideals in the Early Republic', in Burton J. Bledstein and Robert D. Johnston (eds), *The*

Middling Sorts: Explorations in the History of the American Middle Class (New York: Routledge, 2001).

Appleby, Joyce, Lynn Hunt and Margaret Jacob, *Telling the Truth about History* (New York: Norton, 1994).

Archer, Melanie and Judith R. Blau, 'Class Formation in Nineteenth Century America: The Case of the Middle Class', *Annual Review of Sociology*, vol. 19 (1993).

Aresty, Esther, *The Best Behaviour: The Course of Good Manners from Antiquity to the Present as Seen through Courtesy and Etiquette Books* (New York: Simon & Schuster, 1970).

Ariès, Philippe and Georges Duby (eds), *A History of Private Life*: vol. 4, *From the Fires of the Revolution to the Great War* (ed. Michelle Perrot) (Cambridge, MA: Belknap Press, 1990).

Armitage, David, 'Greater Britain: A Useful Category of Historical Analysis?', *American Historical Review*, no. 104 (1999).

Armstrong, Nancy and Leonard Tennenhouse (eds), *The Ideology of Conduct: Essays on Literature and the History of Sexuality* (New York: Methuen, 1987).

Arnstein, Walter L., 'The Survival of the Victorian Aristocracy', in Frederic Cople Jaher (ed.), *The Rich, The Well Born, and the Powerful: Elites and Upper Classes in History* (Urbana: University of Illinois Press, 1973).

Arnstein, Walter L., 'The Myth of the Triumphant Middle Class', *The Historian*, vol. 38 (1975).

Ashelford, Jane, *The Art of Dress: Clothes and Society 1500–1914* (London: National Trust/Laura Ashley, 1996).

Bailey, Peter, *Popular Culture and Performance in the Victorian City* (Cambridge: Cambridge University Press, 1998).

Baltzell, E. Digby, *Philadelphia Gentlemen: The Making of a National Upper Class* (Glencoe, IL: Free Press, 1958).

Banks, J. A., *Prosperity and Parenthood: A Study of Family Planning among the Victorian Middle Classes* (London: Routledge, 1954).

Barcan, A., 'Development of the Australian Middle Class', *Past and Present*, no. 8, (1955).

Beckett, J. V., *The Aristocracy in England 1660–1914* (Oxford: Blackwell, 1986).

Beilharz, Peter, 'Theorising the Middle Class', *Arena*, no. 72 (1985).

Bermingham, Ann and John Brewer (eds), *The Consumption of Culture 1600–1800: Image, Object, Text* (London: Routledge, 1995).

Bledstein, Burton J. and Robert D. Johnston (eds), *The Middling Sorts: Explorations in the History of the American Middle Class* (New York: Routledge, 2001).

Bloom, Allan, *The Closing of the American Mind: How Higher Education has Failed Democracy and Impoverished the Souls of Today's Students* (New York: Simon & Schuster, 1987).

Blumin, Stuart M., 'The Hypothesis of Middle-Class Formation in Nineteenth Century America: A Critique and Some Proposals', *American Historical Review*, vol. 90, no. 2 (1985).

Blumin, Stuart M., *The Emergence of the Middle Class: Social Experience in the American City, 1760–1900* (Cambridge: Cambridge University Press, 1989).

Boot, H. M., 'Real Incomes of the British Middle Class, 1760–1850: The Experience of Clerks at the East India Company', *Economic History Review*, vol. LII, no. 4 (1999).

Bourdieu, Pierre, *Distinction: A Social Critique of the Judgement of Taste* (London: Routledge & Kegan Paul, 1984 [1979]).

Bourdieu, Pierre, *The Logic of Practice* (Cambridge: Polity Press, 1990 [1980]).

Bourdieu, Pierre, *Language and Symbolic Power* (Cambridge: Polity Press, 1991).

Bourke, Joanna, 'Housewifery in Working Class England, 1860–1914', *Past and Present* no. 143 (May 1994).

Bradley, Ian, *The Call to Seriousness: The Evangelical Impact on the Victorians* (London: Jonathon Cape, 1967).

Braembussche, A. A. Van Den, 'Historical Explanation and Comparative Method: Towards a Theory of the History of Society', *History and Theory*, vol. 28, no. 1 (1989).

Branca, Patricia, *Silent Sisterhood: Middle Class Women in the Victorian Home* (London: Croom Helm, 1975).

Brewer, John and Roy Porter (eds), *Consumption and the World of Good* (London: Routledge, 1993).

Briggs, Asa, *The Age of Improvement* (London: Longman, 1959).

Briggs, Asa, 'The Language of "Class" in Early Nineteenth Century England', in Asa Briggs and John Saville (eds), *Essays in Labour History* (London: Macmillan, 1960).

Briggs, Asa and John Saville (eds), *Essays in Labour History* (London: Macmillan, 1960).

Broadbent, James and Joy Hughes (eds), *The Age of Macquarie* (Melbourne: Melbourne University Press, 1992).

Bruchey, Stuart W., *Small Business in American Life* (New York: Columbia University Press, 1980).

Buck, Anne, *Victorian Costume and Costume Accessories*, 2nd edn (Bedford: Ruth Bean, 1984).

Buijs, Gina (ed.), *Migrant Women: Crossing Boundaries and Changing Identities* (Oxford: Berg, 1993).

Burke, Martin J., *The Conundrum of Class: Public Discourse on the Social Order in America* (Chicago: University of Chicago Press, 1995).

Burman, Sandra (ed.), *Fit Work for Women* (London: Croom Helm, 1979).

Bury, Shirley, *An Introduction to Sentimental Jewellery* (London: HMSO, 1985).

Bush, M. L. (ed.), *Social Orders and Social Classes in Europe since 1500: Studies in Social Stratification* (London: Longman, 1992).

Bushman, Richard L., 'American High Style and Vernacular Cultures', in Jack P. Greene and J. R. Pole (eds), *Colonial British America: Essays in the History of the Early Modern Era* (Baltimore, MD: Johns Hopkins University Press, 1984).

Bushman, Richard, *The Refinement of America: Persons, Houses, Cities* (New York: Knopf, 1992).

Bushman, Richard and Claudia Bushman, 'The Early History of Cleanliness in America', *Journal of American History*, vol. 74, no. 4 (1988).

Cain, P. C. and A. G. Hopkins, 'Gentlemanly Capitalism and British Expansion Overseas', parts 1 and 2, *Economic History Review*, vol. 39, no. 4 (1986) and vol. 40, no. 1 (1987).

Campbell, Colin, *The Romantic Ethic and the Spirit of Modern Consumerism* (Oxford: Basil Blackwell, 1987).

Cannadine, David, 'The Present and the Past in the Industrial Revolution', *Past and Present*, no. 103 (1984).

Carson, Barbara G., Ellen Kirven Donald and Kym S. Rice, 'Household Encounters: Servants, Slaves and Mistresses in Early Washington', in Eleanor McD. Thompson (ed.), *The American Home: Material Culture, Domestic Space, and Family Life* (Winterthur, DE: Winterthur Museum, 1998).

Carson, Cary, 'The Consumer Revolution in Colonial British America: Why Demand?', in Cary Carson, Ronald Hoffman and Peter J. Albert (eds), *Of Consuming Interest: The Style of Life in the Eighteenth Century* (Charlottesville: University Press of Virginia, 1994).

Carson, Cary, Ronald Hoffman and Peter J. Albert (eds), *Of Consuming Interest: The Style of Life in the Eighteenth Century* (Charlottesville: University Press of Virginia, 1994).

Carter, Stephen, *Civility: Manners, Morals, and the Etiquette of Democracy* (New York: Basic Books, 1998).

Castronovo, David, *The English Gentleman: Images and Ideals in Literature and Society* (New York: Ungar, 1987).

Chambers Information for the People, vol. 29 (Edinburgh: 1835).

Clark, Clifford E., 'Domestic Architecture as an Index to Social History: The Romantic Revival and the Cult of Domesticity in America, 1840–1870', *Journal of Interdisciplinary History*, vol. 7, no. 1 (1976).

Clark, G. Kitson, *The Making of Victorian England* (London: Methuen, 1962).

Cohen, Robin, *Global Diasporas: An Introduction* (London: University of London Press, 1997).

Corfield, Penelope J., *Language, History and Class* (Oxford: Basil Blackwell, 1991).

Corfield, Penelope J., *Power and the Professions in Britain 1700–1850* (London: Routledge, 1995).

Corfield, Penny, 'The Democratic History of the English Gentleman', *History Today*, vol. 42 (1992).

Cornforth, John, *English Interiors 1790–1848: The Quest for Comfort* (London: Barrie & Jenkins, 1978).

Cott, Nancy F., *The Bonds of Womanhood: 'Women's Sphere' in New England, 1780–1835* (New Haven, CT: Yale University Press, 1977).

Coysh, A. W. and R. K. Henrywood, *The Dictionary of Blue and White Printed Pottery, 1780–1880* (Woodbridge, Suffolk: Antique Collectors Club, 1982).

Crossick, Geoffrey, 'From Gentlemen to the Residuum: Languages of Social Description in Victorian Britain', in Penelope J. Corfield, *Language, History and Class* (Oxford: Basil Blackwell, 1991).

Crossick, Geoffrey and Hans-Gerhard Haupt, *The Petite Bourgeoisie in Europe, 1780–1914: Enterprise, Family and Independence* (London: Routledge, 1995).

Crowley, John E., 'The Sensibility of Comfort', *American Historical Review*, vol. 104, no. 3 (1999).

Cunnington, C. Willet and Phillis Cunnington, *Handbook of English Costume in the Nineteenth Century* (London: Faber, 1959).

Cunnington, C. Willet and Phillis Cunnington, *Handbook of English Costume in the Seventeenth Century* (London: Faber, 1966).

Cunnington, C. Willet and Phillis Cunnington, *The History of Underclothes* (New York: Dover, 1992 [1951]).

Curtin, Emma, 'In Awe of Mrs Grundy: British Gentility and Emigrant

Gentlewomen in Australia, 1830–1880', PhD thesis, LaTrobe University (1995).

Curtin, Michael, *Propriety and Position: A Study of Victorian Manners* (New York: Garland, 1987).

Davidoff, Leonore, *The Best Circles: Society, Etiquette and the Season* (London: Croom Helm, 1973).

Davidoff, Leonore and Catherine Hall, *Family Fortunes: Men and Women of the English Middle Class, 1750–1850* (London: Hutchinson, 1987).

Davidson, Caroline, *A Woman's Work is Never Done: A History of Housework in the British Isles 1650–1950* (London: Chatto & Windus, 1982).

Davidson, Caroline, *The World of Mary Ellen Best* (London: Chatto & Windus, 1985).

Davis, Fred, *Fashion, Culture and Identity* (Chicago: University of Chicago Press, 1992).

D'Emilio, John and Estelle B. Freedman, *Intimate Matters: A History of Sexuality in America* (New York: Harper & Row, 1988).

DeMott, Benjamin, *The Imperial Middle: Why Americans Can't Think Straight about Class* (New York: William Morrow, 1990).

Denholm, David, *The Colonial Australians* (Harmondsworth: Penguin, 1979).

Donegan, Jane B., *'Hydropathic Highway to Health': Women and Water-Cure in Antebellum America* (New York: Greenwood Press, 1986).

Douglas, Ann, *The Feminization of American Culture* (New York: Knopf, 1977).

Douglas, Mary, *Purity and Danger: An Analysis of the Concepts of Pollution and Taboo* (New York: Praeger, 1966).

Douglas, Mary and Baron Isherwood, *The World of Goods: Towards an Anthropology of Consumption* (Harmondsworth: Penguin, 1980).

Drabble, Margaret (ed.), *The Oxford Companion to English Literature* (Oxford: Oxford University Press, 1995).

Earnshaw, Pat, *Lace Machines and Machine Laces* (London: BT Batsford, 1986).

Edwards, Hugh, *Treasures of the Deep: The Extraordinary Life and Times of Captain Mike Hatcher* (Sydney: HarperCollins, 2000).

Elias, Norbert, *The Court Society* (Oxford: Basil Blackwell, 1983 [1969]).

Elias, Norbert, *The Civilizing Process*, trans. Edmund Jephcott (Oxford: Blackwell, 1994 [1939]).

Epstein, Barbara Leslie, *The Politics of Domesticity: Women, Evangelism and Temperance in Nineteenth-Century America* (Middletown, CT: Wesleyan University Press, 1981).

Evans, Joan, *The Victorians* (London: Cambridge University Press, 1966).

Evans-Pritchard, E. E., *The Nuer: A Description of the Modes of Livelihood and Political Institutions of a Native People* (New York: Oxford University Press, 1956).

Ewing, Elizabeth, *Dress and Undress: A History of Underclothes* (London: Bibliophile, 1978).

Faler, Paul, 'Working Class Culture and Politics in the Industrial Revolution: Sources of Loyalism and Revolution', *Journal of Social History*, vol. 9 (1976).

Field, John, 'Wealth, Styles of Life and Social Tone amongst Portsmouth's Middle Class, 1800–1875' in R. J. Morris (ed.), *Class, Power and Social Structure in British Nineteenth-Century Towns* (Leicester: Leicester University Press, 1986).

Fischer, David Hackett, *Albion's Seed: Four British Folkways in America* (New York: Oxford University Press, 1989).

Flugel, J. C., *The Psychology of Clothes* (London: Hogarth Press, 1930).

Fox, Richard Wightman and T. J. Jackson Lears (eds), *The Culture of Consumption: Critical Essays in American History, 1880–1980* (New York: Pantheon, 1983).

Freud, Sigmund, *Civilization and Its Discontents* (New York: Norton, 1962 [1930]).

Friedan, Betty, *The Feminine Mystique* (New York: Norton, 1963).

Gans, Herbert J., *Middle American Individualism: The Future of Liberal Democracy* (New York: Free Press, 1988).

Gash, Norman, *Aristocracy and the People: Britain 1815–1865* (London: Edward Arnold, 1979).

Gay, Peter, *The Tender Passion*, vol. 1, *The Bourgeois Experience* (New York: Oxford University Press, 1986).

Gay, Peter, *The Cultivation of Hatred*, vol. 3: *The Bourgeois Experience* (New York: Norton, 1993).

Gerth, H. H. and C. Wright Mills, *From Max Weber: Essays in Sociology* (New York: Oxford University Press, 1946).

Giedion, Siegfried, *Mechanization Takes Command: a Contribution to Anonymous History* (New York: Norton, 1969 [1948]).

Girouard, Mark, *Life in the English Country House* (Harmondsworth: Penguin, 1980).

Girouard, Mark, *The Return to Camelot: Chivalry and the English Gentleman* (New Haven, CT: Yale University Press, 1981) ch. 2.

Glassie, Henry, *Folk Housing in Middle Virginia* (Knoxville: University of Kentucky Press, 1975).

Gloag, John, *A Short Dictionary of Furniture*, rev. edn (London: George Allen & Unwin, 1969).

Godden, Geoffrey, 'Chinese Export Porcelain', in David Battie (ed.), *Sotheby's Concise Encyclopedia of Porcelain* (Boston: Little, Brown, 1990).

Goffman, Erving, 'The Nature of Deference and Demeanour', in *Interaction Ritual: Essays on Face-To-Face Behaviour* (London: Allen Lane, 1967).

Goldberg, S. L. and F. B. Smith (eds), *Australian Cultural History* (Cambridge: Cambridge University Press, 1988).

Gray, Robert Q., *The Labour Aristocracy in Victorian Edinburgh* (Oxford: Clarendon Press, 1976).

Grazia, Victoria de (ed.), *The Sex of Things: Gender and Consumption in Historical Perspective* (Berkeley: University of California Press, 1996).

Greene, Jack P., *Pursuits of Happiness: The Social Development of Early Modern British Colonies and the Formation of American Culture* (Chapel Hill, NC: University of North Carolina Press, 1988).

Greene, Jack P. and J. R. Pole (eds), *Colonial British America: Essays in the History of the Early Modern Era* (Baltimore, MD: Johns Hopkins University Press, 1984).

Grier, Katherine C., *Culture and Comfort: People, Parlours and Upholstery, 1850–1930* (Rochester, NY: Strong Museum, 1988).

Griffen, Clyde and Sally Griffen, 'Small Business and Occupational Mobility in Mid-Nineteenth Century Poughkeepsie', in Stuart W. Bruchey, *Small Business in American Life* (New York: Columbia University Press, 1980).

Grover, Kathryn (ed.), *Dining in America, 1850–1900* (Amherst: University of Massachusetts Press, 1987).

Guttsman, W. L., *The British Political Elite* (London: Macgibbon & Kee, 1963).

Halévy, Elie, *A History of the English People in 1815* (London: Penguin, 1937).

Halévy, Elie, *The Age of Peel and Cobden: A History of the English People 1841–1852* (London: Ernest Benn, 1947).

Hall, Catherine, 'The Sweet Delights of Home', in Michelle Perrot (ed.), *From the Fires of Revolution to the Great War* (Cambridge MA: Belknap, 1990).

Hall, Catherine, *White, Male and Middle Class* (Cambridge: Polity Press, 1992).

Halttunen, Karen, *Confidence Men and Painted Women: A Study of Middle-Class Culture in America, 1830–1870* (New Haven, CT: Yale University Press, 1982).

Hancock, W. A., *Australia* (London: Ernest Benn, 1930).

Hardyment, Christina, *Behind the Scenes: Domestic Arrangements in Historic Houses* (London: National Trust, 1997).

Harrison, J. F. C., *The Early Victorians 1832–1851* (London: Weidenfeld & Nicolson, 1971).

Hartz, Louis, *The Liberal Tradition in America: An Interpretation of Political Thought since the Revolution* (New York: Harcourt, Brace & Co., 1955).

Hartz, Louis, *The Founding of New Societies: Studies in the History of the United States, Latin America, South Africa, Canada and Australia* (New York: Harcourt Brace & World Inc., 1964).

Hemphill, C. Dallett, *Bowing to Necessities: A History of Manners in the United States, 1620–1860* (New York: Oxford University Press, 1999).

Herskovits, Melville, *The Myth of the Negro Past* (New York: Harper, 1941).

Himmelheber, Georg, *Cast-iron Furniture and All Other Forms of Iron Furniture* (London: Philip Wilson, 1996).

Hirsch, Susan E., *Roots of the American Working Class: The Industrialization of Crafts in Newark, 1800–1860* (Philadelphia: Temple University Press, 1978).

Hirst, John, 'Egalitarianism', in S. L. Goldberg and F. B. Smith (eds), *Australian Cultural History* (Cambridge: Cambridge University Press, 1988).

Hobsbawm, E. J., *The Age of Revolution, Europe 1789–1848* (London: Weidenfeld & Nicolson, 1962).

Hobsbawm, E. J., *Labouring Men: Studies in the History of Labour* (London: Weidenfeld & Nicolson, 1968).

Hobsbawm, Eric, 'The Example of the English', in Jurgen Kocka and Allan Mitchell (eds), *Bourgeois Society in Nineteenth Century Europe* (Oxford: Berg, 1993).

Hollander, Anne, *Seeing Through Clothes* (Viking: New York, 1975).

Hollander, Anne, *Sex and Suits* (New York: Knopf, 1994).

Horn, James, 'British Diaspora: Emigration from Britain, 1680–1815', in *Oxford History of the British Empire*, vol. 2, *The Eighteenth Century*, ed. P. J. Marshall (Oxford: Oxford University Press, 1998).

Horn, Pamela, *The Rise and Fall of the Victorian Servant* (London: Gill & Macmillan, 1975).

Houghton, Walter E., *The Victorian Frame of Mind, 1830–1870* (New Haven, CT: Yale University Press, 1957).

Howe, Daniel Walker (ed.), *Victorian America* (Philadelphia: University of Pennsylvania Press, 1976).

Hudspeth, Wilfred, *Early Van Diemen's Land: Hudspeth Memorial Volume* (Hobart: L.G. Shea, 1954).

Jaher, Frederic Cople (ed.), *The Rich, The Well Born, and the Powerful: Elites and Upper Classes in History* (Urbana: University of Illinois Press, 1973).

Johnston, Paul E., *A Shopkeeper's Millennium: Society and Revivals in Rochester, New York, 1815–1837* (New York: Hill & Wang, 1978).

Johnston, Robert D., 'Historians and the Middle Class', in Burton J. Bledstein and Robert D. Johnston, *The Middling Sorts: Explorations in the History of the American Middle Class* (New York: Routledge, 2001).

Jones, M. G., *The Story of Brushmaking: a Norfolk Craft* (Norwich: Briton Chadwick, 1974).

Joy, Edward T., *English Furniture 1800–1851* (London: Sotheby Parke Bernet Publications, 1977).

Joy, Edward, *Pictorial Dictionary of British Nineteenth Century Furniture Design* (Woodbridge, Suffolk: Antique Collectors Club, 1984).

Joyce, Patrick, *Visions of the People: Industrial England and the Question of Class, 1848–1914* (Cambridge: Cambridge University Press, 1991).

Joyce, Patrick, 'A People and a Class: Industrial Workers and the Social Order in Nineteenth-Century England', in M. L. Bush (ed.), *Social Orders and Social Classes in Europe since 1500: Studies in Social Stratification* (London: Longman, 1992).

Jupp, Peter J., 'The Landed Elite and Political Authority in Britain, c. 1760–1850', *Journal of British Studies*, vol. 29, no. 1 (1990).

Kasson, John F., 'Rituals of Dining: Table Manners in Victorian America', in Kathryn Grover (ed.), *Dining in America, 1850–1900* (Amherst: University of Massachusetts Press, 1987).

Kasson, John, *Rudeness and Civility: Manners in Nineteenth Century Urban America* (New York: Hill & Wang, 1990).

Kelly, Joan, 'The Doubled Vision of Feminist Theory', in Judith L. Newton, Mary P. Ryan and Judith R. Walkowitz (eds), *Sex and Class in Women's History* (London: Routledge & Kegan Paul, 1983).

Kendall, Joan, 'The Development of a Distinctive Form of Quaker Dress', *Costume*, no. 19 (1985).

Kidwell, Claudia B. and Margaret C. Christman, *Suiting Everyone: The Democratization of Clothing in America* (Washington: Smithsonian Institution Press, 1974).

Kingston, Beverley, *My Wife, My Daughter and Poor Mary Ann: Women and Work in Australia* (Melbourne: Nelson, 1975).

Knibiehler, Yvonne, 'Bodies and Hearts', in Geneviève Fraisse and Michelle Perrot (eds), *A History of Women in the West*, vol. 4: *Emerging Feminism from Revolution to World War* (Cambridge, MA: Belknap, 1993).

Kocka, Jurgen and Allan Mitchell (eds), *Bourgeois Society in Nineteenth Century Europe* (Oxford: Berg, 1993).

Koditschek, Theodore, *Class Formation and Urban-Industrial Society: Bradford, 1750–1850* (Cambridge: Cambridge University Press, 1990).

Kolchin, Peter, *American Slavery, 1619–1877* (New York: Hill & Wang, 1993).

Kolodny, Annette, *The Land before Her: Fantasy and Experience on the American Frontiers 1630–1860* (Chapel Hill: University of North Carolina Press, 1984).

Kronos, Sidney, *The Black Middle Class* (Columbus, OH: Charles E. Merrill, 1971).

Kuchta, David, 'The Making of the Self-Made Man: Class, Clothing and English Masculinity, 1688–1832', in Victoria de Grazia (ed.), *The Sex of Things: Gender and Consumption in Historical Perspective* (Berkeley: University of California Press, 1996).

Lambton, Lucinda, *Temples of Convenience and Chambers of Delight* (New York: St. Martin's Press – now Palgrave Macmillan, 1995).

Lane, Terence and Jessie Serle, *Australians at Home* (Melbourne: Oxford University Press, 1990).

Langer, William L., 'The Origins of the Birth Control Movement in England in the Early Nineteenth Century', *Journal of Interdisciplinary History*, vol. 5, no. 4 (1975).

Langland, Elizabeth, *Nobody's Angels: Middle Class Women and Domestic Ideology in Victorian Culture* (Ithaca, NY: Cornell University Press, 1995).

Larkin, Jack, *The Reshaping of Everyday Life, 1790–1840* (New York: Harper & Row, 1988).

Larson, Magali Sarfatti, *The Rise of Professionalism: A Sociological Analysis* (Berkeley: University of California Press, 1977).

Lasdun, Susan, *Making Victorians: The Drummond Children's World 1827–32* (London: Gollancz, 1983).

Laslett, Peter, *The World We have Lost* (London: Methuen, 1965).

Laver, James, *Modesty in Dress: An Inquiry into the Fundamentals of Fashion* (Boston: Houghton Mifflin, 1969).

Lears, T. J. Jackson, 'From Salvation to Self-realization: Advertising and the Therapeutic Roots of the Consumer Culture, 1880–1930', in Richard Wightman Fox and T. J. Jackson Lears (eds), *The Culture of Consumption: Critical Essays in American History, 1880–1980* (New York: Pantheon, 1983).

Lemire, Beverley, *Fashion's Favourite: The Cotton Trade and the Consumer in Britain, 1660–1800* (Oxford: Oxford University Press, 1991).

Levey, Santina, *Lace: A History* (London: Victoria & Albert Museum/W.S. Maney & Sons, 1983).

Lewis, Roy and Angus Maude, *The English Middle Classes* (London: Phoenix House, 1950).

Lewis, William Roger (ed.), *Oxford History of the British Empire*, 5 vols (Oxford: Oxford University Press, 1998).

Loesser, Arthur, *Men, Women and Pianos: A Social History* (London: Victor Gollancz, 1955).

McBride, Theresa M., *The Domestic Revolution: The Modernization of Household Service in England and France, 1820–1920* (New York: Holmes & Meier, 1976).

McCalman, Janet, 'Respectability and Working Class Politics in Late-Victorian London', *Historical Studies*, vol. 19, no. 74 (1980).

McCarthy, Kathleen D., *Noblesse Oblige: Charity and Cultural Philanthropy in Chicago 1848–1929* (Chicago: University of Chicago Press, 1982).

McCracken, Grant, *Culture and Consumption: New Approaches to the Symbolic Character of Consumer Goods and Activities* (Bloomington: Indiana University Press, 1988).

McDannell, Colleen, *The Christian Home in Victorian America, 1840–1900* (Bloomington: Indiana University Press, 1986).

McKendrick, Neil (ed.), *Historical Perspectives: Studies in English Thought and Society* (London: Europa, 1974).

McKendrick, Neil and R. B. Outhwaite (eds), *Business Life and Public Policy* (Cambridge: Cambridge University Press, 1986).

McKendrick, Neil, John Brewer and J. H. Plumb, *The Birth of a Consumer Society: The Commercialization of Eighteenth-Century England* (London: Europa, 1982).

Mahoney, Timothy R., *Provincial Lives: Middle-Class Experience in the Ante-Bellum Middle West* (Cambridge: Cambridge University Press, 1999).

Malchow, H. L., *Gentlemen Capitalists: The Social and Political World of the Victorian Businessman* (London: Macmillan – now Palgrave Macmillan, 1991).

Mangan, J. A. and James Walvin (eds), *Manliness and Morality: Middle Class Masculinity in Britain and America, 1800–1940* (Manchester: Manchester University Press, 1987).

Martin, Ann Smart, 'Makers, Buyers, and Users: Consumerism as a Material Culture Framework', *Winterthur Portfolio*, vol. 28, nos 2–3 (1993).

Martin, Judith, *Miss Manners' Guide to Excrutiatingly Correct Behaviour* (London: Hamish Hamilton, 1983).

Matthews, Glenna, *'Just a Housewife': The Rise and Fall of Domesticity in America* (New York: Oxford University Press, 1987).

Mayer, Arno J., 'The Lower Middle Class as a Historical Problem', *Journal of Modern History*, vol. 47, no. 3 (1975).

Miller, Daniel, *Material Culture and Mass Consumption* (Oxford: Basil Blackwell, 1987).

Miller, Lillian B., *Patrons and Patriotism: The Encouragement of the Fine Arts in the United States, 1790–1860* (Chicago: University of Chicago Press, 1966).

Mills, C. Wright, *White Collar: The American Middle Classes* (New York: Oxford University Press, 1951).

Mingay, G. E., *The Gentry: The Rise and Fall of a Ruling Class* (London: Longman, 1976).

Mintz, Steven, *A Prison of Expectations: The Family in Victorian Culture* (New York: New York University Press, 1983).

Montgomery, Florence M., *Textiles in America 1650–1870* (New York: W.W. Norton, n.d.).

Morgan, Marjorie, *Manners, Morals and Class in England, 1774–1858* (New York: St. Martin's Press – now Palgrave Macmillan, 1994).

Morris, R. J. (ed.), *Class, Power and Social Structure in British Nineteenth-Century Towns* (Leicester: Leicester University Press, 1986).

Morris, R. J., *Class, Sect and Party: The Making of the British Middle Class, Leeds, 1820–1850* (Manchester: Manchester University Press, 1990).

Mudge, Jean McClure, *Chinese Export Porcelain for the American Trade, 1785–1835* (Newark: University of Delaware Press, 1962).

Mukerji, Chandra, *From Graven Images: Patterns of Modern Materialism* (New York: Columbia University Press, 1983).

Nadel, George, *Australia's Colonial Culture: Ideas, Men and Institutions in Mid-Nineteenth Century Eastern Australia* (Melbourne: Melbourne University Press, 1957).

Neale, R. S., *Class and Ideology* (London: Routledge & Kegan Paul, 1972).

Nenadic, Stana, 'Middle-rank Consumers and Domestic Culture in Edinburgh and Glasgow, 1720–1840', *Past and Present*, no. 145 (1994).

Newton, Judith L., Mary P. Ryan and Judith R. Walkowitz (eds), *Sex and Class in Women's History* (London: Routledge & Kegan Paul, 1983).

Nylander, Jane C., 'Everyday Life on a Berkshire County Hill Farm', in Eleanor

McD. Thompson (ed.), *The American Home: Material Culture, Domestic Space, and Family Life* (Winterthur, DE: Winterthur Museum, 1998).

Ogle, Maureen, 'Domestic Reform in American Household Plumbing', *Winterthur Portfolio*, vol. 28, no. 1 (Spring 1993).

Patmore, Coventry, *The Angel in the House* (London: George Routledge & Sons, n.d.).

Peiss, Kathy, *Hope in a Jar: The Making of America's Beauty Culture* (New York: Metropolitan Books, 1998).

Perkin, Harold, *The Origins of Modern English Society, 1780–1880* (London: Routledge & Kegan Paul, 1969).

Perkin, Harold, *The Rise of Professional Society: England since 1880* (London: Routledge, 1989).

Perrot, Michelle, 'The Family Triumphant', in Philippe Ariès and Georges Duby (eds), *A History of Private Life*, vol. 4, *From the Fires of the Revolution to the Great War* (ed. Michelle Perrot) (Cambridge MA: Belknap Press, 1990).

Persons, Stow, *The Decline of American Gentility* (New York: Columbia University Press, 1973).

Pessen, Edward (ed.), *Three Centuries of Social Mobility in America* (Lexington, MA: Heath, 1974).

Pessen, Edward, *The Many-Faceted Jacksonian Era: New Interpretations* (Westport, CT: Greenwood, 1977).

Phillipps, K. C., *Language and Class in Victorian England* (Oxford: Basil Blackwell, 1984).

Pinchbeck, Ivy, *Women Workers and the Industrial Revolution 1750–1850* (London: G. Routledge, 1930).

Pocock, J. G. A., 'British History: A Plea for a New Subject', *New Zealand Journal of History*, vol. 8, no. 1 (1973).

Poovey, Mary, *Uneven Developments: The Ideological Work of Gender in Mid-Victorian England* (Chicago: University of Chicago Press, 1988).

Prochaska, F. K., *Women and Philanthropy in Nineteenth Century England* (Oxford: Clarendon, 1980).

Quinlan, Maurice J., *Victorian Prelude: A History of English Manners, 1700–1830* (Hamden, CT: Archon Books, 1965 [1941]).

Rendall, Jane, *Women in an Industrializing Society: England 1750–1880* (Oxford: Basil Blackwell, 1990).

Ribeiro, Aileen, *The Art of Dress: Fashion in England and France 1750–1820* (New Haven, CT: Yale University Press, 1995).

Rock, H. B. (ed.), *The New York City Artisan, 1789–1825* (Albany: State University of New York Press, 1989).

Rosa, Matthew, *The Silver-Fork School: Novels of Fashion preceding Vanity Fair* (New York: Columbia University Press, 1936).

Rose, Sonya, *Limited Livelihoods: Gender and Class in Nineteenth-Century England* (Berkeley: University of California Press, 1992).

Rosenberg, Carroll Smith, 'The Hysterical Woman: Sex Roles and Role Conflict in Nineteenth-Century America', *Social Research*, vol. 39, no. 4 (1972).

Rosenberg, Carroll Smith, 'The Female World of Love and Ritual: Relations between Women in Nineteenth-Century America', in *Disorderly Conduct: Visions of Gender in Victorian America* (New York: Knopf, 1985).

Rosman, Doreen M., *Evangelicals and Culture* (London: Croom Helm, 1984).

Ross, Robert, *Status and Respectability in the Cape Colony, 1750–1870* (Cambridge: Cambridge University Press, 1999).

Rothstein, Natalie (ed.), *Barbara Johnson's Album of Fashions and Fabrics* (London: Thames & Hudson, 1987).

Rotundo, E. Anthony, 'Learning about Manhood: Gender Ideals and the Middle Class Family in Nineteenth Century America', in J. A. Mangan and James Walvin (eds), *Manliness and Morality: Middle Class Masculinity in Britain and America, 1800–1940* (Manchester: Manchester University Press, 1987).

Rubinstein, W. D., 'Wealth, Elites and the Class Structure of Modern Britain', *Past and Present*, no. 76 (1977).

Rubinstein, W. D., *Elites and the Wealthy in Modern British History: Essays in Social and Economic History* (Brighton: Harvester Press, 1987).

Russell, Penny, 'A Wish of Distinction: Genteel Femininity in Melbourne Society, 1860–1880', PhD thesis, University of Melbourne (1989).

Russell, Penny, *A Wish of Distinction: Colonial Gentility and Femininity* (Melbourne: Melbourne University Press, 1994).

Ryan, Mary, *Cradle of the Middle Class: The Family in Oneida County, New York, 1790–1865* (Cambridge: Cambridge University Press, 1981).

Rybcyzinski, Witold, *Home: The Short History of an Idea* (New York: Viking, 1986).

Scheflen, Albert E., *Body Language and Social Order: Communication as Behavioural Control* (Englewood Cliffs, NJ: Prentice-Hall, 1972).

Schlesinger, Arthur M., *Learning How to Behave: A Historical Study of American Etiquette Books* (New York: Macmillan, 1946).

Scott, Joan, 'Gender: A Useful Category of Analysis', *American Historical Review*, vol. 91, no. 5 (1986).

Seccombe, Wally, 'Patriarchy Stabilised: The Construction of the Male Breadwinner Wage Norm in Nineteenth Century Britain', *Social History*, vol. 11, no. 1 (1986).

Seed, John, 'From "Middling Sort" to Middle Class in Late Eighteenth- and Early Nineteenth-Century England', in M. L. Bush (ed.), *Social Orders and Social Classes in Europe since 1500: Studies in Social Stratification* (London: Longman, 1992).

Seigel, Jerrold, *Bohemian Paris: Culture, Politics and the Boundaries of the Bourgeois Life, 1830–1930* (New York: Viking, 1986).

Sennett, Richard, *The Fall of Public Man* (Cambridge: Cambridge University Press, 1974).

Shackel, Paul A., *Personal Discipline and Material Culture: An Archaeology of Annapolis, Maryland, 1695–1870* (Knoxville: University of Tennessee Press, 1993).

Shammas, Carole, 'The Domestic Environment in Early Modern England and America', *Journal of Social History*, vol. 14, no. 1 (1980).

Shammas, Carole, *The Pre-Industrial Consumer in England and America* (Oxford: Clarendon Press, 1990).

Sombart, Werner, *Luxury and Capitalism* (Ann Arbor: University of Michigan Press, 1967 [1913]).

Spring, David, 'Aristocracy, Social Structure and Religion in the Early Victorian Period', *Victorian Studies*, vol. 6, no. 3 (1963).

Spufford, Margaret, *The Great Reclothing of Rural England: Petty Chapmen and their Wares in the Seventeenth Century* (London: Hambledon Press, 1984).

Stearns, Peter N., 'The Middle Class: Towards a Precise Definition', *Comparative Studies in Society and History*, vol. 21 (1979).

Stearns, Peter N., *Battleground of Desire: The Struggle for Self-Control in Modern America* (New York: New York University Press, 1999).

Stone, Lawrence and Jeanne Fawtier Stone, *An Open Elite? England 1540–1800* (Oxford: Oxford University Press, 1984).

Stone, May, 'The Plumbing Paradox: American Attitudes towards Late Nineteenth Century Domestic Sanitary Arrangements', *Winterthur Portfolio*, vol. 14, no. 3 (Autumn 1979).

Strasser, Susan, *Satisfaction Guaranteed: The Making of the American Mass Market* (New York: Pantheon, 1989).

Susman, Warren I., ' "Personality" and the Making of Twentieth-Century Culture', in John Highman and Paul K. Conkin (eds), *New Directions in American Intellectual History* (Baltimore, MD: Johns Hopkins University Press, 1979).

Sutherland, Daniel E., *Americans and Their Servants: Domestic Service in the United States from 1800–1920* (Baton Rouge, LA: Louisiana State University Press, 1981).

Tait, Hugh (ed.), *The Art of the Jeweller: A Catalogue of the Hull Grundy Gift to the British Museum: Jewellery, Engraved Gems and Goldsmiths' Work*, 2 vols (London: British Museum, 1984).

Tarrant, Naomi E., *The Rise and Fall of the Sleeve, 1825–1840* (Edinburgh: Royal Scottish Museum, 1983).

Tarrant, Naomi, *The Development of Costume* (London: Routledge, 1994).

Tawney, R. H., 'The Rise of the Gentry', *Economic History Review*, vol. 11 (1941).

Taylor, Arthur J. (ed.), *The Standard of Living in the Industrial Revolution* (London: Methuen, 1975).

Thirsk, Joan, *Economic Policy and Projects: The Development of a Consumer Society in Early Modern England* (Oxford: Clarendon Press, 1978).

Tholfsen, Trygve, *Working Class Radicalism in Mid-Victorian England* (London: Croom Helm, 1976).

Thompson, Dorothy, *Queen Victoria: Gender and Power* (London: Virago, 1990).

Thompson, Eleanor McD. (ed.), *The American Home: Material Culture, Domestic Space, and Family Life* (Winterthur, DE: Winterthur Museum, 1998).

Thompson, E. P., 'Time, Work Discipline and Industrial Capitalism', *Past and Present*, no. 38 (1967).

Thompson, E. P., *The Poverty of Theory* (London: Merlin, 1978).

Thompson, E. P., *The Making of the English Working Class* (Harmondsworth: Penguin, 1980 [1963]).

Thompson, F. M. L., *English Landed Society in the Nineteenth Century* (London: Routledge & Kegan Paul, 1963).

Thompson, F. M. L., *The Rise of Respectable Society: a Social History of Victorian Britain 1830–1900* (London: Fontana, 1988).

Thompson, F. M. L., *Gentrification and the Enterprise Culture: Britain 1780–1980* (Oxford: Oxford University Press, 2001).

Toews, John E., 'Intellectual History after the Linguistic Turn: The Autonomy of Meaning and the Irreducibility of Experience', *American Historical Review*, vol. 92, no. 4 (1987).

Tolles, Frederick B., *Quakers and the Atlantic Culture* (New York: Macmillan, 1960).

Tyrrell, Ian, *The Absent Marx: Class Analysis and Liberal History in Twentieth Century America* (New York: Greenwood Press, 1986).

Tyrrell, Ian, 'American Exceptionalism in the Age of International History', *American Historical Review*, vol. 96, no. 4 (October 1991).

Vail, R. W. G., 'Moody's *School of Good Manners*: A Study in American Colonial Etiquette', *Studies in the History of Culture* (Menasha, WN: ACLS, 1942).

Vance, Norman, *The Sinews of the Spirit: The Ideal of Christian Manliness in Victorian Literature and Religious Thought* (Cambridge: Cambridge University Press, 1985).

Veblen, Thorstein, *The Theory of the Leisure Class* (New York: Modern Library, 1934 [1899]).

Vicinus, Martha (ed.), *Suffer and Be Still: Women in the Victorian Age* (Bloomington: Indiana University Press, 1972).

Vickery, Amanda, 'Women and the World of Goods: A Lancashire Consumer and Her Possessions', in John Brewer and Roy Porter (eds), *Consumption and the World of Goods* (London: Routledge, 1993).

Wach, Howard M., 'Culture and the Middle Classes: Popular Knowledge in Industrial Manchester', *Journal of British Studies*, vol. 27, no. 1 (1988).

Wahrman, Dror, *Imagining the Middle Class: The Political Representation of Class in Britain, c.1780–1840* (Cambridge: Cambridge University Press, 1995).

Wainwright, Clive, *The Romantic Interior: The British Collector at Home 1750–1850* (New Haven, CT: Yale University Press, 1989).

Walkley, Christina and Vanda Foster, *Crinolines and Crimping Irons: Victorian Clothes: How They Were Cleaned and Cared For* (London: Peter Owen, 1978).

Wallech, Steven, '"Class versus Rank": The Transformation of Eighteenth Century English Social Terms and Theories of Production', *Journal of the History of Ideas*, vol. 47, no. 3 (1986).

Walsh, Lorena S., Gloria L. Main, Lois Green Carr, Jackson Turner Main and John J. McCusker, 'Forum', *William and Mary Quarterly*, vol. XLV, no. 1 (1988).

Walton, Whitney, *France at the Crystal Palace: Bourgeois Taste and Artisan Manufacture in the Nineteenth Century* (Berkeley: University of California Press, 1992).

Ward, Russel, *The Australian Legend* (Melbourne: Oxford University Press, 1977 [1958]).

Wardle, Patricia, *Victorian Lace* (London: Herbert Jenkins, 1968).

Warner, W. Lloyd, *American Life: Dream and Reality* (Chicago: University of Chicago Press, 1953).

Waterhouse, Richard, *Private Pleasures, Public Leisures: A History of Australian Popular Culture since 1788* (Melbourne: Longman, 1995).

Waters, Malcolm, *Globalization* (London: Routledge, 1995).

Weber, Max, 'Class, Status, Party', in H. H. Gerth and C. Wright Mills, *From Max Weber: Essays in Sociology* (New York: Oxford University Press, 1946).

Weekes, Jeffrey, *Sex, Politics and Society: The Regulation of Sexuality since 1800*, 2nd edn (London: Longman, 1989).

Welter, Barbara, 'The Cult of True Womanhood, 1820–1860', *American Quarterly*, vol. 18, no. 2 (1966).

Wiener, Martin J., *English Culture and the Decline of the Industrial Spirit* (Cambridge: Cambridge University Press, 1981).

Wildblood, Joan, *The Polite World* (London: Oxford University Press, 1965).

Wilkie, Jacqueline, 'Submerged Sensuality: Technology and Perceptions of Bathing', *Journal of Social History*, no. 19 (1986).

Wilkinson, R. H., 'The Gentleman Ideal and the Maintenance of a Political Elite', in P. W. Musgrave (ed.), *Sociology, History and Education: A Reader* (London: Methuen, 1970).

Williams, Neville, *Powder and Paint: A History of the Englishwoman's Toilet* (London: Longman, Green & Co., 1957).

Williams, Raymond, *Keywords: A Vocabulary of Culture and Society* (London: Fontana, 1976).

Williams, Rosalind, *Dream Worlds: Mass Consumption in Late Nineteenth Century France* (Berkeley: University of California Press, 1982).

Wilson, Elizabeth, 'The Bohemianisation of Mass Culture', *International Journal of Cultural Studies*, vol. 2, no. 1 (April 1999).

Wolff, Janet 'The Culture of Separate Spheres', in Janet Wolff and John Seed (eds), *The Culture of Capital: Art, Power and the Nineteenth Century Middle Class* (Manchester: Manchester University Press, 1988).

Wolff, Janet, *Feminine Sentences: Essays on Women and Culture* (Cambridge: Polity Press, 1990).

Wright, Lawrence, *Clean and Decent: The Fascinating History of the Bathroom and Water Closet* (London: Routledge & Kegan Paul, 1960).

Yosifon, David and Peter N. Stearns, 'The Rise and Fall of American Posture', *American Historical Review*, vol. 103, no. 4 (1998).

Young, G. M., *Victorian England: Portrait of an Age*, 2nd edn (Oxford: Oxford University Press, 1953 [1936]).

Young, Linda, 'Life in the English Country House – in Australia: the Case of Martindale Hall', *Heritage Australia*, vol. 9, no. 3 (1990).

Young, Linda, 'Constructing Ancestral Grandeur: The Performance of Two Assemblages of Furnishings', *Public History Review*, no. 1 (1992).

Young, Linda, 'Decency and Necessity: Material Life in South Australia, 1859', *Journal of Interdisciplinary History*, vol. XXV, no. 1 (1994).

Young, Linda, 'The Struggle for Class: The Transmission of Genteel Culture to Early Colonial Australia', PhD thesis, Flinders University of South Australia (1997).

Index